Lecture Notes of the Institute for Computer Sciences, Social Informatics and Telecommunications Engineering 179

More information about this series at http://www.springer.com/series/8197

Enrique Sucar · Oscar Mayora
Enrique Muñoz de Cote (Eds.)

Applications for Future Internet

International Summit, AFI 2016
Puebla, Mexico, May 25–28, 2016
Revised Selected Papers

Springer

Editors
Enrique Sucar
Department of Computer Science
Instituto Nacional de Astrofísica,
    Óptica y Electrónica (INAOE)
Tonantzintla, Puebla
Mexico

Oscar Mayora
CREATE-NET
Trento
Italy

Enrique Muñoz de Cote
Department of Computer Science
Instituto Nacional de Astrofísica,
    Óptica y Electrónica (INAOE)
Tonantzintla, Puebla
Mexico

and

PROWLER.io
Cambridge
UK

ISSN 1867-8211   ISSN 1867-822X (electronic)
Lecture Notes of the Institute for Computer Sciences, Social Informatics
and Telecommunications Engineering
ISBN 978-3-319-49621-4   ISBN 978-3-319-49622-1   (eBook)
DOI 10.1007/978-3-319-49622-1

Library of Congress Control Number: 2016957851

Printed on acid-free paper

This Springer imprint is published by Springer Nature
The registered company is Springer International Publishing AG
The registered company address is: Gewerbestrasse 11, 6330 Cham, Switzerland

Preface

The International 360° Summit on Applications for Future Internet (AFI360) was held in Puebla, Mexico, May 25–28. It included workshops and tutorials, industrial and academic keynotes, demonstrations, and a technical conference. Here we present the accepted works of the technical conference after a double-blind peer-review process. Two paper formats will be presented in this proceedings: a long paper format with a 12-page limit and a short paper format with a four-page limit. Naturally, long papers give a more in-depth view of the problem and contribution while the short papers give a more superficial, but still insightful view.

The technical conference was divided in four tracks: (1) infrastructures and enablers, (2) e-health, (3) smart cities, and (4) IoT applications, covering most topics regarding the future Internet and its applications, from protocols and frameworks to hardware and cloud infrastructures. The usage of the future Internet in the biological and health sciences was viewed as an important theme, as well as the explosion of IoT devices and its applications across fields such as smart cities, health, and agriculture.

October 2016

Enrique Sucar
Oscar Mayora
Adriana Tapus
Juan-Manuel Ahuactzin
Alessandro Farinelli
Enrique Munoz de Cote
Venet Osmani
Alberto Moran
Athena Vakali
Miguel Gonzalez-Mendoza

Organization

Steering Committee

Steering Committee Chair

Imrich Chlamtac   Create-Net, Italy

Steering Committee Members

Enrique Sucar   INAOE, Mexico
Oscar Mayora   Create-Net, Italy
Enrique Munoz de Cote   INAOE, Mexico; PROWLER.io, UK

Tracks

FINE

General Chairs

Athena Vakali   AUTH
Miguel Gonzalez Mendoza   ITESM, Mexico

PC Chairs

Hugo Estrada   INFOTEC, Mexico
Luis Trejo   ITESM, Mexico

PC Vice Chairs

John Garofalakis   UP
Salma Jalife   CUDI

Workshops Chair

Sophia Petridou   UOM

Publication Chair

Oscar Herrera   UAEM, Mexico

Proceedings/Publicity Chair

Ioannis Katakis   UoA

Website Chair

Joanna Alvarado Uribe   ITESM, Mexico

FI-eHEALTH

General Chairs

Alberto L. Morán   UABC, Mexico
Venet Osmani   Create-Net, Italy

TPC Chair

Felipe Orihuela-Espina   INAOE, Mexico

Publications Chair

Enrique García Ceja   Tec de Monterrey, Mexico

SCIFI

General Chair

Juan-Manuel Ahuactzin   T-Systems, Mexico

General Co-chair

Adriana Tapus   École Nationale Supérieure de Techniques Avancées

Program Chair

Robert Laurini   INSA Lyon, France
Jorge Valadez   Universidad Autónoma del Estado de Morelos, Mexico
Luis Muñoz Ubando   Grupo Pluenum

Workshops Chair

Cesar Cárdenas   ITESM Guadalajara, Mexico

FIOTA

General Chair

Enrique Munoz de Cote   INAOE, Mexico; PROWLER.io, UK

General Co-chair

Alessandro Farinelli   University of Verona, Italy

Contents

SCiFI 2016

Towards a Generic Ontology for Video Surveillance 3
  Pablo Hernandez-Leal, Hugo Jair Escalante, and L. Enrique Sucar

Smart Cities for the Rest of Us. 8
  Miguel Ángel Ylizaliturri-Salcedo, J. Antonio García-Macías,
  Raúl Cardenas-Osuna, and Leocundo Aguilar-Noriega

Smart Disaster Response Through Localized Short-Term Cooperation 12
  Youna Jung

Towards a Smart Highway Lighting System Based on Road Occupancy:
Model Design and Simulation. 22
  Ahmad M. Mustafa, Omar M. Abubakr, Ahmed H. Derbala,
  Essam Ahmed, and Bassem Mokhtar

FIoTA 2016

Exploiting Data of the Twitter Social Network Using Sentiment Analysis . . . 35
  David Gonzalez-Marron, David Mejia-Guzman,
  and Angelica Enciso-Gonzalez

Decentralized Control for Power Distribution with Ancillary Lines
in the Smart Grid 39
  Michele Roncalli and Alessandro Farinelli

An Experimental Evaluation of IoT Technologies in Precision Viticulture . . . 51
  Luis Orozco-Barbosa, Francisco Montero García,
  Antonio Brasa Ramos, and Francisco Montero Riquelme

GARMDROID: IoT Potential Security Threats Analysis Through the
Inference of Android Applications Hardware Features Requirements 63
  Abraham Rodríguez-Mota, Ponciano Jorge Escamilla-Ambrosio,
  Jassim Happa, and Eleazar Aguirre-Anaya

Making the Intelligent Home Smart Through Touch-Control Trigger-Action
Programming . . . . ,. 75
  Guan Wang and Michael L. Littman

Optimal Scheduling of On/Off Cycles: A Decentralized IoT-Microgrid
Approach.   79
   Fernando Lezama, Jorge Palominos, Ansel Y. Rodríguez-González,
   Alessandro Farinelli, and Enrique Munoz de Cote

CML-WSN: A Configurable Multi-layer Wireless Sensor Network
Simulator.   91
   Carolina Del-Valle-Soto, Fernando Lezama, Jafet Rodriguez,
   Carlos Mex-Perera, and Enrique Munoz de Cote

Conceptual Model for the Explanation of the Phenomenon of Radical
Innovation in the Disruption of the Internet of Things, on Scales of Smart
Objects, Homes and Cities.   103
   David Soasti Bareta and Gerardo Muñiz

MAIoT - An IoT Architecture with Reasoning and Dialogue Capability.   109
   Juan Carlos Nieves, Daniel Andrade, and Esteban Guerrero

FI-eHealth 2016

An Internet System to Self-monitoring and Assess Feeding in Young
Mexicans.   117
   Miguel Murguía-Romero, Bernardo Serrano-Estrada,
   Itzell A. Gallardo-Ortíz, J. Rafael Jiménez-Flores,
   and Rafael Villalobos-Molina

A Conversational Agent for Use in the Identification of Rare Diseases   128
   Ana Olivia Caballero Lambert, Cesar Horacio Torres Montañez,
   Monica Bueno Martinez, and Marcelo Funes-Gallanzi

Using Intermediate Models and Knowledge Learning to Improve Stress
Prediction.   140
   Alban Maxhuni, Pablo Hernandez-Leal, Eduardo F. Morales,
   L. Enrique Sucar, Venet Osmani, Angelica Muñoz-Meléndez,
   and Oscar Mayora

Sensor Abstracted Extremity Representation for Automatic Fugl-Meyer
Assessment   152
   Patrick Heyer, Felipe Orihuela-Espina, Luis R. Castrejón,
   Jorge Hernández-Franco, and Luis Enrique Sucar

FINE 2016

A Platform for Creating Augmented Reality Content by End Users.   167
   Fernando Vera, J. Alfredo Sánchez, and Ofelia Cervantes

Strategic Learning Meta-model (SLM): Architecture of the Regulation
Model (RM) Based on the Cloud Computing   172
   Rafaela Blanca Silva-López, Oscar Herrera-Alcántara,
   and Jalil Fallad-Chávez

Overview of a Framework for Ubiquitous User Models Interoperability   185
   María de Lourdes Martínez-Villaseñor and Miguel González-Mendoza

Author Index   189

SCiFI 2016

Towards a Generic Ontology for Video Surveillance

Pablo Hernandez-Leal, Hugo Jair Escalante[✉], and L. Enrique Sucar

Instituto Nacional de Astrofísica, Óptica y Electrónica Sta. María Tonantzintla,
Puebla, Mexico
{pablohl,hugojair,esucar}@inaoep.mx

Abstract. Video surveillance is an important problem that has been studied for several years. Nowadays, in the context of smart cities, intelligent video surveillance is an important topic which has several subproblems which need to be solved and then integrated. For example, on one side there are several algorithms for detection, recognition and tracking of objects and people. On the other side, it is necessary to recognize not only objects and persons but complex behaviors (fights, thefts, attacks). To solve these challenges, the use of ontologies has been proposed as a tool to reduce this gap between low and high level information. In this work, we present the foundations of an ontology to be used in an intelligent video surveillance system.

Keywords: Video surveillance · Ontology · Event recognition

1 Introduction

Ontologies are used to represent knowledge and they have different uses. In video recognition and analysis, their main use has been to remove the *semantic gap*, this is, the difficulty of mapping semantic concepts into a set of image and/or spatiotemporal features that can be automatically extracted from video data without human intervention [2]. For example, even when a concept such as "car accident" is an accepted standard linguistic concept, there are thousands of videos that fulfill that linguistic term.

An ontology for analyzing this sort of videos would specify all associated entities and how they relate to each other. Ontologies are basically defined by two parts: entities and its relationships.

There are several works in video surveillance that use ontologies, one of them proposes a multi-camera platform for bank monitoring [3]. The platform follows the steps: (i) Object detection for each camera. (ii) Tracking for each camera to obtain a graph of moving objects. (iii) A fusion of information is used to combine the information from different cameras producing a global graph. (iv) This global graph is used to perform long term analysis (i.e., behavior recognition). (iv) Contextual information can be added (i.e., 3d information).

Previous works have used ontologies to detect objects and events. Some were used together with a rule detection system [7]. In that work, the used data was

© ICST Institute for Computer Sciences, Social Informatics and Telecommunications Engineering 2017
E. Sucar et al. (Eds.): AFI 2016, LNICST 179, pp. 3–7, 2017.
DOI: 10.1007/978-3-319-49622-1_1

part of the PETS (Performance Evaluation of Tracking and Surveillance) 2012 competition where the objective was to estimate the probability of certain events as well as its initial and final times.

Ontologies for specific applications had been designed, for example for analyzing soccer videos [1]. In this ontology each concept is associated with a visual concept. Concepts are clustered by their spatiotemporal similarity and each cluster has a visual prototype (clip, shot, frame or part of a frame).

An approach to use an ontology for video surveillance was presented by San-Miguel et al. where the ontology is based on two levels of knowledge: scene (domain information) and system (analysis information) [6]. In the scene there are three types of entities: (i) events: can be simple or complex, (ii) context: spatial information and (iii) objects: movables and context. In the system part there are different categories: (i) status, (ii) capacity (e.g., input parameters, output) and (iii) reaction (i.e., record event, activate alarm). The authors evaluated the approach in recognizing events such as grabbing and dropping objects.

In this work we contribute with a generic ontology for video analysis, we present the main components and relationships that are needed in a video surveillance environment.

2   Proposed Ontology

The proposed ontology is expected to be used jointly with a surveillance system.

2.1   Ontology Use

In particular, we want to use the ontology to help in the detection of events, and behaviors. An ontology is useful to define all the objects and behaviors that are important in video surveillance. The ontology can help to decide which algorithms to use [6]. Further, it will be interesting to use the ontology as a way to retrieve videos that match specific events [5]. In the context of smart cities there are another set of possible uses of an ontology in video analysis, namely: automatic annotation of videos, automatic extraction of videos and automatic annotation of composed events, among others [1]. Finally, another idea is to use the structure of the ontology together with hierarchical classifiers.

Based on the previous works and with the objective of developing a generic ontology for video surveillance we present our proposal. The ontology was defined using Protégé [4].

2.2   Entities

Entities are divided in three groups: Content, System and Context.

Content. There two important groups: Event and Physical_object. There are two types of Event: Person_Event and Vehicle_Event. Inside Person_Event there are activities such as: Standing, Running, Sitting, Walking, etc. There is also another group for generic events: such as Enter or Exit an area. Examples of Person_event are: Greeting, Fighting or Hugging. Inside Physical_object there are two groups: Movable_object and Fixed_objects (see Fig. 1 (a)).

There are two types of Movable_object: Individual and Multiple_ objects. In the Individual category there are animals (Bird, Mammal), persons (Baby, Adult, Man, Woman), vehicles (Air, Road) and personal objects (Backpack, Hat, Laptop, Camera, Book). A Multiple_object is a group of persons, vehicles or animals.

Fixed objects are considered those that do not change naturally of place, for example: generic (Building, Fence, Furniture, Window, etc.), natural object (Vegetation, Sky, Snow, etc.) and road objects (Sidewalk, Street, Traffic_light, etc.).

System. This group contains information that the video surveillance system will use. There are 4 entities: 3 auxiliary concepts Point, Reaction and Area, and another entity Algorithm.

There are different sub-entities of Algorithm that describe different tasks that are needed in video surveillance: preprocessing, object detection, object recognition, tracking, behavior analysis, among others. Also inside each entity there can be another division depending on what the technique is based on (see Fig. 1 (b)).

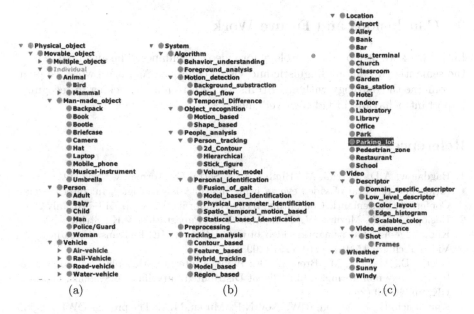

(a)   (b)   .(c)

Fig. 1. Parts of the proposed ontology: (a) Object, (b) System and (c) Context.

Context. Here is where the information regarding the environment is defined (see Fig. 1 (c)). For example weather (`Rainy`, `Sunny`, `Windy`), location (`School`, `Church`, `Parking`, `Bank`, etc.) and information from the video itself (`Frame`, `Shot`, `Descriptor`, etc.).

2.3 Properties

Besides entities, properties are important in an ontology. In particular, there two important types of properties: object properties and datatype properties.

Object Properties. These are defined between instances of entities. An example is `hasArea`. Entities such as `Event` or `Physical_object` have an `Area`. This is useful, for example, when the system detects an object and in the video we want to highlight a box to show that object, this is represented by the object `Area`. Another example is: `hasReaction`. Every `Algorithm` has a possible reaction such as activate an alarm, record the event, or do nothing.

Datatype Properties. The second type of properties relate entities and datatypes (`int`, `float`, `string`, etc.). An example of this type of property is `hasSpeed` which refers to a `Movable_object` that is moving and this speed is represented internally by a `float` value. Another example is the property `hasTitle` which belongs to every `Video` that has a title represented as a `string`.

3 Conclusions and Future Work

In this work we proposed an ontology for video surveillance. The idea is to reduce the semantic gap among linguistic and visual concepts. As future work we plan to combine the ontology with algorithms for detection and tracking to recognize important behaviors in video surveillance.

References

1. Bagdanov, A.D., Bertini, M., Bimbo, A.D., Serra, G., Torniai, C.: Semantic annotation and retrieval of video events using multimedia ontologies. In: International Conference on Semantic Computing, Irvine, California, USA, pp. 713–720, July 2007
2. Dasiopoulou, S., Mezaris, V., Kompatsiaris, I., Papastathis, V.K., Strintzis, M.G.: Knowledge-assisted semantic video object detection. IEEE Trans. Circuits Syst. Video Technol. **15**(10), 1210–1224 (2005)
3. Georis, B., Maziere, M., Bremond, F.: A video interpretation platform applied to bank agency monitoring. In: Intelligent Distributed Surveilliance Systems, London, UK, pp. 46–50 (2004)
4. Knublauch, H., Fergerson, R.W., Noy, N.F., Musen, M.A.: The protégé OWL plugin: an open development environment for semantic web applications. In: McIlraith, S.A., Plexousakis, D., Harmelen, F. (eds.) ISWC 2004. LNCS, vol. 3298, pp. 229–243. Springer, Heidelberg (2004). doi:10.1007/978-3-540-30475-3_17

5. Mezaris, V., Kompatsiaris, I., Boulgouris, N.V., Strintzis, M.G.: Real-time compressed-domain spatiotemporal segmentation and ontologies for video indexing and retrieval. IEEE Trans. Circuits Syst. Video Technol. **14**(5), 606–621 (2004)
6. SanMiguel, J.C., Martínez, J.M., García, A.: An ontology for event detection and its application in surveillance video. In: International Conference on Advanced Video and Signal Based Surveillance, Genova, Italy, pp. 220–225 (2009)
7. Kazi Tani, M.Y., Lablack, A., Ghomari, A., Bilasco, I.M.: Events detection using a video-surveillance ontology and a rule-based approach. In: Agapito, L., Bronstein, M.M., Rother, C. (eds.) ECCV 2014. LNCS, vol. 8926, pp. 299–308. Springer, Heidelberg (2015). doi:10.1007/978-3-319-16181-5_21

Smart Cities for the Rest of Us

Miguel Ángel Ylizaliturri-Salcedo[1], J. Antonio García-Macías[2(✉)],
Raúl Cardenas-Osuna[3], and Leocundo Aguilar-Noriega[1]

[1] Faculty of Chemistry Sciences and Engineering,
Autonomous University of Baja California, Tijuana, B.C., Mexico
{mylizaliturri,laguilar}@uabc.edu.mx
[2] Computer Sciences Department, CICESE Research Center, Ensenada, B.C., Mexico
jagm@cicese.mx
[3] Change Agents Society, Tijuana, B.C., Mexico
info@torolab.org

Abstract. More than half of the world's population live in cities. Smart cities could help to solve the present and upcoming problems that affects the people's well-being. However, developing regions face big challenges, like fighting poverty, jeopardizing the smart cities adoption. In this paper, we propose to design technologies for the problems of our developing regions. We describe our current work, designing and developing a wearable device for measuring poverty trough the analysis of social interaction and outlining its evaluation in the neighborhood of Camino Verde in Tijuana. We conclude by discussing our vision on the importance of designing technologies for our specific problems, culture and way of life.

Keywords: Smart cities · Poverty measurement · Wearable computing · Developing countries

1 Introduction

According to a recent UN report [11], from the current 7.2 billion people world's population, more than half lives in cities, and most of the future growth will occur in the less developed regions. However, urban growth, if well planned, has the potential to improve the people's well-being and managing environmental impact. Indeed, the welfare of the present and future population on the developing regions is a world concern, pointed already in the UN millennium goals [12]. In this scenario, the smart city is a way to achieve it. However, transiting to living in smart cities heavily depends on a costly, highly technified horizon, where both citizens and infrastructure are always connected to the Internet.

In this paper, we first present our vision about how smart cities must become more inclusive. Later, we propose the design of wearable technology for measuring poverty as a complementary mechanism to surveys and census for both, gathering data and empowering citizens on developing regions. Finally, we point to our conclusions and outline our future work.

© ICST Institute for Computer Sciences, Social Informatics and Telecommunications Engineering 2017
E. Sucar et al. (Eds.): AFI 2016, LNICST 179, pp. 8–11, 2017.
DOI: 10.1007/978-3-319-49622-1_2

2   Smart Cities in the Context of Developing Countries

When thinking about Latin-American smart cities, there are a few examples besides capital cities such as Santiago, Mexico City, Bogota, Buenos Aires, and Montevideo, or the recognized efforts of Rio de Janeiro, Curitiba, Medellin or Guadalajara. We observe that this development is being centralized and the progress remains exclusive of just a few regions. With this in mind, we ask ourselves: what is happening with the rest of the region? Which are the opportunities for a city like Oaxaca or Tijuana to being smarter?

We consider that it is not enough to adopt pre-packaged "one size fits all" technologies or replicating developed country models, as they do not realize that each region, and each city, has its particular shape, geography and culture. It is necessary to recognize that becoming a smart city means so much more than creating costly infrastructure [5] to score satisfactorily on the international standards checklists [8]; remarking that our communities have also higher priorities, like fighting poverty, or achieving universal education, and other complex tasks that are still far from being realized.

We strongly believe that answering our questions must be done consciously, gaining knowledge from the city itself, with the participation of the more disadvantaged side of society: those who suffer from the more imperative situations, like poverty. We need to find out not only how to transfer the technology of the developed countries to the cities that need to get smarter, but also to create the appropriate technology for them. We think that this task should also empower citizens to solve their specific neighborhood problems, resulting in improving directly their quality of life.

3   Designing Around Poverty

Poverty is a multidimensional social phenomenon widely spread on the world, especially severe in developing countries. At least in Mexico, three dimensions are used as poverty indicators [6]: the net income compared to a "poverty line" (i.e. the minimum amount of money enough to pay housing, transport and feeding), the access to social services welfare (i.e. education, health, housing, utilities, social security and feeding) and the social inequality.

In the concrete case of Mexico, according to [4], 45.5% of the Mexican population live in poverty conditions. From Mexico's 117.3 million habitants, 41.8 million are living on moderated poverty and 11.5 million on extreme poverty.

Poverty measurements are made typically through census and surveys, resulting in composed welfare indexes. However, obtaining this data and turning it into information is costly, and the periodicity of these studies is relatively low. It is a fact that governments require poverty measurement data in order to identify priority themes, and to establish focalized programs and actions for guaranteeing social and economic development.

4   Measuring Poverty

Eagle et al. [7] showed that the diversity on social ties could be a proxy for measuring the economic well-being of a region. They shaped contact networks, analyzing the source and destiny of all the telephone calls in the United Kingdom and found that the social and spatial diversity between contacts correlate well with the United Kingdom's Index of Multiple Deprivation. Later, [9] studied 5 months of mobile phone data from Cote d'Ivoire, and proposed a linear regression model for estimating poverty, based on the traffic of phone calls between regions, diversity on calls and the introversion of the regions. In a further work [10] focused on the analysis of the mobile phone carriers antennas activity, rather than individuals calls, and they claim that their approach could provide a more detailed information on which specific zones suffers of poverty.

However, the aggregated data from telephone companies are essential for this kind of analysis and it is not always publicly available. The mentioned works also focused on the country or regional level, but do not provide answers at the community level, which is useful to describe how citizens suffer poverty and how their particular problems could be addressed. These works collect data using opportunistic sensing, and we aim to find out how appropriate it is to follow a participatory sensing approach. We are not aware of previous attempts to do this, but we think that a good starting point is to take clues from the sociometer device experiments proposed by [3].

4.1   Reinterpreting the Sociometer

Our idea is to develop a small, portable, and inexpensive device, composed with the necessary sensors to acquire data related to mobility and human interactions. Some of the parameters to be sensed (either directly or inferred) include proximity to others, orientation, and geographical position. Currently we are designing and testing our first laboratory prototypes using the ARM mbed IoT Device Platform [1]. Our approach follows user-centered design techniques, informed through interviews with our stakeholders, as well as participatory and non participatory observation for generating our next prototypes. The form factor for such device should be wearable, in order to be able to carrying it in a keychain ring, using a necklace or maybe incorporated in the design of community clothes.

For designing and testing our device, we closely collaborate with the Agents of Change Society at their project headquarters, the Transborder Farmlab [2], located in the neighborhood of Camino Verde in Tijuana. Camino Verde is a community of about 45,000 individuals, where near to 70% of the families living there are headed by single mothers. Camino Verde was previously known as one of the most dangerous neighborhoods of Tijuana, with the higher indexes on alimentary poverty on the city, suffering also of insecurity and the lack of public services. The Transborder Farmlab opened in 2012 as a community space, where workshops, artistic events and sustainability projects are developed, for empowering citizens to create ideas for increasing their own income and shaping a better quality of life.

5   Conclusions and Future Work

We strongly believe that the smart city discourse would be enriched when it focuses on proposing and designing technologies for the specific problems of developing countries, some of which do not exist or do not affect in the same way the developed countries.

We consider that designing with low cost in mind, should make the transit to the smarter city easier for our developing regions, recognizing our own culture and way of life. We are currently on the stage of designing and testing laboratory prototypes for supporting our wearable device concept. We plan to utilize user-centered design techniques for generating our final prototypes and developing a study into the wild for assessing its usability and utility with the help of the Camino Verde neighborhood community.

We aim to show if our proposed focus would offer new tools for gathering data related with the poverty phenomena and at the same time, to empower citizens' participation. We believe that these tools are essential when deploying smart cities technology in our development regions.

References

1. ARM mbed IoT Device Platform. http://www.mbed.com/en/
2. Cárdenas Osuna, R.: El laboratorio de la granja transfronteriza. Letral, pp. 138–151 (2011)
3. Choudhury, T., Pentland, A.: The sociometer: A wearable device for understanding human networks. In: CSCW 2002 Workshop (2002)
4. Consejo Nacional de Evaluación de la Política de Desarrollo Social, Informe de pobreza en México, 2012, México, DF (2013)
5. Center for Urban Innovation at Arizona State University, Smart cities financing guide: expert analysis of 28 municipal finance tools for city leaders investing in the future, Arizona (2014)
6. Diario Oficial de la Federación, Lineamientos y criterios generales para la definición, identificación y medición de la pobreza. 16 de junio de 2010. México, DF (2010)
7. Eagle, N., Macy, M., Claxton, R.: Network diversity and economic development. Science **328**(5981), 1029–1031 (2010)
8. ISO, ISO 37120:2014 Sustainable development of communities indicators for city services and quality of life (2014)
9. Smith, C., Mashadi, A., Capra, L.: Ubiquitous sensing for mapping poverty in developing countries. In: In Data for Development: Net Mobi 2013 (2013)
10. Smith, C., Mashadi, A., Capra, L.: Poverty on the cheap. In: Proceedings of the 32nd Annual ACM Conference on Human Factors in Computing Systems - CHI 2014, pp. 511–520 (2014)
11. United Nations, Concise Report on the World Population Situation in 2014, New York (2014)
12. United Nations, Millennium Development Goals and beyond 2015. http://www.un.org/millenniumgoals/

Smart Disaster Response Through Localized Short-Term Cooperation

Youna Jung[(✉)]

Department of Computer and Information Sciences, Virginia Military Institute,
Lexington, VA, USA
jungy@vmi.edu

Abstract. As the information and communication technology (ICT) has
advanced, research on smart cities that take advantage of ICT has been extensively
conducted to improve resource management and enhance citizen's quality of life.
Disaster management is a critical component in smart cities to secure citizen's
safety. From experiences with recent disasters such as tsunamis, earthquakes, and
hurricanes, we can easily find evidence that shows an urgent need for intelligent
disaster management systems. In a disaster situation, a disaster response system
must address not only long-term needs that require continuous disaster recovery,
but also short-term needs that require ephemeral cooperation between people and
smart devices nearby. However, existing disaster-responsive applications have
been based on pre-established long-term relationships and focused on communication among human users. To address the limitation of disaster management, in
this paper, the smart disaster response system (DRS) is proposed. The Smart DRS
allows connectivity among users and sensing devices with short-term relationships based on geographical location within. The approach allows effective
sharing of disaster information and immediate cooperation within communities
in a manner that reconciles with requirements of security and privacy.

Keywords: Smart city · Disaster response system · Temporary social network ·
Overlay network · Localized cooperation

1 Introduction

As evidenced by experience from recent natural disasters such as the Tsunami and
earthquake in Japan, and Hurricanes in the USA (Sandy and Katrina) and Haiti (Fay,
Gustav, Hannah, and Ike), it is essential to develop smart disaster response systems in
order to secure citizen's safety in smart cities. In a disaster situation, long-term needs
coexist with short-term needs that must be addressed in a timely fashion. For examples,
people in disaster areas need to continuously receive updated disaster data that are related
to local areas (such as flooded areas nearby or the collapse of the nearest freeway) to
exactly know the situation of the surrounding areas and quickly escape from disaster
areas, as well as related to the overall situation, such as the path of a Hurricane. One of

© ICST Institute for Computer Sciences, Social Informatics and Telecommunications Engineering 2017
E. Sucar et al. (Eds.): AFI 2016, LNICST 179, pp. 12–21, 2017.
DOI: 10.1007/978-3-319-49622-1_3

the short-term needs arise in search and rescue situations, where it is critical to dynamically establish communication between citizens in distress and nearby emergency response personnel.

The ubiquity of smart mobile devices and the advent of online social networks (OSNs) have enabled a paradigm shift in how users interact with each other, allowing unprecedented ease in discovering and communicating with their peers at anytime and anywhere. To respond to disasters using such emerging technologies, some mobile applications have been developed, such as the Shelter Finder App of the Red Cross [1], the Outbreaks Near Me App of the HealthMap [2], the Disaster Alert App of the Pacific Disaster Center [3], the SOS+App [4], and the HelpBridge App of Microsoft [5]. However, current mobile applications focus on sharing or alerting of general emergency events, and do not fully exploit the potential benefits of tapping into mobile devices and OSNs in enhancing the ability of users to organize disaster-responsive communities and cooperate with each other during emergencies. For example, in a search and rescue scenario, a distressed person with a mobile device can potentially use sensor information (GPS coordinates, images and audio) in combination with user-input messages to a disaster community of nearby users as valuable information to assist in their rescue. To this end, the following challenges must be addressed.

1. It is desirable that users are able to establish short-term social relationships to peers that may not be in their circle of friends, such as other users who are nearby within a geographical area. Typical OSNs, however, connect users to friends who are selected by users themselves based on relationships built over a long period of time. In disaster situations, in which short-term relationships with strangers are necessary, users may not be able to effectively discover and communicate with others who may be in the best position to provide help, such as nearby emergency response teams. Existing OSNs are thus fundamentally hindered by these constraints.

2. Existing centralized OSNs may become unavailable during a disaster due to outages in the network. For instance, users may not be able to connect to the central services of Twitter [6] or Facebook [7] in a disaster situation. Furthermore, considerations on performance, capability, and privacy are additional limitations of traditional OSNs, as they require all information to be processed by (and shared with) a provider.

3. Real-time processing and sharing of local disaster data captured by environmental sensors and people in the surrounding areas is essential for effective evacuation and rescue. Furthermore, disaster data must be retained for disaster recovery in the future. However, centralized data management may not be working in a disaster situation.

To meet the challenges above, I propose a smart disaster response system (Smart DRS) that operates on the basis of on-demand collaboration between eligible objects, including smart devices and users nearby, over ad-hoc social networks. The rest of the paper is organized as follows. In Sect. 2, I describe our vision for innovative disaster response and identify the contributions of the Smart DRS. In Sect. 3, I explain an overall architecture and operational flow and then describe an example use case. In Sect. 4, I present evaluation plans and, in Sect. 5, provide a comparison with existing approaches for location-based disaster response. In Sect. 6, I summarize our contributions and future research directions.

2   Disaster Response in Smart Cities

2.1   Requirements for Innovative Disaster Response

To guarantee the safety of citizen, a disaster response system needs to support the following features.

1. **Creation and maintenance of localized disaster community** – As stated earlier, in disaster situations, localized communities can play a key role by enabling people closely located each other to receive sensing information from nearby sensors, share local information, and provide/obtain help to/from nearby people. OSNs have great potential to facilitate wide and rapid dissemination of disaster information and recruitment of nearby people because of its huge user set and, in fact, many location-based social networks (LBSNs) have been proposed. However, existing LBSNs have not much considered relationships between human users and devices such as sensors and mission-oriented cooperation.
2. **On-demand creation and management of ad-hoc localized social networks** – As users are increasingly interacting with peers through OSN services and applications, OSN services that mediate user communication raise major concerns in perform-ance, fault-tolerance, and privacy. Therefore, it is required to dynamically establish and maintain connections between peers without interference of a centralized server.
3. **Localized disaster data management** – For more prompt process and analysis of localized disaster information, distributed management of disaster data management is required. Furthermore, disaster data can be retained even if infrastructures and central data servers are destroyed.

2.2   Disaster Response with the Smart DRS

The Smart DRS allows users to effectively cope with a disaster by discovering essential sensors and users who can give vital information and help and communicating with them using their mobile devices. It dynamically creates ad-hoc social overlay networks that encompass mobile devices of users and sensors to enable real-time information sharing and knowledge creation on top of in a peer-to-peer (P2P) so that it is not constrained by the availability, capability and privacy considerations of central services. The followings are the contributions of the Smart DRS.

1. **Short-term static and dynamic localized disaster community** – The Smart DRS extends the organization and cooperation mechanism of Whistle [8] that creates a large-scale user pool with structured user contexts while minimizing user interfer-ence, searches the most suitable user in real-time, and organizes emergency communities with eligible and available users. Unlike Whistle, in the Smart DRS, environmental sensors can be also a community's members. Basically, the commun-ities are divided into two types, the static community and the dynamic community. A static community is a location-based community that is automatically created by a corresponding a local manager when a disaster occurs, while a dynamic community is a goal-oriented community that is created upon a distressed person's request by

one or more local managers. To organize more effective communities, the Smart DRS searches suitable objects in real-time and search criteria can be varied depending on a community's goal. Once a community is created, members start to communicate and cooperate with each other. Currently, the Smart DRS is supposed to provide four types of cooperation services: (1) Posting (Passive information sharing), (2) Alerting (Active information sharing such as notifying users in disaster area), (3) Donate (Passive cooperation such as donation of water, food, or shelter), and (4) Rescue (Active dynamic cooperation between users and smart devices).

2. **Ad-hoc localized social overlay networks** – The Smart DRS requires instant peer-to-peer (P2P) communication among social peers nearby. To this end, the Smart DRS leverage SocialVPN [9] to incorporate bootstrapping through social connections. SocialVPN is a network overlay technique that embed social links in its topology by providing virtual private IP networking, in order to support mobile peers, unstructured P2P routing, and network resilience. At the networking layer, the overlay can be visualized as a communication system where every participating device (e.g. mobile, desktop, or cloud instances) has virtual private links to each of their social peers that are determined based on their proximity. Such an overlay provides a foundation to address privacy, fault-tolerance and performance concerns. This is because it allows users to leverage OSN services to discover and establish peer relationships, while bypassing the centralized service to communicate with social peers. Direct peer-to-peer communication is important when privacy is desired, when the exposed OSN interfaces are performance-limiting and/or limit scalability (e.g. OSN imposes limits on size or rate of requests), or when the OSN service is unavailable.

3. **Hybrid-decentralized management of disaster data** – A localized disaster communities can take an important role of sharing and retaining of disaster data. In the Smart DRS, each disaster community is able to provide vital information about disaster to community members and store disaster data in a community manager node or member nodes. While localized communities deal with localized data sharing and processing, a centralized disaster management system gathers all disaster data from local communities and conducts a comprehensive analysis on them.

The Smart DRS consists of three response layers as shown in Fig. 1: the physical layer, the localized response layer, and the generic response layer. The physical layer represents our real world, and contains immobile objects (such as local managers and fixed sensors) and mobile objects (such as human and vehicles). Each object is an end node of a disaster-responsive social network and has short-term connections with previously-unknown users and sensors in order to effectively respond to disasters. Ordinarily, each user performs normal social networking tasks – for example, posting a message and making friends through existing OSNs. When a disaster occurs, users, who turn on the proposed disaster response application, are automatically involved in the nearest local community based on their current locations, and are able to communicate with their nearby friends. Furthermore, if necessary, a rescue community consisting of necessary objects can be dynamically created for active cooperation. The major objective of the localized response layer is to manage local communities and local disaster data. In the generic response layer, a centralized disaster management system collects and analyses all disaster data and announces generic disaster situations.

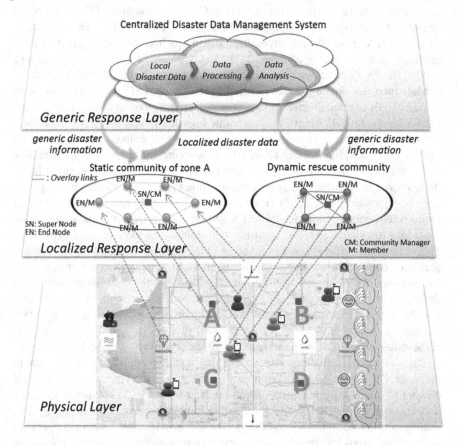

Fig. 1. Disaster Management with the Smart DRS

Unlike existing disaster response applications using pre-established relationships only and focusing on comprehensive analysis on disaster data in a centralized fashion, the Smart DRS allows people to communicate and cooperate with necessary peers regardless of long-term relationships within geospatial proximity and a common goal. With the Smart DRS, distressed people can give and receive vital information as a data provider and consumer, and furthermore actively contribute to the rescue of people in danger. From the perspective of disaster data handling, the Smart DRS employs local managers that govern local communities, initially process local disaster data, and deliver data to the central server. This approach allows providing and storing disaster data associated with certain geospatial area for effective post-disaster management and disaster modeling, even if the connection to the central DRS is damaged.

3 Smart Disaster Response System

3.1 Architecture

The Smart DRS consists of a number of local managers and object applications that are connected through disaster-responsive social networks as shown in Fig. 2.

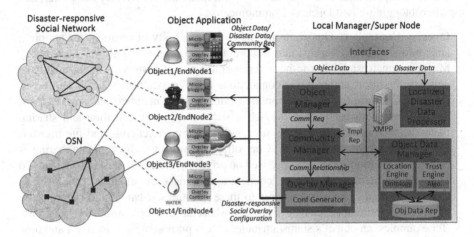

Fig. 2. Overall architecture of Smart DRS

A local manager is a trusted party that complies with laws and regulations relevant to privacy protection and it consists of five components below.

- **Object Manager:** The main task of this component is to handle objects' entrance and leaving by interacting with a local manager's own XMPP server which acts as an OSN server. The Object Manager receives an object's XMPP account when the object enters a zone assigned to a local manager, and shares that account information with the Community Manager and the Object Data Manager.

- **Object Data Manager**: This component manages object-related data, including dynamic location information and trust values of objects. If requested, it searches eligible objects based on objects' conditions in real time.

- **Community Manager**: This component aims to organize a localize disaster –responsive community with most suitable users. When receiving a request, it delivers required information specified in a corresponding template to the Context Manager. If the Object Data Manager returns a set of candidates, it checks availabilities of candidates and creates a member list with only available users.

- **Overlay Manager**: The goal of this component is to dynamically create overlay network configuration files for each member so that members can automatically establish social connections among them. To do so, it gets members' XMPP OSN accounts from the Community Manager, generates virtual IP addresses for members, and then distributes the generated configurations to member's applications.

– **Localized Disaster Data Processor**: The module manages disaster data produced by objects, generates information about local disaster situation, and analyzes disaster risks in near real-time. For better scalability, the Localized Data Processor will leverage existing technologies in big data management and cloud computing to accommodate a sudden burst of data flooding from massive population in the future.

An object application is composed of two components: the Overlay Controller, and the Microblogging-based Disaster Communicator.

– **Overlay Controller**: This controller takes responsibility of creating, maintaining, and removing social overlay links. According to a configuration file that the Overlay Manager sent, it establishes ad-hoc overlay connections between members, maintains network condition, and removes connections when cooperation is terminated.
– **Disaster Communicator**: This communicator displays members and enables them to cooperate with each other through a rich set of communication and sharing methods, such as text messaging, text/audio/video conferencing, and file transfer. Each communicator has an Access Controller that prevents indiscriminate sharing of private information and resources based on privacy policies of users and devices. To facilitate immediate yet secure cooperation in disaster situations, the Access Controller should be able to answer to three questions: what should be protected during cooperation for each type of objects; what can be criteria to authorize an access (for examples, an object's status/attribute, access purpose/action, or role); and how we can enforce security policies in a decentralized manner. As an initial step, the Smart DRS leverages the community-centric property-based access control model (CPBAC) [10], a cooperation-aware access control model for OSN users. Since the CPBAC model considers human users only, a more comprehensive model that can be applied to cooperation between sensors and users should be applied in near future.

3.2 Operational Flow

In a disaster situation, the Smart DRS is operated according to the following operational flow.

1. **Object registration** – An object including a user should register in the Smart DRS before taking or giving cooperative help in disaster situation. A user can sign up with his/her existing OSN account (for example, Facebook or Twitter) and enter additional contexts in the central server. With a user's OSN username received from the Object Manager, the Object Data Manager fetches various user data from an OSN using APIs that the OSN provides. Once the Object Data Manager retrieves all related data from the OSN, the Object Manager creates a sticky object data set, encrypts the sticky data set with its private key, and sends it to the object.
2. **Object joining in a static disaster community** – When a mobile object (such as human users and vehicles) enters the zone of a local manager, it automatically sends a joining request with its sticky data set to a local manager. Information about available local managers may be pre-configured in the application, or discovered by querying nearby devices. The nearest local manager receives the request, decrypts

the object's sticky data set with the public key of the central server, and maintains those data until the object leaves the zone.

3. **On-demand creation of a dynamic rescue community across multiple zones** – When receiving a request for disaster rescue from a user, a Community Manager retrieves a community template selected by the requester from the Template Repository and asks the Context Manager to find out candidates who meet eligibility conditions. In candidate search, the primary criterion is users' locations. If there is no eligible users and the local manager broadcasts the request to neighbor managers. After receiving the candidate lists from neighbors, the Community Manager selects best candidates and sends an invitation to each candidate with information about a rescue community. With only available candidates, it finalizes a list of members, while the Overlay Manager creates configuration files for each member.

4. **Secure and unrestricted cooperation among members** – As soon as a member object receives a configuration file and a member list, it establishes ephemeral social overlay connections between members and runs microblogging communicator. All conversations and resources shared through the communicator are protected from unauthorized accesses of non-members by the Access Controller.

5. **Localized disaster data processing** – The localized disaster data processor extracts disaster situations such as local torrential rainfalls in its zone based on user-generated data and sensing data. Note that the third, fourth, and fifth operations can be operated in parallel.

6. **Community dissolution** – When an object is out of the zone, the Object Manager removes the data related to the object. This may be accomplished by obtaining GPS coordinates from the device. In case of a dynamic community, if a community's goal is achieved, a leader of a community notifies members of the end of cooperation, and in turn each object application removes all overlay connections with a community's members.

3.3 Use Case Scenario

For better understanding, we describe an example use cases of the Smart DRS in case of dynamic cooperation for search and rescue. Let's assume that Bob breaks his leg while escaping a disaster area. He sends a request for emergency rescue with his location to its local manager node. Let's assume that Bob gets injured in the zone C (See the Fig. 1). The local manager of the zone C broadcasts Bob's location and necessary capability/object types into neighbor manager nodes in the zone A, B, and D. After receiving response from neighbors, the manager of the zone C federates responses and dynamically creates a rescue community with eligible objects. Finally, two people who are close to him assist in search and rescue. They all then can escape successfully. Compared to existing passive cooperation through OSNs, the Smart DRS can promote active rescue by creating a dynamic community. To protect Bob's privacy, his rescue request and medical/location information are shared with only a few selected members.

4 Evaluation Plan

To test the performance and reliability of the proposed Smart DRS, I plan to evaluate it in two steps: (1) The individual evaluation that tests each component of the Smart DRS and (2) the integrated evaluation that tests the performance of an integrated DRS based on several example scenarios.

For the individual evaluation, I plan to create the set of synthetic data related to users and devices by randomly selecting values among values actually used for each attribute types of objects. To do this, well-known ontologies (for example, GeoNames [11] ontology for location data) and the occupation profiles of the United States department of Labor will be used. Using the synthetic data set, I will evaluate the accuracy and speed of the candidate search algorithm and the effectiveness of the community management model. To test the organization management model and the cooperation model, I plan to simulate objects' cooperation based on few scenarios including members' failures, and evaluate the goal achievement rate. To measure the performance of the access control, I will check the privacy violations rate of shared data and resources. After completing individual evaluations, I plan to develop a prototype by integrating individual components, and test the overall performance of the prototype from the perspectives of localized disaster data processing and on-demand creation of static and dynamic disaster communities.

5 Related Work

Location-based Social Networks (LBSNs) aim to enable social users to share location-embedded information with friends and also make new friends who are recommended based on similarities in locations in the physical world as well as their location-tagged media content [12]. At present, there is a variety of LBSNs; for example, NeerbyFeed [13], Facebook Places [14], and Sonar [15]. According to the study of TNS in 2012 [16], mobiles users are increasingly using location-based services. Around a quarter uses it to find restaurants and entertainment venues (26%) and one in five is using it to find their friends nearby (22%).

Unlike existing LBSNs that are mainly focusing on sharing of geo-tagged information and recommending nearby friends, the Smart DRS focuses on dynamic organization of local communities and cooperation management within communities. Existing LBSNs process location-embedded data in a centralized manner to find interesting places, events, and people, while the Smart DRS processes location-tagged disaster data in decentralized manner to grasp local disaster situations. Above all, existing LBSNs basically consider human users only. In contrast, the Smart DRS aims to create localized ad-hoc social networks that include computing devices, such as sensors and vehicles, as well as users. Furthermore, existing LBSNs is insufficient for disaster response due to lack of real-time organization and cooperation management mechanisms.

6   Conclusions

To address an urgent need for short-term ad-hoc connectivity between nearby people and sensors in disaster situations, I propose a smart disaster response system that enables distressed people to connect with each other regardless of pre-established relationships, share vital information related to surrounding areas, and rescue distressed people without serious privacy loss. For complete disaster response service, the following work should be conducted in the future.

- Distributed data processing under the constraints of computing resources
- Disaster-specific situation model
- Organization, cooperation, trust, and access control model considering sensors as well as human users
- Resilient peer-to-peer overlay routing in situations where the SocialVPN XMPP service is unavailable, or when Internet connectivity of a subset of devices is restricted and only ad-hoc connections to nearby Internet-connected devices (e.g. over Bluetooth) are available.

References

1. Red Cross Shelter Finder App. http://www.redcross.org/mobile-apps/shelter-finder-app
2. Outbreaks Near Me App. http://healthmap.org/mobile
3. Disaster Alert App. http://www.pdc.org/solutions/tools/disaster-alert-app
4. SOS+App. https://plerts.com/mobile-apps/sos-plus-emergency-alert/
5. HelpBridge App. http://www.microsoft.com/about/corporatecitizenship/en-us/nonprofits/Helpbridge.aspx
6. Twitter. https://twitter.com
7. Facebook. https://www.facebook.com
8. Jung, Y., Figueiredo, R., Fortes, J.: Location-based timely cooperation over social private network. In: 10th International Conference on Collaborative Computing: Networking, Applications and Worksharing (CollaborateCom), 25 October, pp. 388–396 (2014)
9. Juste, P.S., Wolinsky, D., Boykin, P.O., Covington, M.J., Figueiredo, R.J.: SocialVPN: enabling wide-area collaboration with integrated social and overlay networks. Comput. Netw. **54**(12), 1926–1938 (2012)
10. Jung, Y., Joshi, J.B.: CPBAC: property-based access control model for secure cooperation in online social networks. Computer and Security **41**, 19–39 (2014)
11. GeoNames Ontology, http://www.geonames.org/ontology/ontology_ v3.1.rdf
12. Zheng, Y., Zhou, X.: Location-based social networks. In: Zheng, Y., Zhou, X. (eds.) Computing with Spatial Trajectories. Springer, New York (2011). ISBN 978-1-4614-1629-6
13. NeerbyFeed. http://www.nearbyfeed.com
14. Facebook Places. https://www.facebook.com/places
15. Sonar. https://play.google.com/store/apps/details?id=me.sonar.android&hl=en
16. TNS, "Two thirds of world's mobile users signal they want to be found", April 2012. http://www.tnsglobal.com/press-release/two-thirds-world´s-mobile-users-signal-they-want-be-found

Towards a Smart Highway Lighting System Based on Road Occupancy: Model Design and Simulation

Ahmad M. Mustafa, Omar M. Abubakr, Ahmed H. Derbala,
Essam Ahmed, and Bassem Mokhtar[✉]

Department of Electrical Engineering, Faculty of Engineering,
Alexandria University, Alexandria, Egypt
ahm.alexeng@gmail.com, omar.abubakr.alexeng@gmail.com,
eng.ahmedhassanderbala@gmail.com, essam.ahmed.alexeng@gmail.com,
bmokhtar@alexu.edu.eg

Abstract. Energy saving is a major aspect of smart cities, so optimizing highway lighting is essential, as it consumes considerable amounts of energy. However, there is a remarkable potential for reducing this consumption through smart lighting techniques. This paper introduces preliminary design and simulation for a smart highway lighting management system based on road occupancy. Wireless Sensors Network (WSN) detects the presence of vehicles along the road, and controls lamps accordingly. The system is simulated and optimized using a realistic probabilistic model for vehicles traffic, taking the advantage of simulation to provide estimation for expected energy saving rates; in contrary to previous works depending only on rough calculations or real-time results after implementation. According to simulation results, the proposed system can save up to 57.4% of power consumption compared to conventional lighting systems.

Keywords: Smart cities · Smart highway lighting · Energy saving · Wireless sensors network · Traffic modeling · Traffic simulation

1 Introduction

Smart cities-oriented research, towards green computing and information technology, attracts large number of researchers nowadays. One of the main challenges in smart cities is developing smart traffic and lighting management systems, saving more energy and minimizing polluting emissions.

It's essential to optimize highway lighting in smart cities, as it represents a significant portion of energy consumption, especially in densely populated and industrial countries. In the United States for example, 51TWh were consumed in roadway lighting in 2010 [1].

In conventional lighting systems, light was switched on at dusk and switched off at dawn by manual operation, and then smart controller was used to switch street lighting on and off automatically, based on sunrise/sunset times or light intensity of controller surroundings [2]. Most of city street lights use the pattern of "full night-lights, constant illumination lighting", which not only causes much energy waste, but also loss of lamp life [3].

© ICST Institute for Computer Sciences, Social Informatics and Telecommunications Engineering 2017
E. Sucar et al. (Eds.): AFI 2016, LNICST 179, pp. 22–31, 2017.
DOI: 10.1007/978-3-319-49622-1_4

In highways, energy is wasted in lighting the whole road continuously, as not all the road is occupied with vehicles during operation time. One of smart street lighting techniques is controlling street lighting upon road occupancy. When there is less traffic in the road, some lamps can be turned off or dimmed, and the system can still meet the lighting requirements, saving energy and also ensuring traffic safety. The integration of this methodology with other smart lighting techniques [4] will ensure outstanding energy saving levels.

This paper introduces preliminary design and simulation for a smart highway lighting system based on road occupancy. The proposed system uses Wireless Sensors Network (WSN) to detect the presence of vehicles along the road. According to occupancy of the road, the system determines whether to switch on, switch off or dim specific number of lamps. The whole road is divided into sections; when a section is occupied with vehicles, it will be illuminated; otherwise, the lamps will be turned off or dimmed.

The system is simulated and optimized using a realistic probabilistic model for vehicles traffic, including various traffic conditions. Simulation is based on "Nagel-Schreckenberg" discrete model for road traffic simulation [5].

The novelty of this work consists in providing a methodology for using traffic flow model to simulate the behavior of a smart highway lighting system. This methodology provides estimation for energy saving rates expected from the system when applied in real life, as well as other useful analytical data; in contrary to previous works which depend on rough calculations or real-time results after implementation [6, 7]. The same methodology can be very useful in simulating traffic-related solutions, such as Vehicular Cloud Computing (VCC) and Vehicle-to-vehicle (V2V) technologies.

The rest of this paper is organized as follows: Sect. 2 discusses the main idea and structure of our system. Section 3 introduces the mathematical model used for simulation. The simulation setup and the obtained results are presented in Sect. 4. Finally, Sect. 5 concludes the paper and highlights our future work.

2 Main Concept

The idea of our proposed system is based on dividing the road into sections; each section represents the distance between two successive light poles. WSN node is attached to each pole; including a sensor to detect vehicles presence, and a wireless transceiver for communication between nodes.

When a section is momentarily unoccupied with vehicles, the lighting pole on the head of this section is turned off or dimmed; otherwise, the lighting pole will be working in full capacity, as shown in Fig. 1.

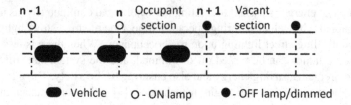

Fig. 1. Nodes distribution along road.

The concept of presence detection depends on counting the number of vehicles occupying a section continuously. Each section has two nodes on its terminals, one responsible for controlling its corresponding lamp, and the other responsible for controlling the next lamp. When a vehicle enters a section "n", the first node increments the counter "C_{-n}" by 1, and when the vehicle leaves the section and enters the next one, the second node decrements the counter "C_{-n}" by 1. Lamp turns off or dims only when counter is equal to 0 (i.e. section is unoccupied). The same process is repeated along the road for all sections. A flowchart for the mentioned process is shown in Fig. 2.

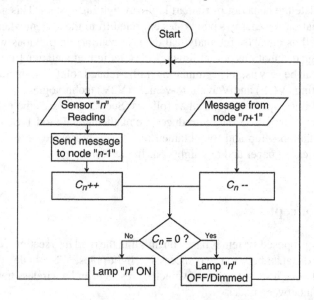

Fig. 2. Flowchart for node process.

This distributed control approach is more efficient and reliable than more centralized approaches [8, 9]. When a node fails, it will have a very limited effect on the whole system (i.e. the preceding section and succeeding section only). This also insures less complexity in communication between nodes.

The data collected by WSN nodes, representing number of vehicles in each section, can be very valuable in monitoring traffic status along the road. Each node can be equipped with a remote communication module (e.g. GPRS module) to send this data to a central traffic monitoring and control server.

3   Mathematical Model

Modeling and simulation are essential procedures when implementing a novel solution, especially when the simulated model involves numerous variables including random ones. This is the case with our intelligent lighting system methodology.

In order to simulate smart lighting system based on road occupancy, a realistic model for traffic flow is a necessity. It's crucial to build a model for traffic flow that captures the characteristics of real traffic, yet sufficiently simple to allow efficient numerical treatment.

The best way to realize a traffic model on computer is discretization of continuous quantities. Continuous analogue numbers could be treated at user programming level by software, but there would be considerable performance degradation [10].

Our simulation is based on the pioneering "Nagel-Shreckenberg" cellular automaton discrete model for traffic simulation. More developed and complex versions of this model can be used in future work to provide modeling for more traffic conditions and scenarios [11].

The "Nagel-Shreckenberg" model is defined on a one-dimensional array of L sites and with open boundary conditions. Each site may either be occupied by one vehicle, or it may be empty. Each vehicle has an integer velocity with values between 0 and v_{max}. For an arbitrary configuration, one update of the system consists of the following four consecutive steps, which are performed in parallel for all vehicles:

1. **Acceleration:** if the velocity v of a vehicle is lower than v_{max} and if the distance to the next car ahead is larger than $v + 1$, the speed is advanced by one $[v \rightarrow v + 1]$.
2. **Slowing down** (due to other cars): if a vehicle at site i sees the next vehicle at site $i + j$ (with $j \leq v$), it reduces its speed to $j - 1$ $[v \rightarrow j - 1]$.
3. **Randomization:** with probability p the velocity of each vehicle is decreased by one $[v \rightarrow v - 1]$.
4. **Car motion:** each vehicle is advanced v sites.

This model was mainly used to simulate traffic in single-lane ring (closed system) or bottleneck situation. To make the model suitable for highway traffic simulation, we use bottleneck situation as following:

1. When the leftmost (site 1) is empty, we occupy it with a car of velocity zero.
2. At the right site (i.e. the end of the street), we delete cars on the right most six sites, thus producing an open boundary [5].

These rules are repeated each time sample of simulation. By the end of the simulation, we have a two-dimensional matrix expressing traffic characteristics through definite road length and simulation time, as shown in Fig. 3. Thus, we can use this matrix to simulate the behavior of our smart lighting system accordingly. When a section (i.e. number of consecutive cells) is empty, the light pole corresponding to it is turned off or dimmed (see Sect. 2).

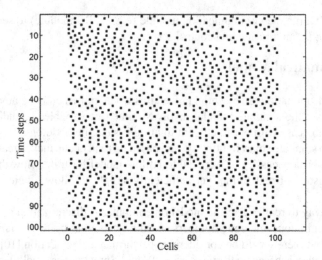

Fig. 3. 100 × 100 cells from traffic matrix, each empty cell is represented as a white pixel, and each occupant cell is represented as a black pixel.

By the end, we will have a new matrix representing the status of each light pole per time sample. This matrix is analyzed to get estimated energy saving levels and other system parameters. This procedure is repeated for different scenarios and cases (i.e. different spacing between light poles, different dimming levels, etc.).

4 Simulation

4.1 Simulation Setup

The model discussed above was implemented in MATLAB, using a PC with Intel Core-i7 2.00 GHz processor, and 8.00 GB of RAM. The following parameters were used:

- L (road length) = 4000 cell. Each cell represents 7.5 m, which is the space occupied by a single vehicle in complete jam [5]. Thus:

$$Road\ length = 7.5\ m \times 4000\ cell = 30\ km \qquad (1)$$

- v_{max} (maximum velocity) = 4 cells/time sample (110 km/h).
- p (probability of each vehicle to decrease its velocity by 1) is 0.2 with uniform distribution. The deceleration rate depends on the road condition and also on the skill and personality of driver [10].
- T_s (time of sample): as the length of one cell is 7.5 m, and maximum velocity (v_{max}) is assumed to be 110 km/h, which is common speed limit in highways, we can deduce time for one sample [5]:

$$1\,hr \rightarrow 110\,km$$

$$T_s \rightarrow 7.5\,m \times v_{max}$$

$$\therefore T_s = 7.5\frac{m}{cell} \times 4\frac{cell}{timesample} \times \frac{60 \times 60}{110 \times 1000}\frac{s}{m} \approx 1\frac{s}{timesample} \qquad (2)$$

- T (total simulation time): total number of samples is 40000, representing 40000 s (i.e. approximately 11 h.).
- ρ (traffic density): initial density is assumed to be 0.15 car/cell. However, density changes w.r.t. time due to the open boundary conditions assumed in simulation. After simulation, density was found to have decreased reaching a mean value of 0.106 car/cell.
- N (number of light poles): equals to number of sections, as each section has 1 light pole.

$$N = 4000\,cell \div 4\frac{cell}{section} = 1000\,section \qquad (3)$$

- h (section length): section length is the distance between two consecutive light poles. Simulation is repeated for different values of h (4, 5 cells), and for treating each two consecutive poles as one section (i.e. $h = 8$, 10 cells).

The discussed parameters are summarized in Table 1.

Table 1. Simulation parameters.

Parameter	Value
Fixed parameters	
L (road length)	4000 cells
v_{max} (maximum velocity)	4 cells/time sample (110 km/h)
p (deceleration probability)	0.2
T_s (time of one sample)	1 s
T (total time)	40000 s
ρ (initial density)	0.15 car/cell
Variable parameter	
h (section length)	4, 5, 8, 10 cells

4.2 Simulation Results

Energy Saving. Before applying the smart lighting system, lamps are ON during the whole operation time, but after applying the system, some lamps will be OFF/dimmed when their sections are empty. Thus the energy saving factor E_o is the ratio between the sum of number of OFF lamps per second after applying system $n(t)$, and sum of number of ON lamps per second, before applying system (i.e. all lamps = N). In Fig. 4, $n(t)$ is plotted against time for section length $h = 4$ cells.

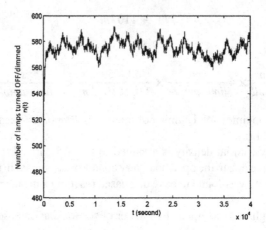

Fig. 4. Number of OFF/dimmed lamps $n(t)$ plotted against time (s), at $h = 4$ cells.

Equation (4) calculates the energy saving factor E_o:

$$E_o = \frac{\sum_{t=1}^{T} n(t)}{N \times T} \tag{4}$$

When simulation was performed according to mentioned parameters at $h = 4$ cells, energy saving factor appeared to be (57.4%), assuming that the lamp will be turned OFF when its section is vacant. This ratio indicates the energy saving achieved after applying the system to conventional lighting systems.

If lamps are dimmed instead of being turned OFF, the energy saving factor will decrease according to dimming level D, knowing that the ratio of LED dimming and energy saving is roughly 1:1 [12]. For example, if lamps are dimmed by 50% instead of being turned OFF, energy saving factor decreases by 50% accordingly, so energy saving factor is (28.7%).

However, the dimming approach seems to be more eligible in practice; taking into account the necessity of providing the driver with sufficient lighting ahead, to ensure safety measures and driver's comfort, as well as the lighting condition of road's neighborhood.

Equation (5) calculates the energy saving factor when lamps are dimmed E:

$$E = D \times \frac{\sum_{t=1}^{T} n(t)}{N \times T} \tag{5}$$

Simulation was repeated for different section lengths h (other parameters unchanged) to study the effect of changing section length on energy saving. When section length (i.e. the separation between two consecutive light poles) was changed to 5 cells (37.5 m), energy saving factor decreased to (46.7%).

Simulation was also repeated for treating every two consecutive light poles as one section (i.e. section length is 8 cells and 10 cells), energy saving factor appeared to decrease at (21%) and (11.6%) respectively.

Figure 5 shows that increasing section length has negative impact on energy saving, which is logical, as increasing section's length means that section is less likely to be unoccupied with vehicles, which means that lamps are less likely to be turned OFF or dimmed.

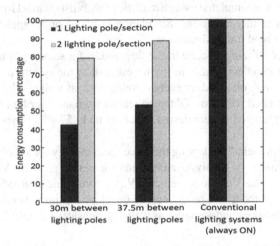

Fig. 5. Energy consumption rates before and after applying the system.

Lamp Switching Frequency. When simulation was performed with the initial param-eters, lamps appeared to be changing their state (ON/OFF or dimmed) with a mean frequency f of 0.70 Hz, which means that the lamp will change its state 42 times per minute. This can only be implemented with systems that use LED lamps with very fast on/off response times [13].

When simulation was repeated for different section lengths h (5, 8, 10 cells), mean lamp switching frequency f was found to be 0.60, 0.28, 0.16 Hz respectively. This shows that when increasing section length, there is a trade-off between energy saving factor E and lamp switching frequency f, as shown in Table 2.

Table 2. Energy saving factor and mean lamp switching frequency for differnt section lengths.

h (Section length)	E_o (Energy saving factor)	f (Lamp switching frequency)
4 cells	57.40%	0.70 Hz
5 cells	46.70%	0.60 Hz
8 cells	21.00%	0.28 Hz
10 cells	11.60%	0.16 Hz

The mentioned results, as well as more results that can be obtained for other system parameters, can play an important role in design and optimization of smart lighting systems, as they give an indication for system's performance in various cases and scenarios.

5 Conclusion

In this paper, a preliminary design for a smart highway lighting system has been introduced. The system was simulated using a realistic probabilistic model for vehicles traffic, including various traffic conditions. Simulation is based on "Nagel-Schreckenberg" discrete model for road traffic simulation.

The concept of utilizing discrete traffic flow model for smart lighting system simulation has shown its effectiveness in giving estimation for system performance. Our simulation results were obtained for energy saving rates, as well as other system parameters at various studied scenarios. Obtained results were used for leveraging the capability of having optimized system design, reaching up to 57.4% of hypothetical energy saving rates.

Our future work includes adapting the same methodology for simulating traffic and resource management in highly dynamic environments, such as Vehicular Cloud Computing (VCC) and Vehicle-to-vehicle (V2V) communication. More mature and complex versions of the traffic model can be developed to provide efficient modeling for more traffic conditions and scenarios as well (e.g. considering multi-lane road traffic).

Acknowledgment. This work is a part of a graduation project at Department of Electrical Engineering, Faculty of Engineering, Alexandria University. We would like to thank all members of the team which yielded this research (Abdullah Nasser, Abdullah Fathy, Ahmed M. Samy, Ayman M. Abdel-Nasser, Ayman Adel and Amr Youssry). We would like also to thank the SmartCI research center at Faculty of Engineering, Alexandria University, Egypt for their support.

References

1. U.S. Department of Energy. http://www.energy.gov/
2. Chunguo, J., Yan, W., Wenyi, S., Xin, S.: Design of street light pole controller based on WSN. In: IEEE 10th International Conference on Electronic Measurement & Instruments (ICEMI), pp. 147–150 (2011)
3. Lian, L., Li, L.: Wireless dimming system for LED street lamp based on ZigBee and GPRS. In: IEEE 3rd International Conference on System Engineering and Modeling (ICSEM), pp. 100–102 (2012)
4. Castro, M., Jara, A.J., Skarmeta, A.F.G., Smart Lighting solutions for Smart Cities. In: IEEE 27th International Conference on Advanced Information Networking and Applications Workshops (INTICO), pp. 1374–1379 (2013)
5. Nagel, K., Schreckenberg, M.: A cellular automaton model for freeway traffic. J. Phys. I France **2**, 2221–2229 (1992)

6. Yusoff, Y., Rosli, R., Kamaluddin, M., Samad, M.: Towards smart street lighting system in Malaysia. In: IEEE Symposium on Wireless Technology and Applications (ISWTA), pp. 301–305 (2013)

7. Mahoor, M., Najafaabadi, T., Salmasi, F.: A smart street lighting control system for optimization of energy consumption and lamp life. In: IEEE 22nd Iranian Conference on Electrical Engineering (ICEE), pp. 1290–1294 (2014)

8. Lavric, A., Popa, V., Sfichi, S.: Street lighting control system based on large-scale WSN: a step towards a smart city. In: IEEE International Conference and Exposition on Electrical and Power Engineering (EPE), pp. 673–676 (2014)

9. Wang, Y., Wang, Z.: Design of intelligent residential lighting control system based on ZigBee wireless sensor network and fuzzy controller. In: IEEE International Conference on Machine Vision and Human-machine Interface (MVHI), pp. 561–564 (2010)

10. Cheon, T.: Discrete Models of Traffic Flow eLectures. http://www.kochi-tech.ac.jp/

11. Chauhan, S., Kumar, L.: Survey paper on traffic flow control using cellular automata. IJIEASR **2**, 1–7 (2013)

12. Biery, E., Shearer, T., Ledyard, R., Perkins, D., Feris, M.: Controlling LEDs. Technical white paper by Lutron Electronics Co. (2014)

13. Lavric, A., Popa, V., Finis, L., Simion, D.: The design and implementation of an energy efficient street lighting monitoring and control system. Przegląd Elektrotechniczny (Electrical Review) **11**, 312–316 (2012)

FIoTA 2016

Exploiting Data of the Twitter Social Network Using Sentiment Analysis

David Gonzalez-Marron[✉], David Mejia-Guzman, and Angelica Enciso-Gonzalez

Instituto Tecnológico de Pachuca, Carretera México-Pachuca Km 81.5,
42080 Pachuca, Hidalgo, Mexico
{dgonzalez,a_enciso}@itpachuca.edu.mx,
davidmejia.05@hotmail.com

Abstract. Social Networks nowadays are producing an enormous quantity of data, this data transformed into information could be useful for the decision support systems. A new emerging technology denominated as Sentiment Analysis or Opinion Meaning extracts the opinion or sentiment of a particular text. The Twitter social network is a source of valuable information in simple text and appropriated to use this technology. In this paper is described the process used to select the most suitable algorithms to analyze tweets for particular words written in Spanish, also the results obtained by every algorithm are reported.

Keywords: Future internet · Social networks · Sentiment analysis · NoSQl databases

1 Introduction

Recently, the growth rate in the volume of data produced has caused the generation of technology to manage this huge quantity of data, most of this data is stored in the internet, and every year this tendency of growth continues.

Social networks are a good source of information because users tend to use the web to establish communication among people who share similar interests. Many enterprises are interested in knowing what their customers think about the products or services received, and a good source of information is the exploitation of data stored in social networks.

According to [1] a social network is defined as, a social structure conformed by organizations or individuals with similar interests that permits the creation of a public or semipublic profile in a delimited system, enabling the creation of a user's list to share connections. It is possible for developers the extraction of data contained in several social networks, as Facebook, Twitter, Google plus and others, this paper is oriented to Twitter because the data produced is a simple chain of up to 140 characters by tweet.

2 Sentiment Analysis

Also known as "opinion mining" consists in the extraction of information produced by users (post, blog, etc.) for study or classification [2]. The process for this sentiment

© ICST Institute for Computer Sciences, Social Informatics and Telecommunications Engineering 2017
E. Sucar et al. (Eds.): AFI 2016, LNICST 179, pp. 35–38, 2017.
DOI: 10.1007/978-3-319-49622-1_5

analysis is constituted by the next parts [3]: (a) Tokenization, (b) Word correction, (c) Words grammatical tagging, (d) Word categorization and identification, (e) Morphological analysis of text, and (f) Text properties extraction.

In social media the immediacy and spontaneity of opinions using an automatic sentiment analysis tool permits the translation of human emotions into data, this data can preserve the emotional content of the message and can be used by the taking decision group to improve services or product's qualities. The most valuable features in sentiment analysis are: Polarity, intensity and subjectivity. The polarity is considering if the comment is (positive, negative or neutral), the intensity is referring to how strong the emotion is expressed, and the subjectivity is about whether the source is objective, biased or subjective.

A brief description describing what polarity must consider to evaluate texts is realized below.

Polarity: [4]

Positive words: Words that express happiness or gratitude, usually are adjectives or verbs
Verbs examples: Love, adore, like, enjoy
Adjectives examples: Beautiful, pretty, well, fascinating, etc.
Negative words: Words expressing anger or sadness, regularly are adjectives or verbs
Verbs examples: Hate, annoy, upset, angry, etc.
Adjectives examples: Ugly, awful, bad, boring, etc.
Neutral words: Words that not express negative or positive emotions, usually are nouns, articles or pronouns.
Nouns examples: School, house, dog, football, etc.
Articles examples: The, a, an, etc.
Pronouns examples: I, you, them
Deniers, Cancellers or inversors: Words contained in a phrase or sentence that change its meaning
Negation adverbs: No, never, neither, etc.
Adversative conjunctions: but, yet, nevertheless, etc.

Twitter was selected by several reasons, below are described the most important reasons why we selected this social network:

- Because it is a microblogging free social network used to publish, share and interchange information in real time.
- It is used by different people to express their opinion.
- It contains a great number of posts related to different topics.
- The members of this social network represent different parts of a society.
- People from different regions and countries, interact in this networks.
- People post information in several languages, but it is of our particular interest the messages produced in Spanish.

3   Sentiment Analysis Algorithms

The process defined to realize sentiment analysis [4], was to select some resources and APIs, prioritizing those who could analyze Spanish sentences and that could interact with the python language, as is described in Table 1.

Table 1. Analyzing characteristics of the sentiment algorithms

Sentiment Analysis APIs and Resources	Resource type	Language	Compatibility with Python 2.7	Selected
NLTK	Library of Python	English	No	No
Diccionario marcado con emociones y ponderado para el español	Dictionary	Spanish	No apply	No
Sentiment140	API	English and Spanish	Yes	Yes
TextBlob	API	English	Yes	No
Sentiment Analysis of Meaning Cloud	API	Spanish	Yes	Yes
Bitext's API	API	English and Spanish	Yes	Yes

In order to validate the best performance of Sentiment Algorithms in Spanish, It was developed a set of 100 sentences in Spanish that allowed us to verify the classification efficiency of the three selected twitter API's, in Table 2, a reduced number of six sentences representing typical expected classification are shown, it was detailed the classification process to obtain the sentence type.

Table 2. Reduced set of sentences to validate sentiment analysis in Spanish

Type sentence	Word type conforming the sentence	Example sentence	Sentence classified words			
			Pos. P.	Neg. P.	Neu. P.	N.I.A.
Simple positive	Pos. P + Neu. P.	Ayer fue un excelente día	Ayer		Ayer, fue, un, día	
Positive with NIA	Neg. P. + Neu. P. + N.I.A.	No estoy enojado		Enojado	Estoy	No
Simple negative	Neg. P + Neu. P.	Odio ir a la escuela		Odio	Ir, a, la, escuela	
Negative with NIA	Pos. P. + Neu. P. + N.I.A.	No me siento bien	bien		Me, siento	No
Simple neutral	Neu. P.	Prueba 1			Prueba, 1	
Neutral complex	Pos. P. + Neg. P. + Neu. P. + N.I.A	No estoy triste pero tampoco estoy feliz	feliz	triste	Estoy, estoy	No, pero, tampoco

Abbreviations description.

Pos. P.: words with positive polarity   **Neg. P.:** words with negative polarity   **Neu. P.:** words with neutral polarity
N.I.A.: words with the ability to deny, cancel, or change the meaning of one sentence

In Table 3 is described the result obtained by each API selected with the set of 100 Spanish sentences. Once selected the meaning cloud algorithm as the best algorithm to classify sentences in twitter, a set of 1000 text posts on Twitter were analyzed automatically with the algorithm and verified manually in order to analyze the efficiency obtained as can be in Figs. 1 and 2.

Table 3. Performance obtained with selected Twitter sentiment analysis tools

Sentences type	Sentences of classify	Sentiment140			Sentiment Analysis of Meaning Cloud			Bitext's API		
		Result		Success	Result		Success	Result		Success
Type sentence	Example sentence	Expected	Obtained		Expected	Obtained		Expected	Obtained	
Simple positive	Ayer fue un excelente dia	Positive	Neutral	No	Positive	Positive	Yes	Positive	Positive	Yes
Positive with NIA	No estoy enojado	Positive	Neutral	No	Positive	Positive	Yes	Positive	Positive	Yes
Simple negative	Odio ir a la escuela	Negative	Neutral	No	Negative	Negative	Yes	Negative	Negative	Yes
Negative with NIA	No me siento bien	Negative	Negative	Yes	Negative	Negative	Yes	Negative	Negative	Yes
Simple neutral	Prueba 1	Neutral	Neutral	Yes	Neutral	Neutral	Yes	Neutral	Neutral	Yes
Neutral complex	No estoy triste pero tampoco estoy feliz	Neutral	Neutral	Yes	Neutral	Neutral	Yes	Neutral	Neutral	Yes
Percentage of success for 100 sentences:		50%			100%			92%		

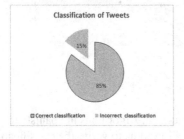

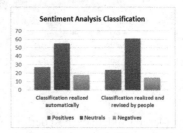

Fig. 1. Tweets classification for sentences   **Fig. 2.** Automatic and manual classification

4 Conclusions

Tweets storage increase at a rate of about 7000 tweets per second [5], and because of this, a strategy for processing and storing information was defined [4], in this work were analyzed only six APIs and resources for sentiment analysis, although. There are many API tools developed for realizing sentiment analysis mainly in English language, the results obtained with the API selected "Sentiment Analysis of Meaning Cloud" were very good, 85% of the tweets analyzed were correctly classified, and the detected errors were mainly caused by slang use, sarcasms and regionalisms in Spanish. The Storage realized in a NoSQL database allowed us to improve the data storage for future analysis, and improves the speed in updates and consults.

References

1. Flores, J., Moran, J., Rodriguez, V.: Las Redes Sociales. USMP (2009). http://www.usmp.edu.pe/publicaciones/boletin/fia/info69/sociales.pdf
2. Análisis de sentimiento: capturando la emoción. 27 de mayo de 2015, de www.daedalus.es Sitio web (2012). http://www.daedalus.es/blog/es/analisis-de-sentimiento-capturando-la-emocion
3. Valverde J.C.: Sistema de extracción de entidades y análisis de opiniones en contenidos Web generados por usuarios. Trabajo de fin de grado. Universidad Autónoma de Madrid. Madrid, España (2013)
4. Gonzalez, D., Mejia, D., Mendoza, M., Enciso, A.: Desarrollo de una aplicación para la extracción de información de la red social Twitter y análisis de sentimientos de Tweets, Revista de Tecnologías de la Información, vol. 2, no. 2, ECORFAN (2015)
5. Internetlivestats (2016). http://www.internetlivestats.com

Decentralized Control for Power Distribution with Ancillary Lines in the Smart Grid

Michele Roncalli and Alessandro Farinelli[(✉)]

Computer Science Department, University of Verona, Verona, Italy
`alessandro.farinelli@univr.it`

Abstract. Energy management is a key topic for today's society, and a crucial challenge is to shift from a production system based on fossil fuel to sustainable energy. A key ingredients for this important step is the use of a highly automated power delivery network, where intelligent devices can communicate and collaborate to optimize energy management.

This paper investigates a specific model for smart power grids initially proposed by Zdeborov and colleagues [12] where back up power lines connect a subset of loads to generators so to meet the demand of the whole network. Specifically, we extend such model to minimize CO_2 emissions related to energy production.

In more detail, we propose a formalization for this problem based on the Distributed Constraint Optimization Problem (DCOP) framework and a solution approach based on the min-sum algorithm. We empirically evaluate our approach on a set of benchmarking power grid instances comparing our proposed solution to simulated annealing. Our results, shows that min-sum favorably compares with simulated annealing and it represents a promising solution method for this model.

Keywords: Smart grid · Decentralized constraint optimization · Factor graphs

1 Introduction

Energy management is a key topic for today's society, and a crucial challenge that governments and societies are facing is to shift from a production system based on fossil fuel to sustainable energy. A key point for sustainable energy is the use of renewable energy sources such as solar, wind and tidal power, biomass, geothermal energy etc. Many of the renewable energy sources (e.g., solar power, wind power and biomass) can be exploited in a decentralized fashion, dramatically changing the current centralised production system. More specifically, decentralized energy is energy generated near the point of use, and is typically produced by small generating plants connected to a local network distribution rather than to the high-voltage transmission system required by the centralised energy production scheme. Technologies for producing decentralized energy are already mature enough for large scale deployment, and in many countries, such as Finland, the Netherlands and Denmark, a significant percentage

© ICST Institute for Computer Sciences, Social Informatics and Telecommunications Engineering 2017
E. Sucar et al. (Eds.): AFI 2016, LNICST 179, pp. 39–50, 2017.
DOI: 10.1007/978-3-319-49622-1_6

of the national electricity production is provided through decentralized energy (respectively 35%, 40% and 50%).

In this context, the vision of an *intelligent electricity delivery network*, commonly called **smart grid**, has been advocated as a key element to achieve decentralized sustainable energy provisioning. The smart grid is a highly automated distribution network that incorporates many different devices, such as smart meters and smart generators. A key element to realize the long term vision of the smart grid is the development of proper ICT infrastructures that enable data transfer and interoperability among all the core components of the smart grid. In this perspective, the internet of things (IoT) provides crucial enabling technologies for the smart grid by proposing a clear set of standard and effective communication protocols that foster the interoperability between different devices [5].

The long term goal of the smart grid is to exploit such ICT infrastructure to optimize the energy management and distribution process, hence minimising carbon emissions and reducing costs to generate electricity. In this perspective a crucial topic is to avoid the overloads of power generation units that may be caused by the fluctuation in demand and by the intermittent generation typical of renewable technologies (e.g., wind).

Within this framework, we will study a specific model for power grids initially proposed by Zdeborov and colleagues [12] where back up power lines (called ancillary lines) connect a subset of loads to several generators. Such loads can then choose which generator to use to meet their demand. In the model proposed in [12] authors focus on a *satisfaction problem*, i.e., the solution is a configuration of loads (i.e., a mapping from load to generators) where no generator in the grid is overloaded (i.e., the demand of the connected load does not exceed the generator maximum production). Figure 1 shows an exemplar situation where 6 loads ($L_{1,1}, \cdots, L_{2,3}$) are connected to 2 generators (G_1, G_2). Dashed arrows represents ancillary lines that could be used by a subset of the loads (i.e., $\{L_{1,1}, L_{1,2}, L_{2,1}, L_{2,3}\}$).

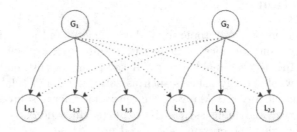

Fig. 1. Diagram depicting a power grid with 2 generators, 6 loads and 4 ancillary lines.

Here, we extend such model by considering that the CO_2 emissions of the generators depend on their production level. Thus, the problem becomes a constrained *optimization problem*, where the goal is to find the configuration of loads that minimizes the total CO_2 emissions in the grid ensuring that no generator is overloaded.

Following the distributed energy management paradigm that underpins the smart grid vision, we propose a decentralized solution approach for this problem. Specifically, we represent the problem discussed above as a Distributed Constraint Optimization Problem (DCOP) which is a widely used framework for decentralized decision making [9]. The DCOP literature offers a wealth of solution approaches ranging from exact algorithms [9,10] to heuristic techniques [3,7,13]. While exact algorithms are guaranteed to return the optimal solution, they all suffer from an exponential element in the computation (and message size/number) that hinders their applicability for the large scale scenarios we consider here (i.e., thousands of variables). In contrast, while heuristic approaches can not guarantee the quality of the retrieved solutions, they have been successfully used in several scenarios [2,4]. Hence, here we employ a standard heuristic approach (i.e., the max-sum algorithm [3]) that has been shown to provide high quality solutions in various application domains. In more detail, following previous work [3,11] we represent the DCOP problem by using factor graphs [6] and we run a close variation of the max-sum algorithm, i.e., the min-sum as we address a minimization problem.

We empirically evaluate our approach on a set of benchmarking power grid problems, created with the procedure proposed in [12]. Results obtained over a wide range of problem instance have been analyzed by considering different measures such the final cost (i.e., CO_2 emissions), steps required to converge to a solution and total run time. Our proposed approach has been compared to simulated annealing, a well known centralized method for optimization. Overall the empirical analysis shows that the min-sum algorithm can solve large instances (i.e., up to 20000 generators) in seconds and that it provides a significantly smaller cost when compared to simulated annealing, hence being a promising approach for our model.

2 Background

In this section we discuss necessary background detailing the DCOP formalism, factor graphs and the max-sum approach.

2.1 Distributed Constraint Optimization Problems

Distributed constraint optimization problems ($DCOP$) are a generalization of COP for distributed frameworks. A DCOP is a tuple $\langle \mathcal{A}, \mathcal{X}, \mathcal{D}, \mathcal{R} \rangle$, where $\mathcal{A} = \{a_1, \ldots, a_s\}$ is a set of agents and $\mathcal{X} = \{x_1, \ldots, x_n\}$ is a set of variables, each variable x_i is owned by exactly one agent a_i, but an agent can potentially own more than one variable. The agent a_i is responsible for assigning values to the variables it owns. $\mathcal{D} = \{D_1, \cdots, D_n\}$ is a set of discrete and finite variable domains, and each variable x_i can take values in the domain D_i. Then, $\mathcal{R} = \{r_1, \ldots, r_m\}$ is a set of cost functions that describe the constraints among variables. Each cost function $r_i : D_{i_1} \times \cdots \times D_{i_{k_i}} \rightarrow \Re \cup \{\infty\}$ depends on a set of variables $\mathbf{x_i} \subseteq \mathcal{X}$, where $k_i = |\mathbf{x_i}|$ is the arity of the function and ∞ is used to represent hard constraints. Each cost function assigns a real value to each possible valid assignment of the variables it depends on and ∞ to non valid assignments.

For a minimization problem, the goal is then to find a variable assignment that minimizes the sum of cost functions:

$$\arg\max_{\mathbf{x}} \sum_i r_i(\mathbf{x_i}) \tag{1}$$

2.2 Factor Graphs and Min-Sum

A *Factor Graph* is a bipartite graph that encodes a factored function, e.g. functions that can be expressed as a sum of components, such as the function reported in Eq. 1. A factor graph has a *variable node* for each variable x_i, a *factor node* F_j for each local function r_j, and an edge connecting variable node x_i to factor node r_j if and only if x_i is an argument of r_j.

Factor graphs represents a very convenient computational framework for several optimization techniques such as max-sum, max-prod, and the min-sum algorithm that we use in this work.

In more detail, the min-sum algorithm belongs to the Generalized Distributive Law (GDL) framework [1], a family of techniques frequently used to solve probabilistic graphical models (e.g. to find the maximum a posteriori assignment in Markov random fields or compute the posterior probabilities) [2]. If applied to constraint networks in tree form, min-sum provides the optimal solution, but when applied to more general networks (i.e. networks which contain loops) optimality (and convergence) can be no longer ensured. However, empirical evidence shows that GDL-based algorithms are able to find solution very close to the optimal in several problems.

Min-sum operates directly on a factor graph representation of the problem iteratively exchanging messages between variable nodes and function nodes. The key idea in the algorithm is that new messages are computed and passed between the nodes in the graph until a stop condition is verified. There can be many convergence criteria (e.g. messages convergence, solution convergence, etc.). In our approach we focused on the messages convergence, as our tests revealed this criterion to be the best choice for our problem scenario. Moreover, to deal with not satisfiable instances we consider a maximum number of message computation steps, if this maximum number of steps is reached the algorithm states that it could not find a valid solution.

3 Problem Formulation

In this section we first detail the model for controlling the power distribution with ancillary lines proposed in [12], then we present our proposed extension and our factor graph formalization of such problem.

3.1   Model for Power Distribution with Ancillary Lines

The model for power distribution proposed in [12] is composed by two types of elements: a set of M *generators* and a set of *loads*. A generator G_i has a fixed maximum energy production value and without loss of generality, we normalize this to 1, thus no more than one unity of energy can be absorbed by all the loads connected to G_i.

A load is a component of the grid that is not able to produce energy for itself or for other nodes in the network. The power consumption rate varies across the loads, but for each load it is a constant that can not be controlled. This value is drawn from a uniform probability distribution with support on the interval $(0, 1)$. The center of the distribution is set to $\bar{x}$ (that represents the *mean value* and x is the consumption rate). The width of the distribution is Δ. Thus, given a load l_j, its power consumption rate is a value drawn uniformly in the set $[\bar{x} - \frac{\Delta}{2}, \bar{x} + \frac{\Delta}{2}]$. This power can be absorbed by only one generator at time, i.e. if a load is connected to several generators, only one link can be active. Each generator is connected to D distinct loads, thus the total number of loads is $(M \cdot D)$.

A power grid is then a graph forest composed by M trees. Among this forest, R *ancillary lines* for each generators are added. In more detail, $(R \cdot M)$ new links are created to interconnect the grid. These links are added in two simple steps: (1) R loads are chosen from each generator; (2) for each load chosen in the first step, connect it to another generator in such a way that, at the end of the process, every generator is connected to $(D + R)$ loads.

The final result is a bipartite graph with the following properties: (i) M nodes corresponding to the generator set; (ii) $M \cdot D$ nodes corresponding to the load set; (iii) $M \cdot (D - R)$ loads are connected to only one generator; (iv) $(M \cdot R)$ loads are connected to two generators; (v) every generator is connected to $(D + R)$ loads; (vi) no load in the net is connected to more than 2 generators. Hence the free parameters that define an instance of the power grid model are M, D and R.

In Fig. 1 shows an exemplar instance of a power grid when $M = 2$, $D = 3$ and $R = 2$. Loads $L_{1,3}$ and $L_{2,2}$ are single connected, so they can use only the generator they are connected to (respectively generator G_1 and generator G_2). The remaining loads ($L_{1,1}, L_{1,2}, L_{2,1}$ and $L_{2,3}$) are connected to both the generators, so they can use energy from G_1 or from G_2 (never concurrently).

3.2   Formalization of CO_2 emissions in the power grid

As mentioned before, Zdeborov and colleagues in [12] focus on a *satisfaction problem*, aiming to find a mapping from loads to generators, where no generator in the grid is overloaded.

Here, we extended their model considering the CO_2 emissions for each generator and aiming to minimize the total emission for the grid.

Specifically, following [8], the CO_2 emission function is proportional to the energy produced by the generators. In more detail, the CO_2 emission function is: $CO_2 = mult \cdot energy$ where *energy* is the ratio of energy that the generator must produce with respect to its maximum energy production value (which as mentioned above is set to 1); *mult* represent a feature of the generator, that expresses the unit of CO_2 emitted by the generator for each unit of energy produced. In our experiments we choose *mult* randomly in a range $[1, 5]$.

3.3   From Power Grid to Factor Graph

Our factor graph model of a power grid with ancillary lines consider a variable node for each load L_i and a factor node for each generator G_j. In more detail, the variable node x_i, that corresponds to load L_i, has a domain that contains a value for each possible generator G_j which the load L_i can connect to. Moreover, the scope for the factor node F_j, corresponding to generator G_j, is the set of variable nodes $\{x_i, \dots, x_k\}$ that correspond to loads that can get power from G_j.

For example, consider the power grid in Fig. 1. The corresponding factor graph is shown in Fig. 2 (left), while the correspondence between nodes and generators/loads is summarized in Fig. 2 (right).

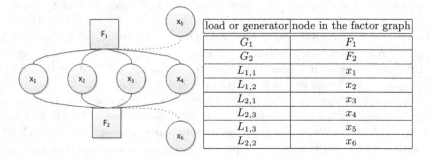

load or generator	node in the factor graph
G_1	F_1
G_2	F_2
$L_{1,1}$	x_1
$L_{1,2}$	x_2
$L_{2,1}$	x_3
$L_{2,3}$	x_4
$L_{1,3}$	x_5
$L_{2,2}$	x_6

Fig. 2. Left: example of factor graph for the power grid in Fig. 1. Right: correspondence between nodes and generators

Consider the dotted edge from x_5 to F_1 and from x_6 to F_2. In a *naïve* model, x_5 would be connected to F_1 and x_6 to F_2 but, since their domains contain only one value, they can be safely removed from F_1 and F_2. In practice, variable with a single value can be considered meaningless because its value is already known. Specifically, x_5 is removed from F_1, which is modified to consider the consumption of the load represented in x_5 for any possible value of its other arguments. Since x_5 can be connected only to F_1, it means that for every possible value of x_1, x_2, x_3 and x_4 the total energy that generator G_1 can produce is $(1 - energy\ required\ by\ L_{1,3})$.

4   Results and Discussion

In this section we first detail our empirical methodology and then discuss obtained results.

4.1   Empirical Methodology

Our goal is to empirically evaluate the proposed min-sum approach in power grid instances that have the same characteristics as the benchmarking test suite proposed in [12]. In that work authors use two different algorithms (i.e., walkgrid and belief propagation), but since here we extend their model considering an optimization problem (and not satisfaction) we do not compare min-sum to such algorithms but instead use a simulated annealing procedure. Simulated annealing is a well known, powerful approach for finding a global minimum of a cost function.

To create the power grid instances, we follow the procedure described in [12], fixing $D = 3$ $R = 2$ and $\Delta = 0.2$. Then we vary $M \in \{200, 1000, 2000, 10000, 20000\}$ and $\bar{x}$ between 0.29 and 0.3 with a step of 0.01.

With this parametrization, the factor graph obtained from a power grid with M generators, has M function nodes and $(M \cdot R)$ variable nodes (as described in Sect. 3.3, only loads connected to two generators are mapped to variable nodes). Hence, at each iteration of the min-sum algorithm $(2R \cdot M)$ messages from variables to functions and $(2R \cdot M)$ messages from functions to nodes are sent.

We create 100 different power grid instances for all possible values of input parameters. For all instances the consumption rate x of each load is drawn from the uniform probability distribution centered in $\bar{x}$ and with width set to Δ.

Our metrics to evaluate the solution techniques are the final cost (the lower the better), the total run time and the amount of iterations required to get a response. The halting condition for min-sum is either message convergence or a maximum number of iterations (set to 300).

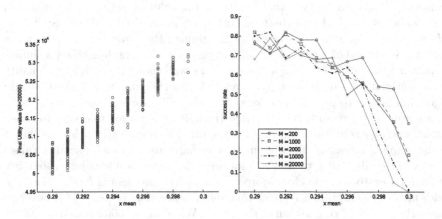

Fig. 3. Left: cost values varying $\bar{x}$ and with $M = 20000$, Rigth: success rate varying both $\bar{x}$ and M

4.2   Results

Figure 3 (left) reports the final cost value when $M = 20000$ (i.e., the biggest value for M) varying the value of $\bar{x}$. The graph reports the obtained cost value for all repetitions that result in a valid configuration (i.e., no generator is overloaded given the min-sum mapping from loads to generator). The graph shows that when the values of $\bar{x}$ increases the number of valid solution decreases (i.e., when $\bar{x} = 0.299$ the number of points in the graph is significantly less than the number of points when $\bar{x} = 0.29$). Moreover, there are no points when $\bar{x} = 0.3$, thus there are no solution for the 100 power grid problems created for the maximum value available for $\bar{x}$. Notice that, there is no guarantee that if min-sum is not able to find a solution, then the problem is not-satisfiable. However, bigger values of $\bar{x}$ result in power grid instances where loads generally require more energy. Hence it is more likely that there is no valid configuration for the power grid, this is confirmed by results obtained with simulated annealing (not reported here in the interest of space).

Figure 3 (right) reports the success rates varying both M and $\bar{x}$, where the success rate is number of valid solutions/total number of instances. As mentioned before, the success rate heavily depends on $\bar{x}$, however, there is also a dependency with respect to M when large values of $\bar{x}$ are used (approximately $\bar{x} >= 0.28$). This happens because bigger values of M result in bigger power grids, where the probability of having at least on generator overloaded increases. Thus, when $\bar{x} = 0.3$ the power grid is not-satisfiable most likely when $M = 20000$ then when $M = 200$. Moreover, M has a strong influence on the absolute value of the final cost (i.e., CO_2 emissions) because, when all other parameters are fixed, bigger networks will generate more energy and hence create more CO_2 emissions. Hence to analyse the quality of the solution returned by min-sum with for we report in Fig. 4 the final cost value normalized with respect to the M parameter (here, and in the following graphs, the error bars represent the confidence interval of a t-test with 95% accuracy). This graph exhibits a similar trend w.r.t the one in Fig. 3. Specifically, the graph shows that while the quality of the optimal solution is strongly correlated with the growth of $\bar{x}$, the min-sum algorithm is able to provide solutions of good quality for large scale systems.

Figure 5 (left) reports the run time (in milliseconds) for min-sum to finish (either finding a solution or stating that the problem is not-satisfiable). As shown in the graph, $\bar{x}$ influences the time used. This happens because for smaller values of $\bar{x}$ it is usually easier to find a solution, since there is a smaller probability to have generators overloaded. Moreover, when the problem is *harder* (i.e., the loads mean consumption is higher), min-sum require more iterations to converge, hence the growth of time shown in the graph. When $M = 10000$ and $M = 20000$, from $\bar{x} = 0.298$ time peaks to its maximum value: this is the case for not-satisfiable problems, when the min-sum stops by reaching the maximum number of iterations.

The graph also shows a linear dependency between M and time: this can be easily observed in the cases when $M = 10000$ and $M = 20000$, where when $\bar{x} = 0.3$ the case $M = 20000$ requires approximately double the time required

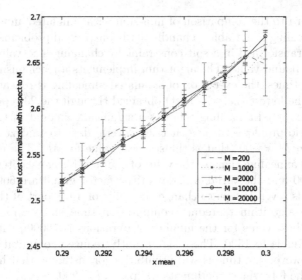

Fig. 4. Final cost value (normalized with respect to M).

by the case $M = 10000$. This can be explained by considering that the number of messages sent for each iteration by the min-sum algorithm is $4R \cdot M$.

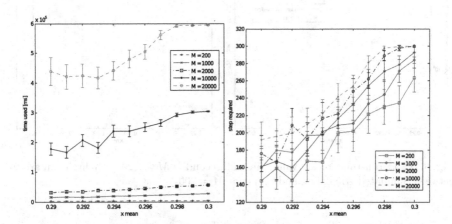

Fig. 5. Left: mean values for run time varying both $\bar{x}$ and M, Right: steps required.

The steps required by the min-sum algorithm are shown in Fig. 5 (right). The graph shows a similar trend between steps required when M changes. For example consider $M = 200$ and $M = 20000$ when $\bar{x} = 0.296$: M grows 100 times, and the steps required change from 190 to 250. The growth is sub-linear. There is a stronger dependency between step required and $\bar{x}$: thus, when the problem is *harder* a bigger number of iterations is necessary to find a solution.

We now turn to the comparison of min-sum with simulated annealing. Since simulated annealing is not able to handle hard-constrained problem, every hard-constraint is transformed in a soft-constraint by changing $+\infty$ values to a pre-defined upper bound value. The algorithm implements a mechanism of random restart: for 20 times, the execution of simulated annealing is repeated, and the final value is the lowest (i.e., the best) obtained through the 20 repetitions.

Overall, simulated annealing requires a significant amount of time to solve these power grid problems. In fact, it takes several days to analyze all the 1100 instances when $M = 200$ (that is the smallest value for M). The main issue is that simulated annealing changes the value of one variable at each iteration: thus, when $M = 200$ and the variable nodes in the factor graph are 600, simulated annealing needs several steps to change the value of a big part of the variables. We tuned the algorithm to reduce computation time and we found that for $M = 200$ the best value for the number of iterations is 100000 with an initial temperature equals to 1500. These significantly reduced computation time (to few hours), however run time is still prohibitive for instances that have a larger M, hence in the following experiments we fixed $M = 200$.

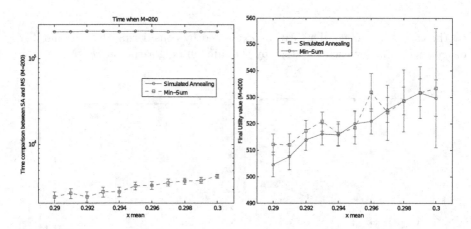

Fig. 6. Left: run-time mean value (in milliseconds) $M = 200$, Right: comparison between Simulated Annealing and min-sum $M = 200$

Figure 6 (left) confirms a significant difference in run time in favour of min-sum. Moreover, Fig. 6 (right) reports a comparison between the mean values of the cost obtained by min-sum and Simulated Annealing. The graph shows that min-sum is generally comparable to simulated annealing and sometimes gives better results.

Figure 7 provides a more refined comparison between the performance of min-sum and simulated annealing. This chart (best viewed in colors) reports a percentage of the outcomes for the two algorithms. As previously mentioned, min-sum is in generally better. Moreover, a more detailed analysis of this results reveals that if both min-sum and simulated annealing terminate, than min-sum does never provide a solution of higher cost with respect to simulated annealing.

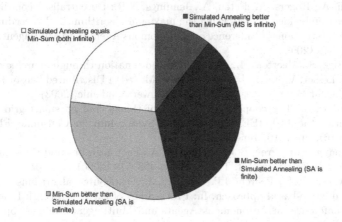

Fig. 7. Cake graph for comparing min-sum and Simulated Annealing results (Color figure online)

5 Conclusions and Future Work

In this paper we considered the model for power distribution with ancillary lines proposed in [12]. We extend such model to consider CO_2 emission and we propose a decentralized solution approach based on a DCOP formalization of the problem and the min-sum algorithm.

We empirically evaluate our approach on a set of benchmarking power grid instances built according to the procedure proposed in [12] and we compare the results obtained by min-sum with simulated annealing. Our results, suggests that min-sum favorably compares with simulated annealing and it provides a promising method for a distributed implementation of this model.

This work lays the basis for several interesting future directions. For example an interesting aspect is to further extend the power grid model to better describe realistic situations. A first extension might be to consider loads that can produce energy (e.g., renewable sources) and handle the optimization problems related to storing the excess of power created by such prosumers. Another interesting aspect would be to consider in the optimization process other important factors for energy distribution such as energy prices, government regulations and load/production forecasting.

References

1. Aji, S., McEliece, R.: The generalized distributive law. IEEE Trans. Inf. Theory **46**(2), 325–343 (2000)

2. Farinelli, A., Rogers, A., Jennings, N.: Agent-based decentralised coordination for sensor networks using the max-sum algorithm. Auton. Agent. Multi-agent Syst. **28**(3), 337–380 (2014)
3. Farinelli, A., Rogers, A., Petcu, A., Jennings, N.R.: Decentralised coordination of low-power embedded devices using the max-sum algorithm. In: Proceedings of the Seventh International Conference on Autonomous Agents and Multiagent Systems, pp. 639–646 (2008)
4. Fitzpatrick, S., Meertens, L.: Distributed coordination through anarchic optimization. In: Lesser, V., Ortiz Jr., C.L., Tambe, M. (eds.) Distributed Sensor Networks: A Multiagent Perspective, pp. 257–293. Kluwer Academic (2003)
5. Karnouskos, S.: The cooperative internet of things enabled smart grid. In: Proceedings of the 14th IEEE International Symposium on Consumer Electronics (ISCE2010), pp. 7–10, June 2010
6. Kschischang, F.R., Frey, B.J., Loeliger, H.A.: Factor graphs and the sum-product algorithm. IEEE Trans. Inf. Theor. **47**(2), 498–519 (2006)
7. Maheswaran, R.T., Pearch, J.P., Tambe, M.: Distributed algorithms for dcop: a graphical game-based approach. In: Proceedings of the Seventeenth International Joint Conference on Autonomous Agents and Multi-agent Systems, pp. 432–439 (2004)
8. Miller, S., Ramchurn, S.D., Rogers, A.: Optimal decentralised dispatch of embedded generation in the smart grid. In: Proceedings of the 11th International Conference on Autonomous Agents and Multiagent Systems, pp. 281–288 (2012)
9. Modi, P., Shen, W.M., Tambe, M., Yokoo, M.: Adopt: asynchronous distributed constraint optimization with quality guarantees. Artif. Intell. **161**(1–2), 149–180 (2005)
10. Petcu, A., Faltings, B.: Dpop: a scalable method for multiagent constraint optimization. In: Proceedings of the Nineteenth International Joint Conference on Artificial Intelligence, pp. 266–271 (2005)
11. Pujol-Gonzalez, M., Cerquides, J., Meseguer, P., Rodríguez-Aguilar, J.A., Tambe, M.: Engineering the decentralized coordination of UAVs with limited communication range. In: Bielza, C., Salmerón, A., Alonso-Betanzos, A., Hidalgo, J.I., Martínez, L., Troncoso, A., Corchado, E., Corchado, J.M. (eds.) CAEPIA 2013. LNCS (LNAI), vol. 8109, pp. 199–208. Springer, Heidelberg (2013). doi:10.1007/978-3-642-40643-0_21
12. Zdeborov, L., Decelle, A., Chertkov, M.: Message passing for optimization and control of a power grid: model of a distribution system with redundancy. Phys. Rev. E Stat. Nonlinear Soft Matter Phys. **80**(4), 046112 (2009)
13. Zhang, W., Wang, G., Xing, Z., Wittenburg, L.: Distributed stochastic search and distributed breakout: properties, comparison and applications to constraint optimization problems in sensor networks. Artif. Intell. **161**(12), 55–87 (2005)

An Experimental Evaluation of IoT Technologies in Precision Viticulture

Luis Orozco-Barbosa[1][(✉)], Francisco Montero García[2],
Antonio Brasa Ramos[2], and Francisco Montero Riquelme[2]

[1] Albacete Research Institute of Informatics,
Universidad de Castilla La Mancha, 02071 Albacete, Spain
Luis.Orozco@uclm.es

[2] School of Agronomics Engineering, Universidad de Castilla La Mancha, 02071 Albacete, Spain
{Antonio.Brasa,Francisco.Montero}@uclm.es

Abstract. There is no doubt that the introduction of IoT-assisted applications will become an invaluable asset to optimize farm performance. Through the data collected by sensors deployed in the fields together with other sources of information and facilities, farmers will have at their disposal a set of tools allowing them to make informed decisions on the day-to-day operation. Since 2005, a multidisciplinary team of researchers from the Albacete Research Institute of Informatics and the School of Agronomical Engineers of the University of Castilla La Mancha (UCLM) has been exploring the use of information and communication technologies in the agricultural industry. This paper reports on the main findings acquired through the deployment and experimental evaluation of IoT technologies in a vineyard. Our results also provide insight into future directions on the use of IoT technologies in precision viticulture.

Keywords: IOT · Wireless sensor networks · Web-based applications · Precision agriculture

1 Introduction

Latest developments of IoT technologies have spurred the interest on their application to numerous and diverse sectors [1]. It is now widely recognized that the use of IoT technologies in the agriculture sector will allow the monitoring and control of agricultural products during the whole life cycle: from farm to fork. IoT technologies should therefore help farmers on their day-to-day operations and management planning processes. The design process of IoT-based systems for the agricultural sector should start by identifying those areas where their introduction may have an impact on improving the overall food chain, such as, decreasing the use of water and fertilizers, lowering ecological footprints and economic costs as well as increasing food security. The activation of irrigation systems and pesticide sprayers can be timely and wisely planned based on the information extracted from the data gathered by wireless sensor nodes. In the case of viticulture, the selection of the best grapes will be largely based on

© ICST Institute for Computer Sciences, Social Informatics and Telecommunications Engineering 2017
E. Sucar et al. (Eds.): AFI 2016, LNICST 179, pp. 51–62, 2017.
DOI: 10.1007/978-3-319-49622-1_7

the information extracted from the data automatically collected by the sensors throughout the season.

Since 2005, our research team at the Universidad de Castilla La Mancha has been involved on the design and implementation of information-and-communications-technologies solutions for the agriculture industry [2]. Our activities have mainly focused on the introduction of IoT technologies into an important sector in Castilla La Mancha: vine growing. The main goals of our early activities have comprised the development and deployment of full operational wireless sensor networks for the data capture, processing and visualization of environmental parameters: temperature, soil and air humidity among others. Farmers have been provided with friendly user interfaces allowing them to visualize the data collected by the sensors deployed in vineyards. Various visualization tools have been developed in order to assist farmers on their decision making tasks.

Current efforts are focusing on developing tools offering valuable information to grape growers and wine producers. Our main goals go a step ahead on assisting farmers and IoT specialists on the deployment and use of IoT technologies in viticulture. From a farmer's point of view, the data collected should provide valuable information on parameters affecting the quality of the grapes. As for the IoT specialists, experimental trials allow them to gain invaluable experience on the design and deployment of IoT system in vineyards.

In this paper, we present the results obtained from the design and experimental evaluation of an IoT-based system deployed in a vineyard. Our results show that the deployment of wireless networks and other computer-based systems in a vineyard requires cost-effective and reliable solutions. Throughout the integration of networks of sensors, Internet-based services and machine intelligence principles, IoT sets the basis to the development of invaluable sources of information to winegrowers.

In Sect. 2, we start by motivating the use of IoT technologies in precision viticulture. We then review the main organization and relevant parameters of a vineyard to be taken into account when developing an IoT precision viticulture solution. Section 3 describes the overall architecture of our proposed IoT solution for precision viticulture. We also identify the vineyard features to be taken into account when defining the network layout of a precision viticulture application. Section 4 describes the methodology and challenges involved in the planning and deployment of a wireless network composed of power-constrained devices (sensor nodes). Section 5 describes the information made available to winegrowers and IoT specialists. Section 6 draws our conclusions and future work plans.

2   IoT-Based Precision Viticulture

2.1   Rationale

In traditional viticulture, winegrowers overlooked the natural variability within a vineyard and applied identical treatment to all plots. In fact, winegrowers did not count with the tools allowing them to monitor and manage each and every plot. Precision viticulture is a differentiated management approach aiming to meet the real needs of each plot within a vineyard [3]. Its ultimate goal is to maximize the grape yield and quality while minimizing environmental impacts and risks. Nowadays, precision viticulture makes use of information and communications technologies that help in the monitoring and control of various vine growth parameters. Monitoring tools have been developed using remote and land sensing instrumentation. For many years, remote sensing have been used on the monitoring of vineyards. Remote sensing is an image acquisition technique capable of describing the vineyard status by detecting the sunlight reflected from the vegetation indices and soil. The actual platforms used in remote sensing have evolved throughout the years. Satellite images have been used in precision agriculture for more than 40 years. However, their resolutions and the limitation of capturing the images from different angles prevent their use for precision viticulture due to the dimensions and orientation of the vines and natural slopes of the land [3, 4]. Furthermore, costs of the images are only economically feasible for large areas. Remote sensing has benefit from recent developments in the area of unmanned aerial vehicles (UAVs) and sensor technologies. UAV applications in remote sensing offer highly flexible and timely monitoring, due to reduced planning time. UAV imaging systems are particularly suitable for vineyards of medium to small size (1–10 ha), especially in vineyards characterized by high fragmentation due to the heterogeneity in training systems, grape varieties, slopes and elevation.

Regarding current land sensing instrumentation being used in precision viticulture, solutions are being implemented around wireless sensor networks (WSN), land vehicle and portable devices [5]. Numerous initiatives around the world have made use of WSNs to monitor important biophysical factors such as solar radiation, soil moisture, and temperature regimes [2, 3]. Up to date, most solutions have explored the feasibility of deploying a wireless network in a vineyard and developing data visualization tools.

In this work, we undertake the implementation of an IoT solution integrating a monitoring tool comprising a wireless sensor network, UAVs and a data processing and visualization engine. From the end-user's point-of-view, the ultimate goal of our proposal is to develop tools allowing winegrowers to gain access to the data being collected. Throughout a friendly user interface, winegrowers can consult and process the data collected by the WSN and UAVs. Among the data processing tools, winegrowers can through a friendly interface carry on statistical analysis, analyze the data collected by all or some of the sensors.

From the IoT specialist's point-of-view, our work analyzes the challenges when planning the deployment of an IoT system in a vineyard. Based on our past experience, we start by characterizing the organization of a vineyard and identify the main parameters of interest to winegrowers. We then describe the overall architecture of our proposal. Throughout a study case, we undertake the definition of the wireless sensor network having been implemented in our experimental trial.

2.2 Vineyard Characterization and Parameters

In this section, we describe the main features characterizing a vineyard. We also motivate the main parameters to be captured by the sensor and UAVs. Recall that precision viticulture aims to address the needs of each individual crop. In a vineyard, production depends on two factors: climatic conditions and management practices. The sensitivity of the grape quality to the climatic conditions varies with the phenological stage of the crop making necessary a proper planning of the actions to be performed by the wine-growers throughout the season.

The choice of the training system is one of the first and most important management decisions to be made when planting a vineyard. Vine training consists of the fixed supports upon which the plant develops providing sufficient aeration and sun exposure to the grape. Besides providing the basis for the management of the vegetation cover, training systems have also been designed to facilitate the viticulture tasks, such as, the pruning and the application of pesticides. The management of the vegetation cover in a vineyard is closely linked to the impact of the climatic conditions on the natural processes of transpiration, photosynthesis and respiration. The ultimate goal when installing a training system is therefore to match the vineyard design to the anticipated vine vigor and climatic conditions. Nowadays, training systems range from single to divided curtain systems and employ both horizontal and vertical canopy division [1]. Figure 1 depicts one of the most commonly-used training systems in Southern Europe, namely, the sprawl systems. It is therefore common practice that within a vineyard, different training systems may be used for each crop. For the purpose of this work, we will consider that the vineyard is divided into crops characterized by the use of a given type of training system.

Fig. 1. Sprawl training system

As for the type of sensors to be installed at each network node and the UAVs, the most relevant climatic parameters are:

- Temperature: Particularly in the month prior to maturity, plays an important role in the quality of the grape. Generally, the higher the temperature fluctuation around the average, better characteristics in terms of flavor, aroma and pigment for a specific level of maturation.
- Relative humidity: It is another major parameter affecting the quality of the grape; very high or very low humidity levels adversely affect fruit development. The heat and water vapor released from the canopy change the temperature and humidity

conditions. In turn, these changes modulate the flow of heat and water vapor from the soil and vegetation. Low humidity causes stomatal closure even if the soil moisture is sufficient, an increase in the potassium concentration in grapes and, consequently, a decrease in acidity, and therefore must quality.

- Radiaton: In general, higher levels of radiation in both intensity and duration, higher yield, acidity and/or sugar content, and fewer leaf area required for cultivation. However, often high levels of radiation is accompanied by thermal variability and low levels of relative humidity, so it is convenient the proper handling of the cover to prevent excessive or inadequate exposure to sunlight.

All of the above parameters should be monitored throughout the season using a wireless sensor network. The main challenge for the network designer remains on the number of nodes and their location within the vineyards.

Another relevant parameter to be monitored is the variability of temperatures of the grape clusters and the canopy in order to derive the plant water stress. Such measurements are taken at various stage of development of the grape. Measurements are taken under a range of environmental conditions and on sunlit and shaded canopies to illustrate the variability of temperatures and derived stress indices. In our study, we have integrated this source of information using UAVs equipped with a thermographic camera.

3   IoT System Architecture and Functions

Figure 2 depicts the overall system configuration implemented as part of our research efforts. The system has been implemented using off-the-shelf components. More precisely, we have used a WSN manufactured by Memsic [6]. Each sensor node has been equipped with three different environmental sensor, namely temperature, humidity

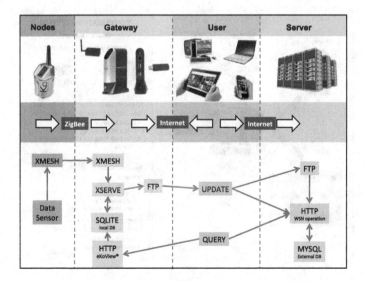

Fig. 2. IoT system architecture

and solar radiation. The WSN comprises all the routing and configuration functions. The main challenge when deploying the network remains on determining the number of nodes and their placement within the vineyard. This issue will be addressed in Sect. 4. Another major task has to do with the integration of the WSN and the UAV into the overall system architecture allowing for the rapid and accurate retrieval of the data collected by the sensors.

The end-user gets access to all the functions provided by the server using a friendly user interface implemented to operate in multiple platforms, i.e., from mobile devices to desktop computers. Figure 3 depicts the main functions implemented in the server. They have been organized into three main blocks:

- Data synchronization and verification: This module is in charge of ensuring the quality of the data collected by the sensors. One issue relates to the temporal reference of the data collected by the sensors. Each sensor reports asynchronously the various metrics every 15 min, i.e., the sensor nodes are not globally synchronized. This issue could have been solved using a clock synchronization mechanism [7], however since our application does not have strict timing requirements an alternative solution had to be found. Our proposal simply associates to a time epoch the data collected from all the nodes during a time window of 15 min. Furthermore, the data gaps are interpolated using the neighboring measurements.
- Data Visualization: This is one of the main functions of our proposal consisting of a series of visualization tools. These tools provide the means to visualize the data captured in various formats. Section 4 provides the main features of the data visualization tools.

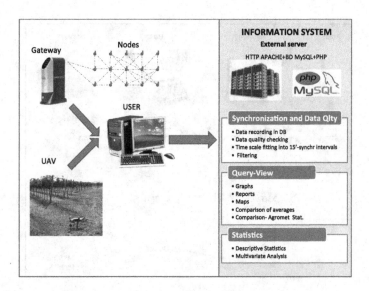

Fig. 3. IoT system functions

- Statistical Analysis: The statistical analysis comprises two parts. First, a comparative analysis of the behavior of the humidity and temperature of the nodes. It allows to compare these two parameters between nodes or groups of nodes. Second, a multivariate analysis used to determine the impact of the temperature and relative humidity over the agronomic conditions, i.e. water stress.

4   IoT Network Infrastructure

One of the main challenges when implementing an IoT solution for precision viticulture concerns the effective deployment of a WSN. By effective deployment, we mean that network has to be designed to capture the variability of the vineyard to be monitored [8, 9]. The structure, number and location of the nodes have therefore to be properly planned to meet the application requirements.

The node structure concerns the sensors to be actually installed at each node. This is dictated by the climatic parameters to be monitored. In the case of our experimental system, the monitoring of the humidity and temperature in the immediate vicinity of the grape clusters should allow us to highlight the variability of the plot. The number and location of sensor nodes should respond to: (1) the criteria of variability of the test area, and (2) the technical requirements in terms of connectivity and operability, i.e., the network should be properly dimensioned to guarantee the reliable and cost-effective transfer of the data being collected. From the above discussion, it is obvious that the planning of the network involves as a first step a characterization of the vineyard to be monitored. In the following, we should illustrate the major tasks required on the design and deployment of an IoT network infrastructure for precision viticulture.

Figure 4a depicts the plot composition of the experimental vineyard. As shown in the figure, the vineyard consists of ten plots with a total area of 12.27 ha. A plot is identified by its perimeter boundaries and by the tuple: grape variety and training system (see Fig. 4a). The training system is a major parameter affecting the production and quality of the grapes. As shown in the figure, five different grape varieties are grown, namely, Cabernet Sauvignon (CS), Syrac (Sy), Graciano (G), Cencibel (C-T) and Petit Verdot (PV); and four different types of training systems are installed, namely espalier (ESP), espalier with manual clamps (ESP-tp), spraw (SPW) and vertical axe (EV).

Once having identified the various plots composing the vineyard, it is necessary to take a closer look at other variability features of the vineyard. The row orientation of the vines is another major agronomic variability parameter to be taken into account. As for the natural parameters to be considered, these include the soil, slopes and microclimate. In our case, we have considered the topographic characteristics of the vineyard, i.e., slopes. Based on the 1-m level curves topographic description of the vineyard, we developed a Digital Elevation Model (DEM) resulting into eight zones shown in Fig. 4b.

Once having completed the above viticultural zoning process, we proceed to define the number and location of the network nodes. According to their technical specifications, the nodes being deployed have a medium transmission range of 125 m [10]. However, we should bear in mind that in order to capture the variability of the vineyard, each plot should count with at least one node. Furthermore, to ensure a robust network

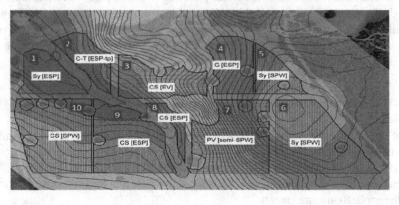

(a)

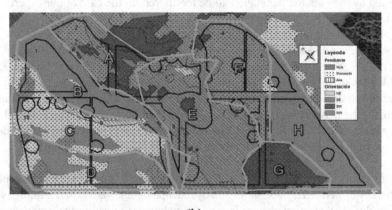

(b)

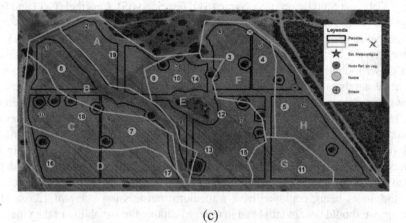

(c)

Fig. 4. Experimental vineyard (a) Plots, (b) Zones and (c) Network layout

deployment, we will have to install more nodes in those zones characterized by steep slopes, e.g., zone E. This is mainly due to the higher variability of the climatic parameters in such areas. Table 1 provides the list and distribution of the nodes deployed in the vineyard. Figure 4c depicts the location of the network nodes, number from 3 to 5 and 7 to 19. Each sensor node was placed as close as possible to a grape cluster of a plant. This should allow us to get an accurate estimate of the solar radiation perceived by the grapes.

Table 1. WSN nodes

Grape variety	Training	Zone	Nodes
Syrah	espalier	B	1
Syrah	sprawl	F	1
Syrah	sprawl	H	1
Syrah	sprawl	G	1
Cabernet	espalier	C	1
Cabernet	espalier	D	1
Cabernet	sprawl	C	1
Cabernet	sprawl	D	1
Cabernet	vertical axe	E*	3
Graciano	espalier	F	1
Cencibel	espalier*	A	1
Petit Verdot	semi sprawl	E*	3

As shown in Fig. 4c, the vineyard counts with a climatic station, denoted in the figure by a star. Furthermore, we have installed an extra node whose sensor always remains exposed to the solar radiation. By comparing the data collected by the extra node and the climatic station with the data captured by the sensor nodes we should be able to evaluate the effectiveness of our system. Our main goal is to show that the data collected by the network effectively captures the natural variability of the vineyard.

5   Data Processing and Visualization

As already mentioned, the system prototype comprises a set of data processing and visualization tools. In this section, we present some of the major services of our system prototype. Rather than describing the mode of operation of the user interface, we focus our efforts on highlighting the quality of the information provided by our proposal. We also provide an example of the information provided by the UAV. We finally present the system management tools: an essential element to guarantee the wide acceptance of a novel IoT system applied to precision viticulture.

Figure 5a depicts the temperature reported by the climatic station and by sensor nodes 3, 4 and 5 during a two-day period. From the results, it is clear that the temperature values reported by the sensors and the climatic station are quite different during the hottest periods. The fact that during these periods the values reported by the station are lower than the ones provided by the nodes can be explained by the fact that the climatic station is located at the top of the hill. These results clearly show the effectiveness of our IoT solution on capturing the natural variability of a vineyard.

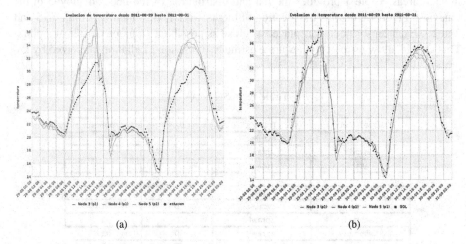

(a)   (b)

Fig. 5. Temperature: (a) Sensor nodes and climatic station; (b) Sensor nodes vs. reference node

Figure 5b shows the values reported by the three aforementioned sensor nodes and the reference nodes. As expected, the values reported by the reference node are higher than the values reported by the sensor nodes. In the case of node 5, the values reported by this node are in very close to the ones reported by the reference node. This result can be explained by the fact that the node 5 has been placed closer to the reference node and in a flat area. Figure 5b shows that during August 29, the temperature reported by node 5 were particularly higher that the one reported by the reference node. In a real setup, the winegrower may take corrective actions based on this piece of information, such as fixing the training system of the plant.

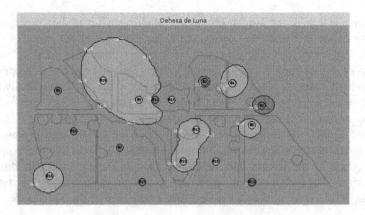

Fig. 6. Georeferenced temperature map

Georeferenced climatic maps are one of the most relevant visualization tools of our IoT solution. This powerful tool allows the user to generate maps with both spatial and temporal components. The system comprises a friendly user interface allowing the user to choose the climatic parameter and time period of the data to be visualized. The maps are based on the mean values reported during the period of time of interest. Figure 6 shows a sample georeferenced map generated based on the data captured by the nodes. We based the interpolation used to generate the maps on the Inverse Distance weighted method (IDW). This algorithm is one of the simplest and most commonly used. Thanks to its property of spatial dependence, the IDW method is based on the assumption that the value of an attribute at some unvisited point is a distance-weighted average of the data points occurring within the neighborhood surrounding the unvisited point [11].

Figure 7 shows a sample thermal and optical image taken by the UAV making part of our proposed solution. The UAV has been equipped with a portable thermal camera SDS-Infrared hotfind-D. As previously explained, our system incorporates these images into its database. The thermal measurement of the grape clusters under different exposure conditions allow winegrowers to determine the temperature differences that may exist between them and the rest of vegetative organs: an important parameter having a direct impact on the quality of the grapes.

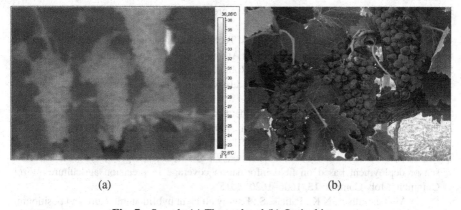

(a)   (b)

Fig. 7. Sample (a) Thermal and (b) Optical image

6   Conclusions

In this work, we have undertaken the design of an IoT system applied to precision viti-culture. We have argued that the design of an IoT solution requires a careful planning of the two main system elements: the sensor network and the information system. The design of the network requires not only having a clear understanding of the main goals of the end application, but equally important to consider the technical constraints of the network technology. As for the design of the information system, a set of tools should be integrated including the storage, processing and visualization of the data collected by the sensors. Our immediate research efforts will be focused on:

- Development of a tool allowing us to easily define the IoT network layout. Our main goal is to develop a tool facilitating the configuration and reconfiguration of the network based on the quality of the results reported by the system.
- Development and evaluation of additional data processing and visualization tools. One of the first tasks will be to incorporate pattern-matching tool applied to the prevention and detection of anomalous situations.

Acknowledgements. This work has been partially sponsored by the Spanish Ministry of Economy and Competitiveness under grant number TIN2015-66972-C5-2-R; and by the Regional Council of Castilla-La Mancha, under grant number POII11-0334-9283.

References

1. Miorandi, D., Sicari, S., De Pellegrini, F., Chlamtac, I.: Internet of things: vision, applications and research challenges. Ad Hoc Netw. **10**(7), 1497–1516 (2012)
2. Olivares Montes, T., Orozco Barbosa, L., López Camacho, V., Pedrón, P.: WISEVINE: wireless sensor network applied to vineyards. In: Proceedings of ACM International Workshop on Real-World Wireless Sensor Networks (ACM REALWSN06), Uppsala, June 2006
3. Matese, A., Di Gennaro, S.F.: Technology in precision viticulture – a state of the art review. Int. J. Wine Res. **7**, 69–81 (2015)
4. Pérez Verdú, J.L., Feliu Jofre, A.: Manual of Techniques for Sustainable Mountain Viticulture LIFE-PRIORAT Project. Fundació Fòrum Ambienta (2007). www.forumambiental.com
5. Ruiz-Garcia, L., Lunadei, L., Barreiro, P., Robla, J.I.: A review of wireless sensor technologies and applications in agriculture and food industry: state of the art and current trends. Sensors **9**, 4728–4750 (2009). Basel
6. http://www.memsic.com/wireless-sensor-networks/
7. Sundararaman, B., Buy, U., Kshemkalyani, A.D.: Clock synchronization for wireless sensor networks: a survey. Ad Hoc Netw. **3**(3), 281–323 (2005)
8. An, W., Ci, S., Luo, H., Wu, D., Adamchuk, V., Sharif, H., Wang, X., Tang, H.: Effective sensor deployment based on field information coverage in precision agriculture. Wirel. Commun. Mob. Comput. **15**, 1606–1620 (2015)
9. Pande, M., Choudhari, N.K., Pathak, S.: Energy efficient hybrid architecture and positioning of sensors in WSN for precision agriculture. In: Proceedings of the CUBE International Information Technology Conference (CUBE 2012), pp. 198–203. ACM, New York
10. http://www.memsic.com/wireless-sensor-networks/
11. Shepard, D.: A two-dimensional interpolation function for irregularly-spaced data. In: Proceedings of the 1968 ACM National Conference, pp. 517–524

GARMDROID: IoT Potential Security Threats Analysis Through the Inference of Android Applications Hardware Features Requirements

Abraham Rodríguez-Mota[1], Ponciano Jorge Escamilla-Ambrosio[2(✉)],
Jassim Happa[3], and Eleazar Aguirre-Anaya[2]

[1] Instituto Politécnico Nacional, Escuela Superior de Ingeniería Mecánica y Eléctrica,
Unidad Zacatenco, Av. IPN S/N, 07738 México D.F., Mexico
armesimez@gmail.com
[2] Instituto Politécnico Nacional, Centro de Investigación en Computación,
México D.F., Mexico
pescamilla@cic.ipn.mx
[3] Department of Computer Science, University of Oxford, Oxford OX1 3QD, UK
http://www.esimez.ipn.mx/

Abstract. Applications and services based on the Internet of Things (IoT) are increasingly vulnerable to disruption from attack or information theft. Developers and researchers attempt to prevent the growth of such disruption models, mitigate and limit their impact. Meeting these challenges requires understanding the characteristics of things and the technologies that empower the IoT since traditional protection mechanisms are not enough. Moreover, as the growth in mobile device market is pushing the deployment of the IoT, tools and mechanisms to evaluate, analyze and detect security threats in these devices are strongly required. In this context, this paper presents a web tool, named GARMDROID, aimed to help IoT software developers and integrators to evaluate IoT security threats based on the visualization of Android application hardware requests. This procedure is based on the static analysis of permissions requested by Android applications.

Keywords: Internet of Things · Android · Security threats

1 Introduction

The Internet of Things (IoT) promises to extend "anywhere, anyhow, anytime" computing to "anything, anyone any service". Each person and thing has a locatable, addressable, and readable counterpart on the Internet. Such highly-distributed nature and use of fragile technologies, such as limited-function embedded devices in public areas, create weak links that malicious entities can exploit [1]. Consequently, a number of different factors may arise and lead to different types of security exposures, among them consistently defects, bugs and

© ICST Institute for Computer Sciences, Social Informatics and Telecommunications Engineering 2017
E. Sucar et al. (Eds.): AFI 2016, LNICST 179, pp. 63–74, 2017.
DOI: 10.1007/978-3-319-49622-1_8

logical flaws are causes of commonly exploited software vulnerabilities [2]. Therefore, the challenge is to prevent the growth of such models or at least to mitigate
and limit their impact.

Traditional IoT protection mechanisms, such as lightweight cryptography,
secure protocols, and privacy assurance are not enough. In this sense, research
must be oriented to analyze current security protocols and mechanisms, and
decide whether such approaches are worth integrating into the IoT as is or if
adaptation or entirely new designs will better accomplish security goals. Since
attacks could involve various layers of the device infrastructure, they could
include applications running on smartphones or tables, cloud services (firmware
included), and network service stacks on WiFi modules (as well as the firmware
and application layer on the host processor) [1].

In IoT mobile applications, new vulnerabilities continue to emerge as IoT
becomes a more attractive target. In terms of the nature of mobile devices,
their vulnerability surface share attributes with traditional client/server and
Web applications. However the type of information that is trusted on mobile
devices creates some unique attack vectors as well. For example, privacy violation
weaknesses occurring on mobile devices can lead to the disclosure of location,
sensitive images, and data entered from the keyboard or displayed on the screen
and other personal information [2].

Taking into account that in recent years Android OS has become one of the
principal sharers in the global mobile devices market [3], our research has focused
on the analysis and detection of security threats in Android applications. This
paper presents a subset of functionalities of an Android malware hybrid analysis
and detection software system, currently under development. Although GAR-
MDROID has a bigger aim, oriented to integrate static and dynamic malware
analysis, since static analysis is usually the first approach to malware analysis, we
focus this discussion on the capabilities of GARMDROID to provide quick feedback to developers producing a visualization of app's permissions and features
requirements which, as discussed later on, result very handy in the identification of potential threats or bad designed software. This system has been named
GARMDROID as a result of the fusion of the words GARM and Android (in
Norse mythology, Garm is a dog described as a blood stained watchdog that
guards Hel's gate [4]).

2   Android Overview

An Android device can have a wide variety of sensors. Android's sensing capabilities are derived from the available hardware on Android devices and from
creative use of it. A capability may use values directly from hardware that can
measure physical quantities or it may use hardware that the user typically inter-
acts with, such as the camera and microphone. A capability may even use a
combination of hardware and server-based processing, such as speech recognition. Whatever the source, the resulting data can inform an application (app)
about the device's state and the environment in which it resides [5].

In any app, acquiring sensor data requires similar code. Each kind of data requires different boilerplate. In many cases, is not trivial to initialize the API and acquire the data. Once an app can initialize and acquire sensor data, it needs to utilize the APIs to collect the data while the app is running. Data can be collected in different ways depending on how an app uses it. For example, location tracking is a common use of location sensors, in this case some apps need to persistently track location while an app performs other tasks. In the case of speech recognition, such app needs to have other components besides actually running the speech recognizer. An app also needs to allow the user to activate speech and mediate turn taking between when the user can speak and when the app is listening [5].

In this sense, a <uses-feature> element contained in an *AndroidManifest.xml* file, declares a single software feature that is used by an application. The purpose of declaring these elements is to inform any external entity of the set of hardware and software features on which an application depends. The element offers a required attribute that lets developers specify whether the application requires and cannot function without the declared feature, or whether it prefers to have the feature but can function without it. Because feature support can vary across Android devices, the declaration of these elements serves an important role in letting an application describe the device-variable features that it uses [6].

Declaring features is for informational purposes only. The Android system itself does not check for matching features support on the device before installing an application. However, other services (such as Google Play) or applications may check the declarations in the application as part of handling or interacting with the application. When a user searches or browses for applications using the Google Play application, the service compares the features needed by each application with the features available on the user's device. If all of an application's required features are present on the device, Google Play allows the user to see the application and potentially download it. If any required feature is not supported by the device, Google Play filters the application so that it is not visible to the user and not available for download [6].

An explicitly declared feature is one that an applications declares in a <uses-feature> element. The feature declaration can include an *android:required=["true"—"false"]* attribute (if the code is being compiled against function API level 5 or higher), which lets the developer specify whether the application absolutely requires the feature and cannot function properly without it, or whether the application prefers to use the feature if available, but it is designed to run without it. In general, if an application is designed to run on Android 1.6 and earlier versions, the *android:required* attribute is not available in the API and Google Play assumes that any and all feature declarations are required [6].

An implicit feature is one that an application requires in order to function properly, but which is not declared in the manifest file. Strictly speaking, every application should always declare all features that it uses or requires, so the absence of a declaration for a feature used by an application should be considered an error. However, as a safeguard for users and developers, Google Play looks for implicit features in each application and sets up filters for those features, just as it would do for an explicitly declared feature. Google Play attempts to discover an application's implied feature requirements by examining other elements declared in the manifest file, specifically, <*uses-permission*> elements [6].

If an application requests hardware-related permissions, Google Play assumes that the application uses the underlying hardware features and therefore requires those features, even though there might be no corresponding features declarations. For such permissions, Google Play adds the underlying hardware features to the metadata that it stores for the application and sets up filters for them [6].

3   Android Threats

The way people experience and interact with devices is changing. More and more gadgets and devices are being added to the Internet of Things ecosystem everyday. The interconnection between these gadgets and devices has the potential to create remarkable, new user experiences [7]. However, novel technology can lead to exposures, as the implications of new technologies can sometimes be difficult to guess and avenues of attack can be unexpected until observed in practice [2].

Mobile application vulnerabilities continue to evolve as Android devices become attractive targets. Mobile devices contain sensors and actuators of types not historically common in personal computers or servers, which collect and transmit private information about the user of the device. The list of sensors that can reveal sensitive information include cameras, microphones, accelerometers, gravity sensors, rotational vector sensors, gyroscopes, magnetometer, Global Positioning System (GPS) sensors, Near-Field Communication (NFC), light sensors, M7 tracking chips, barometers, thermometers, pedometers, heart-rate monitors, and fingerprint sensors [2].

Privacy-violation weaknesses occurring on mobile devices can lead to the disclosure of location, sensitive images, data entered from the keyboard or displayed on the screen and other personal information. While smartphones can be used for viewing, manipulating, and storing local data, these devices also allow users to interact with a world of interconnected resources from the convenience of their hands. Through communication protocols, both sensitive and benign data is shared between remote services in different devices [2]. In the context of Android, privacy violation weaknesses can be related to a set of security risks, Fig. 1 presents 10 of the biggest Android security risks.

Additionally, it must also be considered that insecure deployment combines various configurations, settings, and states that result in unnecessary weaknesses. For mobile applications this may include not using technologies of content protection such as PlayReady DRM, not checking to determine if the application is running on a compromised device, or exhibiting properties that may indicate malicious intent [2].

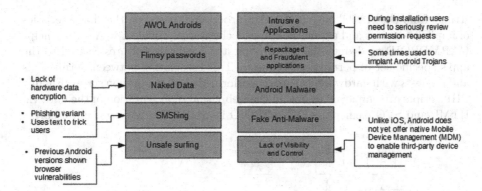

Fig. 1. Android security risks, based on [8].

3.1 Android Malware Analysis

Malware analysis is a process in which the malware is taken apart for study-ing its code structure, operation and functionality. It is conducted with specific objectives which include: to understand the vulnerability that was exploited, to study the severity of the attack and counteracting measures, to penetrate into the compromised data in order to investigate its origin and to obtain information about other compromised machines [9]

Detection techniques for Android malware use statically extracted data from the manifest file or from Android API function calls, as well as dynamically obtained information from network traffic and system call tracing [11]. Most of current systems used to detect malicious code are largely based on syntactic signatures and employ static analysis techniques. Static analysis techniques can be evaded by malware applications using techniques such as polymorphism and metamorphism, since syntactic signatures are ignorant of semantics of instruc-tions [12].

4 GARMDROID

GARMDROID is based on the capabilities provided by the Android SDK tool set, specifically the Android Asset Packaging Tool (AAPT) which is contained as part of the *platform tools* set. In this implementation clients can upload malware samples and request analysis via a Web interface. Figure 2a presents a general representation of the Web system.

During analysis, once an android application file (.apk) has been uploaded by a user, GARMDROID uses a set of bash and python scripts to command AAPT to extract the contents of the app's AndroidManifest.xml file and to filter out the important strings. In this case, as shown in Fig. 2b, the system's software stack includes Java at the bottom layer as it is required to run the AAPT. Python and Bash programming is on top of the AAPT layer since a set of python and bash scripts are used to filter out permissions and feature-request strings from the AAPT output. Further processing, based on the characteristics of implicit features and explicit features declarations provided by Android, helps GARMDROID to deduce the set of requested hardware features related to the app's specific set of permissions requests. This association between permissions and requests with hardware features is performed also by a python script. Finally, PHP scripts are employed to obtain the web visual representation of the data via HTML and SVG elements. GARMDROID is available at www.garmdroid.org.

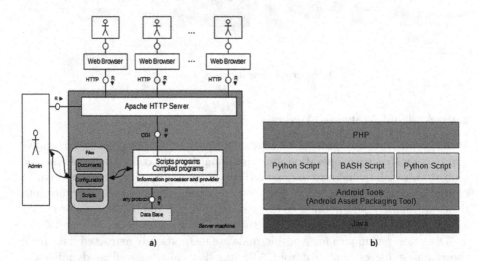

Fig. 2. System representation, (a) Web system and (b) software stack

Figure 3 shows the main page of the system from where users can upload files and see the results after file processing. Once the application file is processed the tool displays the name, mime type, size and md5 hash value of the file. Additionally, permissions and features are identified and displayed. In the case of permissions, Fig. 4a, it has been selected to visualize the requested permissions as a matrix of dots where permissions requested by the application under analysis are indicated as red dots. Features have been represented as icons in order to facilitate visualization: Audio, Bluetooth, Camera, Infrared, Location, Microphone, NFC, Sensors (Accelerometer, Barometer, Compass, Gyroscope, Light, Proximity, Step Counter, Step Detector), Screen, Telephony, Television, Touchscreen, USB and WiFi, see Fig. 4b.

5   Results

In this section a set of results obtained after processing a group of Android applications using GARMDROID is presented. Our results take form of five different case scenarios (apps). In each case GARMDROID presents an inference of the set of hardware features requested by the app under analysis, plus the set

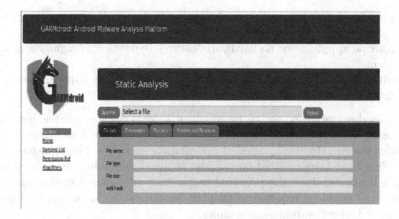

Fig. 3. GARMDROID welcome page

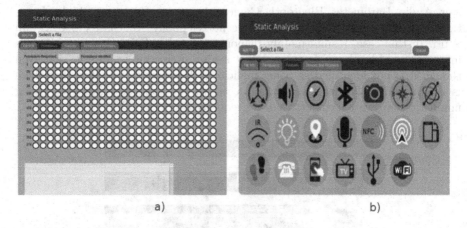

Fig. 4. (a) Permissions tab, additionally to the dot matrix representation, in which hovering over a circle provides the full permission name, a textbox element at the bottom of the tab also displays the identified permissions; (b) Features tab, representing hardware features as icons which change its background color to red if they are requested by the file under analysis. (Color figure online)

of permissions requests. These cases serve a two-fold purpose: to demonstrate GARMDROID operation and direct the discussion towards observations which can lead to identify security threats in IoT-oriented Android applications. In brief, the five cases presented and conclusions drawn can be summarize as follow:

1. Hardware-Test app: granting high volume of permissions and access to hardware features may increase security risks.
2. Lighting app: inconsistency between app's functionality and hardware features requests must raise security concerns.

3. IR remote control apps: excessive hardware feature requests may imply security risks.
4. Gyroscope app: little or no hardware features requests may signify a security problem.
5. Hardware-Test app: problems inferring hardware features requests may imply security risk or app design problems.

In this description it has to be assumed that applications have been analyzed using VirusTotal [13], and in all cases where identified as benign, unless otherwise stated. Moreover, detailed information such as application name and hash values have been omitted on purpose to avoid misleading users from using such applications, since the provided results are only demonstrative and further analysis could be required to properly identify some of the applications as malware or bad software design samples.

Firstly, a Hardware-Test application was analyzed, see Fig. 5. As it can be observed the analysis shows that this application requests access to Accelerometer, Audio, Barometer, Bluetooth, Camera, Compass, Gyroscope, Light, Location, Microphone, NFC, Proximity, Screen, Telephony, Touchscreen, USB and WiFi. In this case, results mainly demonstrate GARMDROID's capability to infer requested hardware features, but it is also interesting to observe that even though it is not identified as being malicious, it is easy to visualize that there is a high risk in allowing this kind of access to any application, due to the big number of hardware elements that are requested.

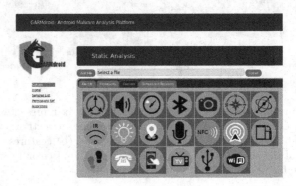

Fig. 5. Features requests for a selected Hardware-Test application.

Secondly, Fig. 6 shows the features requested by an allegedly lighting app. The results may raise suspicion since the application requests not only access to the camera (assuming that the lighting functionality is provided by using the camera flash functionality) but to Location and WiFi features as well.

Thirdly, a couple of Infrared Remote Control apps were analyzed, see Fig. 7. In this case we observed that there is a big difference between the set of features requested which may be a reason to promote a further analysis over the application requesting more than the IR feature (Bluetooth and WiFi).

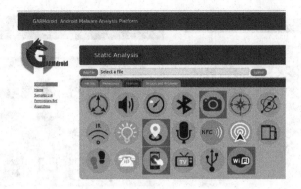

Fig. 6. Features requested by a lighting app.

Fig. 7. Comparison between features-requests by two different Remote-Control Infrared apps.

The following case, see Fig. 8 presents an application advertised as capable to provide gyroscope data. Interestingly, none permission was requested and only the touch screen request is made. At this stage there was no evidence to define whether these characteristics are related to a security threat or a poor design, but provides a strong reason to think that further analysis is required.

As our final case, a Hardware-Test app is presented which requested features but not following the Android specification (Upper case text was used where the specification indicates lower case). This case was detected as a result of a further analysis of the app after observing that no features were indicated on the GAMDROID features tab. Although more information would be required to determine whether the application represents a threat or not, there is an indication of a bad software design. Figure 9 illustrates these results.

Finally, after analyzing four IoT oriented apps samples (home automation type) results were compared with those obtained from analyzing 369 Fake-Installer Android malware samples, see Fig. 10. In this respect, although the selected IoT samples set is small, after comparing the results it can be observed that a request for telephony hardware is not a common feature for home

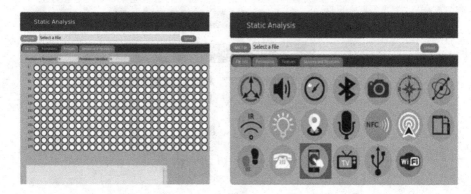

Fig. 8. Gyroscope application which does not request any permission but request the touch screen feature only.

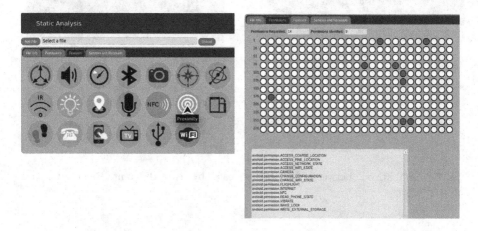

Fig. 9. Hardware-Test app with anomalous feature-request declarations.

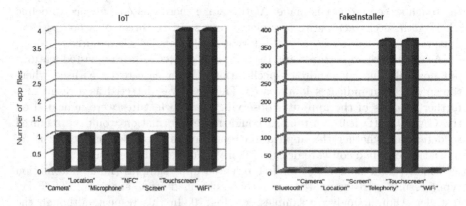

Fig. 10. Features requested by IoT Android Samples (home automation type) and applications identified as FakeInstaller malware

automation apps. From the point of view of developers it can be assumed as a good indication that further analysis is required.

6 Conclusions

Despite the fact that openness has been an important factor in Android fast positioning into the mobile market, it is clear that it implies certain security challenges. In the case of the Internet of Things (IoT) the growing adoption of devices and solutions that incorporate Android has brought those challenges into the realm of the IoT. Therefore, in order to guarantee high security levels IoT developers need to get more involved in the analysis and detection of security threats.

Since IoT development requires a vast and detailed knowledge of diverse technological aspects it is always difficult to count with personnel experienced in those many areas. Consequently, the use and development of new tools and analysis techniques that facilitate or simplify in some extent security analysis are becoming important research and development areas. This paper presented a proof-of-concept that demonstrates visual representations of some application's static features that could help developers to direct security analysis.

Although only a part of the system under development is described in this paper, it is considered that the features provided currently represent a useful asset for software development in the IoT area when compared with other options currently in the marked. As an example, the identification of "suscpicious" hardware features requests discussed in this paper only required from a user a quick review of the visual information, whether a similar analysis using raw analysis data, e.g. from VirusTotal, would require more effort reading all permissions identified and selecting those that could let to infer the hardware features. It must be considered that this task can be performed easily for few samples but it becomes error prone as the number of permissions per app and apps under analysis increases.

In terms of the results presented in this work, it can be concluded that visualization of features requested by an Android app may provide a simple and quick overview of the app's real intentions. This, combined with the knowledge of the permissions requested by the application, provides a good reference for developers that are faced with the decision of whether or not to reuse code, install a new application, grant permissions, define features requests, among other tasks. Further analysis and development is planed in this research in order to integrate these results with others from more elaborated techniques, such as machine learning, in order to provide a more detailed and holistic analysis. Some work in this direction is in progress at our research institution.

Acknowledgments. This material is based on work supported by the Mexican National Council of Science and Technology (CONACYT) under grant 216747. Also the authors acknowledge support from IPN under grant SIP-20161697.

References

1. Roman, R., Najera, P., Lopez, J.: Securing the Internet of Things. IEEE Computer **44**(9), 51–58 (2011)
2. Childs, D., Gilliland, A., Gorenc, B., Goudey, H., Gunn, A., Hoole, A., Lancaster, J., Muthurajan, S., Wook, Oh, J., Tsipenyuk O'Neil, Y., Park, J., Petrovsky, O., Sechman, J., Shah, N., Sotack, T., Svajcer, V.: The HPE Cyber Risk Report 2015. HP (2015)
3. Gartner: Gartner Says Worldwide Smartphone Sales Recorded Slowest Growth Rate Since 2013, 6 January 2016. http://www.gartner.com/newsroom/id/3115517
4. Wikipedia: Garmr. 15 November 2015. https://en.wikipedia.org/wiki/Garmr
5. Milette, G., Stroud, A.: Professional Android Sensor Programming. Wiley, Indianapolis (2012)
6. Android developers: uses-features, 10 December 2015. http://developer.android.com/intl/es/guide/topics/manifest/uses-feature-element.html
7. Embarcadero: Internet of Things Solutions, 2 January 2016. https://www.embarcadero.com/solutions/internet-of-things
8. Phifer, L.: Top 10 Android Security Risks, 14 May 2015. http://www.esecurityplanet.com/views/article.php/3928646/Top-10-Android-Security-Risks.htm
9. Kendall, K.: Practical Malware Analysis, 07 May 2015. https://www.blackhat.com/presentations/bh-dc-07/Kendall_McMillan/Paper/bh-dc-07-Kendall_McMillan-WP.pdf
10. Childs, D., Gilliland, A., Gorenc, B., Goudey, H., Gunn, A., Hoole, A., Lancaster, J.: Cyber Risk Report 2015 Hewlett-Packard. Technical report, HP Security Research (2015)
11. Afonso, V., de Amorim, M., Grgio, A.R.A., Junquera, G., de Geus, P.: Identifying Android malware using dynamically obtained features. J. Comput. Virology Hacking Tech. **11**, 9–17 (2015)
12. Moser, A., Kruegel, C., Kirda, E.: Limits of static analysis for malware detection. In: Computer Security Applications Conference 2007, ACSAC 2007, pp. 421–430 (2007)
13. VirusTotal, 05 December 2015. https://www.virustotal.com/es-mx/

Making the Intelligent Home Smart Through Touch-Control Trigger-Action Programming

Guan Wang[✉] and Michael L. Littman

Brown University, Providence, RI 02912, USA
{wang,mlittman}@cs.brown.edu

Abstract. We introduces a new UI model of Trigger-Action Programming (TAP), that allows users to program through touch-control interfaces to create complicated tasks easily. We present three different user interfaces (UI), for each user interface, we analyze its advantages, limitations, and potential utility. We explain how our UIs can mitigate the problems of TAP caused by ambiguity and demonstrate why our UIs will benefit people without programming backgrounds.

Keywords: Trigger-action programming · Touch-control interface · Smart home · End-user programming

1 Introduction

Trigger-action programming (TAP) makes it possible for people with non-technical backgrounds to write programs in a high-level way. Existing tools, such as IF-THIS-THEN-THAT (IFTTT), enable users to control real devices and virtual services in an intelligent way by creating online tasks remotely. The user interface of IFTTT builds a "rule" as a one-dimensional "IF-A-Then-B" structure. To create a TAP rule, a user chooses from the list of applications supported by IFTTT and decides what A and B should be. This design enables autonomy in devices and services. An example rule is "IFit rains tomorrowTHENsend me an email". However, many useful tasks in real life have a higher-level of complexity that cannot be represented by the simple logic of "IF-A-THEN-B".[1]

On the other hand, research has shown that there are sometimes differences between a user's real intent, his semantic expression, and the program created by the user [2]. To mitigate this problem, which is caused by ambiguity, misunderstanding, and oversimplification of TAP systems, we introduce our own UIs that uses touch control to help end-users build TAP programs of higher complexity in an easy and accurate way.

2 Related Work

Our research builds upon previous investigations of TAP for context-aware systems, and more general end-user programming. Dey et al. discovered through

© ICST Institute for Computer Sciences, Social Informatics and Telecommunications Engineering 2017
E. Sucar et al. (Eds.): AFI 2016, LNICST 179, pp. 75–78, 2017.
DOI: 10.1007/978-3-319-49622-1_9

their visual programming system iCAP that users often specified actions in a TAP-like manner when they are asked to think of behaviors for context-aware applications. [3] Pane et al. also stated similar conclusion that consistency exists between users' mental models and the IF-THEN style specification. [4] Other researchers have also discovered obstacles in applying TAP in smart homes. Newman et al. presented that designing rules which perform actions based on future states is often difficult, especially for none-programming-background users. [5] Ur et al. discussed the problem of users creating rules that require multiple events and conditions to occur at once, and their study showed that there are certain amount of goals in "smart homes" can not be done by the simple IF-A-THEN-B structure. [1] Conducting two studies to examine user's interpretations of TAP rules, Huang et al. claimed that there could be a significant discrepancy between a rule expressed in an IF-THEN style and the performance expected by the user who created the rule. [2] Other studies have also inspired our work, Ghiani et al. mentioned in their paper that lacking feedback could be a hindrance in TAP systems, and that contributed our idea of the "rehearse" function.

3   UIs

There are two purposes of our design: Enabling complex tasks to be constructed easily; Mitigating the problems caused by ambiguity. Given the trend toward mobile devices, we design our UIs based on touch control, making it easy and comfortable for users to create and edit tasks with smart phones or tablets. The design of our touch-control technology, "drag-and-link", is inspired by previous work such as the research project "Math Tutor" [6]. For each interface, users can use their fingers to click, drag, and link between objects in a two-dimensional space. The system checks the validity of the current program automatically, and will display a "REHEARSE" button in the top-right corner whenever a task is completed with no error. By clicking the button, the user will see a rehearsal of the program that he has just made, allowing him to tell whether the performance matches his interpretation.

Figure 1 shows the user experience of 3 UI. In UI 1, the interface is an unconstrained two-dimensional space. The search bar at the top allows the user to query applications. The bottom bar contains two rows of buttons, where the first row has "IF, THEN, WHENEVER, AS LONG AS, WHILE, AFTER", and the second row is "AND, OR, NOT". By adding these functional words, we enhance the original IFTTT statement model to allow the expression of higher-level tasks. The user can click anywhere on the screen to get a menu of icons of supported applications and services. After all icons are placed, the user can use his finger to link between them. If the link is valid, it will be shown as a purple arrow starting from the origin icon to the target icon. Whenever a syntactically valid task is detected by the system, the rehearse button appears.

UI 2 is an updated model of UI 1. We noticed that time is one of the most important features in TAP. Adding time features to each trigger and action

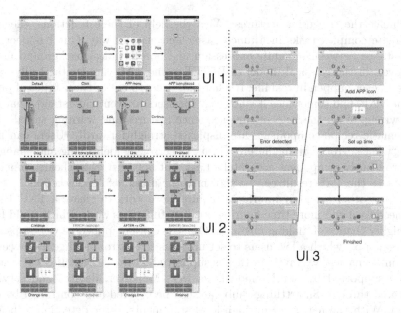

Fig. 1. User experience flow of UI 1, UI 2, and UI 3 (Color figure online)

reveals: (1) When a TAP ends; (2) The duration of a TAP; (3) Inherent conflicts like "IF-It's 6 pm-THEN-email me at 5 pm"; (4) Possible ambiguities by helping the user understand the time sequence better. UI 2 can detect logical errors that are syntactically valid, but do not make sense in real life. When the user wants to add an application icon, he will need to set up two features: The duration is represented as a rectangle attached to the bottom of the app icon; The time that the app starts is activated as a rectangle attached to the right of the app icon. The default setting of duration is "instantaneously", which means that if no duration number is given, the app will run and only run once instantaneously. Similarly, the rule will be activated ever since it's checked in by default.

UI 3 comes with a unique feature, a timeline, which shows the time sequence directly and obviously. By clicking at the screen, a timeline will appear, which allows the user to drop pins (APP icons) onto it. For each pin, the user can slide it to the right to activate the feature of duration. Once the system detects a valid TAP, a rehearse button will appear similar to the behavior of other 2 UIs.

4 Discussion

Our UIs mitigate the problems of ambiguity via using time features, and higher-level statements. The original IFTTT expression cannot deal with situations like: (1) what to do when a TAP ends; (2) how long each trigger or action should last; (3) how many times will a TAP execute; and (4) recipes with more than one trigger. In our UIs, we use "AND, OR, NOT" to represent the logic functionality. We also introduce "AFTER, WHILE, AS LONG AS, WHENEVER" to enhance the triggering features. With the help of these functions, the user can create complex tasks in a much easier and simpler way. Our UIs decrease the distance between semantic expression and non-technical background users. Moreover, in the classical model of IFTTT, some TAPs are syntactically valid but can never happen in real life. It's hard for users to notice these types of problems in TAP, and sometimes it's not easy for users to even understand what has gone wrong. With the help of time-sequence features and warning signals, the problematic recipe components are displayed straightforwardly. Users can now learn "what's wrong" immediately and fix the error by identifying and changing the erroneously component accurately. Last, but not least, the rehearse function guarantees the TAP result can be shown to the users before checked in.

On the other side, our interfaces require more work to create a TAP. Users may need to spend more time figuring out how functions work, which could lead to a higher chance of making mistakes. Our UIs can be applied to web-apps and universal apps, which allow users to set up tasks to control intelligent devices at home in a smart way. Anything that is supported by the current IFTTT system will be supported by our UI models as well. Moreover, devices and services connected through Smartthings hub can also be covered and controlled by our system. With the nature of its high-level statements, error detection, rehearse functionality, our UIs can be a useful tool to introduce classical programming.

Acknowledgement. Members of the Brown UPOD Research Group provided valuable feedback. Stephen Brawner came up with suggestions. Blase Ur, Tushar Bhargava, Jiyun Lee, Diane Schulze, and Jared Cohen also gave helpful feedback.

References

1. Ur, B., McManus, E., Pak Yong Ho, M., Littman, M.L.: Practical trigger-action programming in the smart home. In: Proceedings of the SIGCHI Conference on Human Factors in Computing Systems, pp. 803–812. ACM, April 2014
2. Huang, J., Cakmak, M.: Supporting mental model accuracy in trigger-action programming. In: Proceedings of the 2015 ACM International Joint Conference on Pervasive and Ubiquitous Computing, pp. 215–225. ACM, September 2015
3. Dey, A.K., Sohn, T., Streng, S., Kodama, J.: iCAP: interactive prototyping of context-aware applications. In: Fishkin, K.P., Schiele, B., Nixon, P., Quigley, A. (eds.) Pervasive 2006. LNCS, vol. 3968, pp. 254–271. Springer, Heidelberg (2006). doi:10.1007/11748625_16
4. Pane, J.F., Myers, B.A.: Studying the language and structure in non-programmers' solutions to programming problems. Int. J. Hum. Comput. Stud. **54**(2), 237–264 (2001)
5. Newman, M.W., Elliott, A., Smith, T.F.: Providing an integrated user experience of networked media, devices, and services through end-user composition. In: Indulska, J., Patterson, D.J., Rodden, T., Ott, M. (eds.) Pervasive 2008. LNCS, vol. 5013, pp. 213–227. Springer, Heidelberg (2008). doi:10.1007/978-3-540-79576-6_13
6. Wang, G., Bowditch, N., Kwon, M., Zeleznik, R., Laviola, J.: A tablet-based math tutor for beginning algebra. In: 2015 Workshop on the Impact of Pen and Touch Technology on Education (WIPTTE 2015), Redmond, WA, 28-30 April (2015)

Optimal Scheduling of On/Off Cycles:
A Decentralized IoT-Microgrid Approach

Fernando Lezama[1]([⊠]), Jorge Palominos[1], Ansel Y. Rodríguez-González[1],
Alessandro Farinelli[2], and Enrique Munoz de Cote[1]

[1] Instituto Nacional de Astrofísica, Óptica y Electrónica, 72840 Puebla, Mexico
{f.lezama,jpalominos,ansel,jemc}@inaoep.mx
[2] University of Verona, 37134 Verona, Italy
alessandro.farinelli@univr.it

Abstract. The current energy scenario requires actions towards the
reduction of energy consumptions and the use of renewable resources.
To this end, the energy grid is evolving towards a distributed architecture called Smart Grid (SG). Moreover, new communication paradigms,
such as the Internet of Things (IoT), are being applied to the SG providing advanced communication capabilities for management and control. In this context, a microgrid is a self-sustained network that can
operate connected to the SG (or in isolation). In such networks, the
long-term scheduling of on/off cycles of devices is a problem that has
been commonly addressed by centralized approaches. In this paper, we
propose a novel IoT-microgrid architecture to model the long-term optimization scheduling problem as a distributed constraint optimization
problem (DCOP). We compare different multi-agent DCOP algorithms
using different window sizes showing that the proposed architecture can
find optimal and near-optimal solutions for a specific case study.

Keywords: Multi-agent · Smart Grid · IoT · Microgrid · Optimization

1 Introduction

The current world scenario including global warming, increase in carbon emissions, and the growing world population and power demand has led to governments, energy utilities, and research centers to take concrete actions towards the
reduction of energy consumptions and the use of renewable resources [1].

Due to this, the electric grid has evolved over the last decades to a highly
automated energy network, widely known as Smart Grid (SG). The SG is an
advanced power network that incorporates two-way communication for efficient
control, reliability and safety [2]. Moreover, the SG abandons the centralized
nature of the traditional electric grid towards a decentralized architecture in
which the electricity is produced in a distributed way, and customers can be
producers and consumers (i.e., prosumers) at the same time [3].

In this scenario the concept of microgrid provides a complementary solution
to achieve more efficient energy management in small areas [4]. A microgrid is a

E. Sucar et al. (Eds.): AFI 2016, LNICST 179, pp. 79–90, 2017.
DOI: 10.1007/978-3-319-49622-1_10

small self-sustained power network, with local distribution and local generators that uses renewable energy (such as solar, wind, biomass, among others). Moreover, a *smart* microgrid can be seen as an independent home management system that uses a combination of the electric home network and the Internet to manage home appliances and local generators in an intelligent and efficient way. Both energy consumption and generation should be considered to save energy cost at the user end [5]. In addition, a key element for a microgrid is peer-to-peer communication and plug-and-play functionalities, allowing distributed control and scalability without significant modifications of the grid.

Different technologies used in other industrial applications, such as sensor or wireless networks, can be adopted for the communication of the devices within the SG. Nevertheless, to reduce the number of communication protocols and to handle a significant amount of data, the Internet of things (IoT) arises as one of the most recent enablers of the SG, and it is expected to continue playing a crucial role in the evolution of the SG [2,6].

Figure 1 shows a SG and a microgrid as a home management system. One of the main problems to tackle in a microgrid is the control and management of resources through the scheduling of on/off cycles of devices. A trivial solution can be to turn on the micro generators all the time and storage the exceeded energy in batteries. The main problem with this trivial solution is that life cycle of generators and batteries is drastically reduced, and there is a cost associated with excessive energy generation. For this reason, a more efficient solution to minimize the cost involves the scheduling of on/off cycles of the devices (also known as the dispatch problem) in the microgrid.

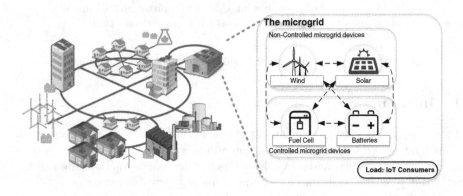

Fig. 1. Smartgrid and microgrid.

The optimal scheduling of on/off cycles of devices in the microgrids can be done in two ways, centralized and decentralized [7]. The centralized approach has the advantage of treating the system as a whole, hence allowing global optimization. However, a centralized approach lacks flexibility since adding new devices to the system implies the recalculation of the entire scheduling, and robustness because losing the central unit shut down all the system [8–10]. On the other hand, the decentralized approach is more flexible, allowing the addition of new devices and performing the optimization in a distributed way according to the tendency of intelligent distribution networks (i.e., the SG).

So far, the decentralized approach has been applied to the optimization scheduling for a particular time without considering long-term optimization [11–13]. However, recently several efforts have been devoted to extend the Distributed Constraint Optimization Problem (DCOP) model so to take system dynamics into consideration. The most prominent approach in this perspective is the Dynamic DCOP model (D-DCOP), where the system evolution is modeled as a sequence of canonical DCOPs computing a new solution each time the system changes (trying to re-use as much as possible the previous solution) [14].

While D-DCOP techniques introduce dynamism to DCOPs, they generally do not capture the sequential nature of the problem: they simply react to changes but do not plan for the best sequence of actions.

Moreover, in many real applications, we also need to take into account the uncertainty related to system dynamic. Recently Markov models have been used to capture the coupling aspect of D-DCOPs in which the DCOP in the next time step is a function of the value assignments in the current time step [15]. A major challenge with this interesting approach is that the problems become rapidly intractable when the size of the problem (e.g., the number of variables for the underlying DCOP) grows.

In this paper, we propose to solve optimal scheduling of on/off cycles for a home microgrid as a multi-agent decentralized approach explicitly considering long-term optimization into account. To this end, each controllable device is modeled as an independent agent with the ability of peer-to-peer communication with other devices (i.e., other agents) in the microgrid. Specifically, we model the problem as a DCOP and we use different off-the-shelf approaches to solve such problem[1].

In more detail, we consider Synchronous Branch and Bound (SynchBB), Distributed Pseudotree-Optimization Procedure (DPOP), Memory-Bounded DPOP (MB-DPOP) and Asynchronous Forward Bounding (AFB) [16], applied to the long-term optimization task.

We compare the performance of such algorithms against the optimal solution returned by a centralized approach. Moreover, we compare the run time, the number and the size of messages for the DCOP algorithms. To solve the long-term optimization problem while maintaining the model tractable, we split the problem into time windows. The results show that, even when the multi-agent distributed approach provides optimal and near-optimal solutions for small window sizes, it pays a large computational cost associated with the interaction of agents for large window sizes.

---

[1] We implemented the DCOP algorithms in FRODO2 and JaCoP. Both available in http://frodo2.sourceforge.net and http://www.jacop.eu respectively.

2   Problem Formulation

We model the microgrid as an IoT-microgrid architecture shown in Fig. 2. This IoT-microgrid architecture has two main blocks. The first block is composed of generators (G) and storage devices (S) (bottom right side of Fig. 2). The generators and storage devices can be grouped as controlled (e.g., fuel cell generators and batteries) and non-controlled (e.g., generators dependent on weather conditions) devices. The second block correspond to the Load formed by IoT consumers (C) (bottom left side of Fig. 2). Such IoT consumers can be different smart appliances, such as smart metering infrastructure, sensors, and other smart devices used for home automation.

The two blocks (i.e., generators and storage devices, and IoT consumers) are linked together and have a connection to external entities, such as the cloud and the SG respectively (upper side of Fig. 2). From the cloud, weather predictions and other information, such as temperature or electric load forecasting, can be retrieved from devices for management and control. Consumers and non-controlled devices provide information as input for the optimization task while the controllable devices can perform actions to modify the conditions of the IoT-microgrid.

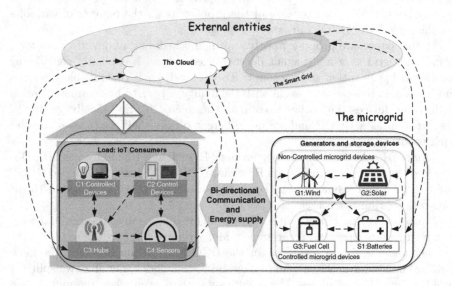

Fig. 2. IoT-microgrid architecture.

In the following, $P_{type,i}(t)$ refers to the production or quantity of energy provided by generators $i = \{1, 2..., N_{type}\}$ of some type of energy $type = \{1, 2..., N\}$ (e.g., wind or solar predictions provided by the cloud) at time t. $P_{BC,j}(t)$ and $P_{BD,j}(t)$ correspond to the energy charge/discharge status respectively of battery $j = \{1, 2, ..., M\}$ at time t. $P_{UE(t)}$ and $P_{EE(t)}$ is the amount of undelivered and exceeded energy at time t. Finally, C is the cost associated with the production or use of each energy.

Our objective is to minimize the cost of generated (E_{gen}) and storage energy ($E_{storage}$), while at the same time keep the balance between production and consume ($E_{disbalance}$) into the microgrid. The objective function is defined as:

$$Minimize \quad f = \sum_{t=1}^{T}(E_{gen}(t) + E_{storage}(t) + E_{disbalance}(t)) \quad (1)$$

where:

$$E_{gen}(t) = \sum_{type=1}^{N}\sum_{i=1}^{N_{type}} P_{type,i}(t) * C_{type,i}(t) \quad (2)$$

$$E_{storage}(t) = \sum_{j=1}^{M}(-P_{BC,j}(t) * C_{BC,j} + P_{BD,j}(t) * C_{BD,j}) \quad (3)$$

$$E_{disbalance}(t) = P_{UE}(t) * C_{UE} - P_{EE}(t) * C_{EE} \quad (4)$$

Subject to the following constraints:

– Kirchhoff law or power balance:

$$\sum_{type=1}^{N}\sum_{i=1}^{N_{type}} P_{type,i}(t) + \sum_{j=1}^{M} P_{BD,j}(t) + P_{UE} = Load(t) + \sum_{j=1}^{M} P_{BC,j}(t) + P_{EE}(t); \forall t \quad (5)$$

where $Load(t)$ is the energy required for all the consumers at time t. Prediction of the $Load$ can be provided by the cloud in the IoT-microgrid architecture.
– Energy type production limits at time t

$$P_{type,i}(t) \leq P_{lim_{type,i}}; \quad \forall type, i, t \quad (6)$$

– Storage, charge and discharge battery limits at each time t

$$P_{Storage,j}(t) \leq P_{lim_{Storage,j}}; \quad \forall j, t \quad (7)$$

$$P_{BD,j}(t) \leq P_{lim_{BD,j}} * X(t); \quad \forall j, t, X \in 0,1 \quad (8)$$

$$P_{BC,j}(t) \leq P_{lim_{BC,j}} * Y(t); \quad \forall j, t, Y \in 0,1 \quad (9)$$

where $P_{Storage,j}$ is the maximum power capacity of the jth battery, and X and Y are boolean variables used to avoid that the jth battery charge and discharge at the same time (i.e., $X(t) + Y(t) \leq 1; \forall t$).
– Charge and discharge limits at time t considering period $t-1$

$$P_{BD,j}(t) - P_{Storage,j}(t-1) \leq 0; \forall j, t \quad (10)$$

$$P_{BC,j}(t) + P_{Storage,j}(t-1) \leq P_{lim_{Storage,j}}; \forall j, t \quad (11)$$

– State balance of the battery

$$P_{Storage,j}(t) = P_{Storage,j}(t-1) - P_{BD,j}(t) + P_{BC,j}(t); \forall j, t \quad (12)$$

This formulation can be optimally solve using Mixed-integer linear programming in a centralized fashion [7]. Different from [7], in the next section we present a long-term decentralized approach that allows solving the problem using agents and DCOP algorithms.

3　Long-Term Multi-agent Optimization

As stated in Sect. 2, in this paper we consider a microgrid with consumers, generators and storage devices. For simplicity, in this section we consider a microgrid with only one solar generator, one wind generator, one fuel cell generator, and one storage device (i.e., one battery). We also assume perfect predictions of solar and wind generation. Moreover, the consumers are grouped all together as a joint *Load*, also known in advanced.

With these considerations, in Fig. 3 we present a distributed multi-agent model for the long-term optimization scheduling of on/off cycles. In this model, agents are the elements (e.g., the fuel cell generator (FC), battery charge (BC) and battery discharge (BD)) that can perform an on/off action to optimize the total cost of energy production in the long-term. These agents receive information of the *Load* and weather conditions (i.e., consumers and renewable energy generation) as input, and perform optimization in a distributed way.

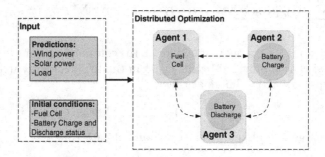

Fig. 3. Multi-agent distributed model.

The decentralized multi-agent architecture enables to treat the problem as a DCOP, allowing the use of distributed multi-agent algorithms such as AFB, DPOP, MB-DPOP, and SynchBB.

The multi-agent algorithms to solve DCOP (e.g., AFB, DPOP, MB-DPOP and SynchBB) distribute the processing among agents. However, optimally solving a DCOP is known to be an NP-complete problem, hence solving the long-term optimization problem directly will be impractical even for a short optimization horizon.

For this reason, we propose to split the problem in time windows. In this way, for a period T, we can solve the problem by dividing such period T in $N_{windows} = T/n$, where n is the size of the window. This means that for a size

$n = 1$ we will solve T windows, for $n = 2$ we will solve T/2 windows and so on. Figure 4 shows the scheme of optimization in time windows. The input for the fist window corresponds to initial conditions of the microgrid (e.g., the battery could start with an initial charge of 100 W, and the fuel-cell generator in off state ready for being activated).

Then, optimization for that window is done by using any of the algorithms to solve the DCOP (e.g., AFB, DPOP, MB-DPOP and SynchSBB). The result obtained in that window is used as input for the next window. The process is repeated sequentially until a solution for the long-term period T is obtained.

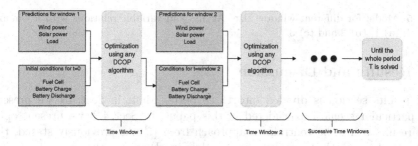

Fig. 4. Optimization using time windows.

One disadvantage of this approach is that the optimal solution cannot be guaranteed and depends directly on the size of the window chosen. Small time windows (e.g., size 1) are solved fast since the optimization is done without knowledge of the future, keeping the information and variable relations low. However, the quality of the solution may not be good enough because of the lack of global vision for the conditions of the successive periods (e.g., wasting all the resources in the current time without considering the demand for the successive time).

It is expected that the quality of the solution improves by increasing the size of the windows. However, as shown in Fig. 5, the number of variables grows significantly with the size of the windows, hence resulting into an exponential growth in the search space of the number of possible configuration to explore. With this in mind, a trade-off between running time (i.e., small sizes) and quality of the solution (i.e., large sizes) has to be considered when solving the long-term optimization problem.

Heuristics and pre-processing strategies can be applied to reduce the configuration search space significantly reducing the run time of the approach in the average case. Nevertheless, in this paper the main objective is to propose a decentralized architecture for the long-term optimization hence the use of such heuristics is out of the scope and will be considered as future work.

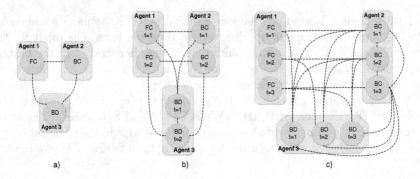

Fig. 5. Model for different window size. Agents and variable relations with a window size of: (a) 1, (b) 2 and (c) 3.

4 Results and Discussion

The results section is divided into three parts. First, in Sect. 4.1 we present the particular scenario considered in this paper. In Sect. 4.2, we present optimal results using the centralized approach from [7]. As previously stated, the centralized approach is less flexible to scalability. However, the optimal solution using such centralized approach is taken as a benchmark. Finally, in Sect. 4.3 we present the results obtained with our decentralized long-term optimization approach.

4.1 Case Study

The reported results consider the Budapest Tech case study presented in [7]. This scenario considers a microgrid with one wind generator (W), one solar generator (S), one fuel cell generator (FC), and one battery. Energy costs are considered constants for simplicity. Such costs and power limits are presented in Table 1.

Table 1. Costs of energy generation and production limits taken from [7].

Costs	Production limits
$C_W = 0.4$ W/h	$P_{lim_W} = 400$ W
$C_S = 0.4$ W/h	$P_{lim_S} = 150$ W
$C_{FC} = 0.9$ W/h	$P_{lim_{FC}} = 80$ W
$C_{BC} = 0.4$ W/h	$P_{lim_{Storage}} = 200$ W
$C_{BD} = 0.6$ W/h	$P_{lim_{BD}} = [0 - 50]$ W
$C_{UE} = 1.5$ W/h	$P_{lim_{BC}} = [0 - 200]$ W
$C_{EE} = 0$ W/h	

Also, the optimization of on/off cycles was done for a period of 24 h (i.e., $T = 24$) in intervals of 1 h. The first 4 columns of Table 2 present the forecast of wind energy (P_W), solar power (P_S), and the joint *Load* at each time t used as an input of the optimization task. Also, we considered that the battery starts fully charged with 100 W.

4.2   Centralized Optimal Solution

We solved the scheduling problem from a centralized perspective as an mixed-integer linear programming (MILP) using Java and ILOG CPLEX. Table 2 shows two different configurations of the controllable devices for the analyzed scenario. Each column has the configuration of fuel cell power (P_{FC}), battery charge (P_{BC}), battery discharge (P_{BD}), undelivered energy (P_{UE}), exceeded energy (P_{EE}), and the cost associated with such configuration at each time t. The total cost of the solution for the long-term optimization in a period T = 24 h is also reported.

We noticed that there were different configurations with the same global optimal value. The problem of multiple configurations that satisfied all the restrictions with minimum cost is known as the degenerated problem [17]. Different configurations were found varying the order in which the restrictions were considered, or the version of CPLEX solver.

The execution times were in the order of 70 mS with a standard deviation of 10 mS after 1000 experiments. We used a PC with Processor Intel(R) Core(TM) i7-4770 @ 3.40 GHz and 16 GB of RAM.

4.3   Decentralized Long-Term Scheduling Results

In this section, we present the results of the proposed decentralized approach for the scenario presented in Sect. 4.1. The optimization procedure was done for different window sizes as explained in Sect. 3. The experiments were run 100 times each. We present the mean value and standard deviation (Std) of those 100 experiments for different DCOP algorithms (i.e., AFB, DPOP, MB-DPOP, and SynchBB).

In general, in this model for an arbitrary window size (WS) and considering 3 agents (i.e., FC, BC, and BD), the number of variables is $3*WS$, the number of constrains is $3*WS + battery_{status}*WS$, and the domain size is $FC^{WS}_{domain}*$ $BC^{WS}_{domain}*BD^{WS}_{domain}$. It can be notice that the domain of each variable grows exponentially along the window size, making the problem not tractable for large window sizes.

Table 3 shows the results of various window sizes reporting the percent error (i.e., the percent error between the long-term decentralized approach and the optimal solution found with the centralized approach of Sect. 4.2), running time, the total number of messages and the total size of messages. It can be seen that DPOP, MB-DPOP, and SynchBB have the same performance. This is because these three algorithms are exact. These three approaches provide an error of 3.64 % for a window size of 1. The error decreases when the window size increases to 2. On the other hand, AFB algorithm found the optimal value for window sizes 3, but the time required to reach the solution was approximately nine

Table 2. Results obtained using Java-ILOG CPLEX. Two optimal configurations.

t	P_W	P_S	Load	P_{FC}	P_{BC}	P_{BD}	P_{UE}	P_{EE}	Cost	P_{FC}	P_{BC}	P_{BD}	P_{UE}	P_{EE}	Cost
1	130	0	160	0	0	30	0	0	70	0	0	30	0	0	70
2	150	0	140	0	10	0	0	0	56	0	0	0	0	10	60
3	140	0	150	0	0	10	0	0	62	0	0	10	0	0	62
4	160	0	120	0	40	0	0	0	48	0	0	0	0	40	64
5	100	0	110	0	0	10	0	0	46	0	0	10	0	0	46
6	120	5	100	0	25	0	0	0	40	0	0	0	0	25	50
7	150	10	170	0	0	10	0	0	70	0	0	10	0	0	70
8	180	30	180	0	30	0	0	0	72	0	0	0	0	30	84
9	170	60	200	0	30	0	0	0	80	0	0	0	0	30	92
10	160	100	220	0	0	0	0	40	104	0	0	0	0	40	104
11	120	130	230	0	20	0	0	0	92	0	0	0	0	20	100
12	130	140	240	0	5	0	0	25	106	0	0	0	0	30	108
13	150	150	240	0	0	0	0	60	120	0	50	0	0	10	100
14	176	140	230	0	0	0	0	86	126.4	0	50	0	0	36	106.4
15	185	130	220	0	0	0	0	95	126	0	50	0	0	45	106
16	120	100	210	0	0	0	0	10	88	0	10	0	0	0	84
17	130	60	210	20	0	0	0	0	94	0	0	20	0	0	88
18	140	30	220	0	0	50	0	0	98	0	0	50	0	0	98
19	170	10	230	0	0	50	0	0	102	0	0	50	0	0	102
20	190	5	240	25	0	20	0	0	112.5	45	0	0	0	0	118.5
21	120	0	250	80	0	50	0	0	150	80	0	50	0	0	150
22	170	0	200	30	0	0	0	0	95	30	0	0	0	0	95
23	130	0	190	60	0	0	0	0	106	60	0	0	0	0	106
24	150	0	180	0	0	30	0	0	78	0	0	30	0	0	78
								Total	2141.9					Total	2141.9

Table 3. Comparison of DCOP algorithms for long-term optimization. Running time are shown in seconds. Messages size are shown in MegaBytes.

Percent error								
Window	AFB	Std	DPOP	Std	MB-DPOP	Std	SynchBB	Std
Size 1	6.34 %	0.0	3.64 %	0.0	3.64 %	0.0	3.64 %	0.0
Size 2	8.30 %	8.3	0.42 %	0.0	0.42 %	0.0	0.42 %	0.0
Size 3	0 %	—	—	—	—	—	—	—
Time								
Size 1	8.1	0.1413	17.3	0.2218	17.2	0.1941	12.3	0.2815
Size 2	2101.3	13.3349	176.6	0.5569	296.7	56.9301	2741.2	137.5269
Size 3	757754.7	—	—	—	—	—	—	—
Number of messages								
Size 1	52785	5.5959	480	0.0	528	0.0	107076	0.0
Size 2	314767	394.3478	628	0.0	688	0.0	5492875	0.0
Size 3	185255337	—	—	—	—	—	—	—
Total size of messages								
Size 1	2.6	$3.87 * 10^{-4}$	0.8	$7.58 * 10^{-6}$	0.8	$6.75 * 10^{-6}$	2.6	$8.56 * 10^{-6}$
Size 2	28	0.0396	2.8	$8.35 * 10^{-6}$	2.9	$8.98 * 10^{-6}$	154.7	0.0
Size 3	2351.7	—	—	—	—	—	—	—

days (e.g., 757754 s). The other three algorithms did not finish the optimization procedure after those nine days. Such behavior can be explained because a small window size (i.e., 1 and 2) does not provide enough information to the agents, limiting the capacity to find the global optimal solution in the long-term. With a window size 3, the agents have sufficient information to find the optimal solution in the long-term but the optimization procedure takes more time since there are more variables to handle by the agents and the search space is too large. The exponential increase in complexity can be also appreciated in the number and size of messages exchanged by the agents in the optimization process.

The results also open research directions for the use of multi-agent systems in the long-term optimization. For instance, it is clear the necessity of faster procedures of search, allowing agents to handle large window sizes and improve the quality of the solutions.

5   Conclusions and Future Work

In this paper, using the concepts of IoT and microgrids, we proposed a distributed architecture of agents for a decentralized management of smart devices. By doing that, the problem of scheduling on/off cycles can be treated as a DCOP, and different multi-agent algorithms can be used to find the solution. Also, knowing that multi-agent algorithms typically do not integrate temporality in their frames due to the large size of variables and search space, we proposed the use of optimization windows to solve the long-term optimization problem sequentially.

Results show that the distributed architecture and time window can be used to find solutions comparable to the optimal for the long-term optimization. Small size windows boost the optimization speed by losing information, limiting the capability of DCOP algorithms. Large window sizes provide more information leading even to the optimal solutions (i.e., with AFB and window size 3), but the search space increases as well, making the optimization task complex. A trade-off must be taken into account between efficiency (i.e., speed) and efficacy (i.e., better solution) when the optimization is performed.

As further work, this paper opens new research directions in different areas. Regarding the DCOP representation, one direction could be the formulation of distributed problems considering time in a compact and natural way. The creation of new restrictions would be needed to include time specifying where and how the variables are connected through time. Another direction, regarding the variable domain of a multi-agent system, will require the develop of new techniques that help to reduce the domain size in challenging scenarios. A way to attack such problem could be through heuristics that help algorithms to find efficiently optimal or near-optimal solutions. Another option would be the implementation of pre-processing techniques to reduce the domain of variables before the application of the optimization algorithms.

References

1. Gungor, V., Sahin, D., Kocak, T., Ergut, S., Buccella, C., Cecati, C., Hancke, G.: A survey on smart grid potential applications and communication requirements. IEEE Trans. Ind. Inf. **9**(1), 28–42 (2013)
2. Yan, Y., Qian, Y., Sharif, H., Tipper, D.: A survey on smart grid communication infrastructures: motivations, requirements and challenges. IEEE Commun. Surv. Tutorials **15**(1), 5–20 (2013)
3. Karnouskos, S.: The cooperative internet of things enabled smart grid. In: IEEE International Symposium on Consumer Electronics (2010)
4. Vega, A., Santamaria, F., Rivas, E.: Modeling for home electric energy management: a review. Renew. Sustain. Energy Rev. **52**, 948–959 (2015)
5. Han, J., sic Choi, C., Park, W.K., Lee, I., Kim, S.H.: Smart home energy management system including renewable energy based on ZigBee and PLC. IEEE Trans. Consum. Electron. **60**(2), 198–202 (2014)
6. Karnouskos, S.: Smart houses in the smart grid and the search for value-added services in the cloud of things era. In: IEEE International Conference on Industrial Technology, pp. 2016–2021, February 2013
7. Morais, H., Kádár, P., Faria, P., Vale, Z.A., Khodr, H.M.: Optimal Scheduling of a renewable micro-grid in an isolated load area using mixed-integer linear programming. Renew. Energy **35**, 151–156 (2010)
8. Bazmohammadi, N., Karimpour, A., Bazmohammadi, S.: Optimal operation management of a microgrid based on MOPSO and differential evolution algorithms. In: IEEE Iranian Conference on Smart Grids, pp. 1–6 (2012)
9. Chaouachi, A., Kamel, R.M., Andoulsi, R., Nagasaka, K.: Multiobjective intelligent energy management for a microgrid. IEEE Trans. Ind. Electron. **60**(4), 1688–1699 (2013)
10. Su, W., Wang, J., Roh, J.: Stochastic energy scheduling in microgrids with intermittent renewable energy resources. IEEE Trans. Smart Grid **5**(4), 1876–1883 (2014)
11. Hiremath, R., Shikha, S., Ravindranath, N.: Decentralized energy planning; modeling and application - a review. Renew. Sustain. Energy Rev. **11**(5), 729–752 (2007)
12. Logenthiran, T., Srinivasan, D., Khambadkone, A.M.: Multi-agent system for energy resource scheduling of integrated microgrids in a distributed system. Electr. Power Syst. Res. **81**(1), 138–148 (2011)
13. Miller, S., Ramchurn, S.D., Rogers, A.: Optimal decentralised dispatch of embedded generation in the smart grid. In: Proceedings of the International Conference on Autonomous Agents and Multiagent Systems, pp. 281–288 (2012)
14. Petcu, A., Faltings, B.: Superstabilizing, fault-containing distributed combinatorial optimization. In: Proceedings of the National Conference on Artificial Intelligence, pp. 449–454 (2005)
15. Nguyen, D.T., Yeoh, W., Lau, H.C., Zilberstein, S., Zhang, C.: Decentralized multi-agent reinforcement learning in average-reward dynamic DCOPs. In: Proceedings of the International Conference on Autonomous Agents and Multi-agent Systems, pp. 1341–1342 (2014)
16. Petcu, A.: A Class of Algorithms for Distributed Constraint Optimization, vol. 194. IOS Press, Amsterdam (2009)
17. Chvatal, V.: Linear Programming: Series of Books in the Mathematical Sciences. W.H. Freeman, New York (1983)

CML-WSN: A Configurable Multi-layer Wireless Sensor Network Simulator

Carolina Del-Valle-Soto[1]([✉]), Fernando Lezama[2], Jafet Rodriguez[1],
Carlos Mex-Perera[3], and Enrique Munoz de Cote[2]

[1] Campus Guadalajara, Facultad de Ingeniería, Universidad Panamericana,
Prolongación Calzada Circunvalación Poniente 49, 45010 Zapopan, Jalisco, Mexico
`{cvalle,arodrig}@up.edu.mx`
[2] Instituto Nacional de Astrofísica, Óptica y Electrónica, 72840 Puebla, Mexico
`{f.lezama,jemc}@inaoep.mx`
[3] Telemática Telemetría y Radiofrecuencia, 44190 Guadalajara, Jalisco, Mexico
`carlosmex@ttr.com.mx`

Abstract. Wireless Sensor Networks (WSNs) have large applications
in environments where access to human cannot be constant or where
reliable and timely information is required to support decisions. WSNs
must show high reliability, robustness, availability of information, monitoring capabilities, self-organization, among other aspects. Also, engineering requirements, such as low-cost implementation, operation, and
maintenance are necessary. In this context, a simulator is a powerful tool
for analyzing and improving network technologies used as a first step
to investigate protocol design and performance test on large-scale systems without the need of real implementation. In this paper, we present a
Configurable Multi-Layer WSN (CML-WSN) simulator. The CML-WSN
simulator incorporates a configurable energy model to support any sensor specification as a one of its main features. The CML-WSN simulator
is useful because it allows exploring prototypes with much less cost and
time compared to the requirements needed in real networks implemen-
tations.

Keywords: Wireless Sensor Networks · Network simulator · C++ ·
Object-oriented programming

1 Introduction

Nowadays, from the most fundamental electrical appliances like toasters to the
most advanced devices like industrial machines, devices have the capability of
communicating with each other due to the advances in technology. This communication is enabled by a network that connects each device so they can work
together towards a common goal such as reducing the risk in a manufacturing
process. In order to control all the devices, sensors are required to determine
when is safe to operate and which one should be selected. A wireless sensor
network (WSN) is the compound of nodes which collaborate in a common task.

© ICST Institute for Computer Sciences, Social Informatics and Telecommunications Engineering 2017
E. Sucar et al. (Eds.): AFI 2016, LNICST 179, pp. 91–102, 2017.
DOI: 10.1007/978-3-319-49622-1_11

These nodes have certain sensory capabilities and wireless communication that allow building ad-hoc networks (i.e., without pre-established physical structure or central administration) [1].

One of the main problems about ad-hoc systems is that there is no infrastructure, so the routes change dynamically. This dynamic change is due to fading, interference, disconnection of nodes, obstacles, node movements, among others. In consequence, problems such as quality of services, mobile battery-perishable, security, reliability of routes and further more appear and cause packet loss [2].

The majoring of this work focuses on engineering and telecommunications, specifically in the WSN field. The use of network simulators provides a more accurate perception of topologies, technologies, transmission media, channel design and pieces of equipment that best suit to the application that is being designed. Moreover, network simulation plays a significant role in areas such as engineering and research.

In this paper, we present a Configurable Multi-Layer WSN (CML-WSN) simulator. The CML-WSN is based on discrete events and implemented in C++. The simulator was intended to overcome some of the limitations presented in other simulators. This new approach allows the user to operate in more than a single layer, specifically in the Physical, MAC, and Network layers. Furthermore, its design permits the inclusion of different routing protocols and functionalities which translates into a scalable software.

The goal of creating CML-WSN simulator is to have the ability to manipulate parameters as needed and observe different network behaviors. Implementing a new simulator from the ground up allows a better view of the nodes, change features and models, and analyze several kinds of statistics needed to study the performance of routing protocols and its influence on the network. The only requirement is to have the data sheet of the wireless sensor chip which the user wants to use. The simulator will provide the energy consumption from the primary task of a node in the network, some of the usual tasks are starting, shutting down, receiving, transmitting, switching, CSMA (Carrier Sense Multiple Access/Collision Avoidance) algorithm and microcontroller.

Another purpose of CML-WSN is to deploy large networks with low costs considering real parameters. The results of a simulation can provide good scalability projections. Besides, our CML-WSN employs an energy model as close to the activity of a common node to optimize future decisions.

Also, with the simulation process, the time can be compressed or expanded allowing an increase or decrease of the speed of the research phenomena. In other words, the design allows the user to easily create and modify highly complex and different scenarios based on large amounts of various input parameters like power of reception and transmission locally and globally, size of the packet, packet's transmission rate, buffer storage size, routing protocol, sampling time, energy model, states of each node and others.

The chosen programming language was C++ due to its fast performance and ease to compile in multiple platforms making it a tool that students, network technicians, and researchers can use to analyze and design better WNS networks.

2   Related Work

WSNs are extensively studied with several network simulators that analyze various performance and power consumption parameters. However, the use of these simulators is intended to study certain topologies or already defined and parameterized environments. The comparison between WSN simulators is out of the scope of this paper. However, in this section we give a brief overview of some of the main-stream WSN simulators highlighting their main characteristics to put in context our CML-WSN. For an extensive comparison of WSN simulators, the reader can refer to [3–6].

NS-2 [7] is a discrete-time simulator that can support multiple protocols for wired, wireless and satellite networks in all layers. This software contains modules that cover a broad group of applications, protocols, routing, transport, different types of links and routing strategies and mechanisms. However, the simulator is not easy to understand and operate, and it was not specifically designed for WSNs simulation.

OPNET (OPtimized Network Engineering Tool) [8,9] Modeler permits to model and simulate communication systems. It allows to design and study networks, devices, protocols, and applications, providing flexibility and scalability. In addition, it simulates diverse networks where it can involve a large number of protocols and specific variables that the user can modify and study. Although it offers a C++ simulation class library and GUI support, it is too slow for MAC protocol simulations and does not have a good wireless mobility model.

Among other network simulators, one of them is TOSSIM [10], which estimates the energy consumption while considering the batteries lifetime of the devices and set realistic scenarios with common platforms. TOSSIM [10] is a TinyOS based interrupt-level discrete event simulator. It simulates only sensor applications ported to the i386 architecture, so it is only compatible with TinyOS. It does not capture CPU time neither energy consumption.

Consequently, one of the best ways to calculate a more precise energy saving model for WSNs is having extensive knowledge of the variables that affect the energy consumption of sensors and in what proportion. In a network, there are many variables that directly or indirectly affect energy consumption, eg., retransmissions of packets, collisions, and so on. Besides, the use of the channel is a variable that directly affects the MAC layer algorithm since nodes have to wait a lot of time if the channel is continuously busy. Moreover, control packets used by protocols significantly increase the amount of packets flowing in the network which causes collisions and, although nodes in WSN are designed to handle low processing, storing large routing tables usually translates into the sensors spending more energy in the development and maintenance. Another important factor is the establishment of links among nodes, which is proposed by a routing protocol. If the links are few, is more likely that some fail and cause others to become bottlenecks for traffic [11].

This overview enables us to propose a network simulator based on an event-driven system where we have an approach to the Physical, MAC and Network layers. The proposed CML-WSN simulator allows the implementation of any topology, several routing protocols, observe and count collisions and retransmissions and establish a model to evaluate energy consumption power techniques.

3   Simulator Overview

In this section, we give a brief overview of our CML-WSN simulator architecture. Our proposed tool is a discrete event simulator implemented in C++ for WSNs. The CML-WSN simulator allows users to create network topologies, configure devices, inject packets and change network settings.

Figure 1 shows the general overview of the CML-WSN simulator. It consists of three blocks: inputs, the discrete event simulation of the WSN through a scheduler, and outputs. Despite the simplicity of the general structure, the simulator provides the ability to debug, test and analyze algorithms in a controlled environment for networking research. Some of the features of the CML-WSN simulator are:

– Viewing code: Window displays the machine code at runtime.
– Debug On: Ability to enable or disable the debugger.
– Step by step execution mode.
– Run/Stop program execution.
– Profile: Displays usage statistics system.
– Traffic monitoring capabilities.
– Energy model required for adequate analysis of the entire platform.
– Physical Layer: 802.15.4 physical layer is split into two sub-layers: PHY data service and PHY management which are responsible for transmitting and receiving messages through the physical environment.
– MAC Layer: Here CSMA/CA algorithm and detection carrier were implemented.
– Network Layer: It is composed for the routing protocol.

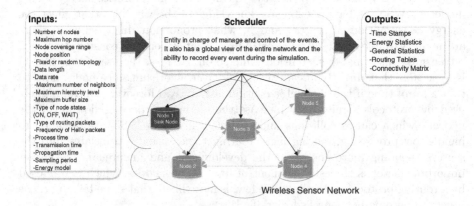

Fig. 1. General overview of CML-WSN simulator.

Besides, the core of the network simulator is composed of two main objects: the node and the scheduler. In the next subsections, we explain the structures of these two objects in the CML-WSN simulator.

3.1 Node Structure

The Node is an autonomous entity (object) that has properties and functions such as transmit, receive, turn on and off, listen, switch and so on. In the CML-WSN simulator, the node is an independent entity that performs many tasks during the simulation period. Figure 2 shows the node behavior during a simulation. Nodes are turned on and off, consume energy, listen to the channel, send and receive packets, have input and output packet queues and manage routing tables. All these tasks are performed by functions that accept input parameters and have output variables.

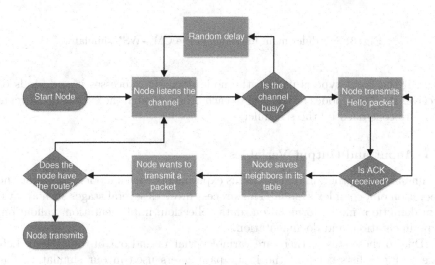

Fig. 2. Basic structure of a node in the CML-WSN simulator.

All the node tasks and interactions are organized and supervised by an external entity called network scheduler. The scheduler is described in next subsection.

3.2 Scheduler Structure

The scheduler is the entity responsible for control and management of all events during simulations. Moreover, it has a global vision of the entire network. Figure 3 shows the scheduler events and actions. The scheduler organizes the events as a queue and performs actions by times. The scheduler is responsible for handling these events regardless of category. Each event is distributed and carried to the node. Then, the node processes the event depending on the type

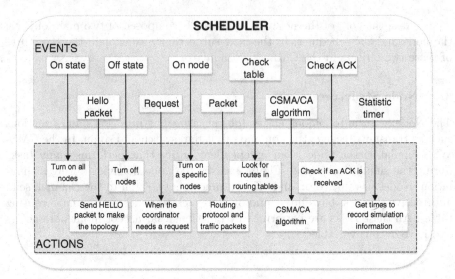

Fig. 3. Scheduler main functions in the CML-WSN simulator.

(e.g., if the event type is packet, the node opens it, processes it and sends or receives it). Thus, nodes are related to each other through the exchange of events that are controlled by the scheduler.

3.3   Input and Output Variables

A simulator is a program that performs experiments with a model mimicking the operation of a complex system. This process involves several stages such as: system definition, model formulation, data collection, implementation, validation, experimentation, and documentation.

Due to these stages, there are variables that in and out of the system. Left side of Fig. 1 lists some of the input parameters used in our simulator. The inputs can be read from a .txt file. Notice that the input parameter list includes different data allowing the user to modify the conditions of the simulation. Right side of Fig. 1 shows the outputs after simulation ends. The output consists in 5 .txt files with general information of the simulation process, and also with useful stats for analysis.

The first output file contains the data about individual per node and network. Also, it provides the stats for global consumption of each kind of energy used on the main tasks of the nodes. The second file includes the number of delivered packets, received packets, types of packets, packets loss due to a collision or interference in the channel and much more by each node and the whole network. The third file has the routing tables used by each node according to the rules of the selected routing protocol. The fourth file consists of the connection matrix between the nodes which will help verify the information about the neighbors of each node in the network. The fifth and last file includes the general resulting parameters from the processes of each node and the time data when the operations were executed.

The resulting collection of stats provides insights into the working procedure of each routing protocol such as the redundancy in the tables in case a path is inaccessible. This output from the simulator is a set of .txt files formatted to be easy to read by the user. The main reason to select this type of file was to allow a simple interaction with the data and to be able to create graphics with ease. Moreover, the data collected from the files allows the gathering of routing metrics such as the number of attempts to listen the channel, retransmissions of packets, delay times, overhead, special packets from the routing protocol, among others.

4   Framework and Functionality

One of the most important features in WSNs is the ability of a node to process and manage the network traffic and make decisions about processing received data.

Likewise, a node can make decisions as a function of collected data, and if they have low relevance, the node will not generate unnecessary traffic thus saving battery and avoiding possible congestion on the network. These decisions are made based on a routing protocol and can be improved or adapted to the network conditions through a network simulator that optimizes certain parameters before the implementation. Current available simulators were not suitable for high investigation level because of the lack of flexibility for modifications or impossibility to incorporate new protocols.

Therefore, we designed and implemented a network simulator based on events using the C++ language. The simulator was conceived with the paradigm of "object-oriented programming", where nodes are autonomous entities (objects) that have properties and functions. Simulation events are managed by a planner (i.e., the scheduler) who serves as "tasks organize" for objects involved in the simulation. Some advantages of having made the simulator in C++ was the speed and the capability of managing various classes as separate entities.

4.1   Physical Layer

One of the main problems about ad-hoc systems is there is no infrastructure, so the routes change dynamically. This is due to fading, interference, disconnections, obstacles, node movements, etc. In consequence, issues such as quality of services, mobile battery-perishable, security, reliability of routes appear and cause packet loss. These factors (e.g., noise, fading, shading and modulation signal) generate interference. As a basic Physical layer, we propose a percentage of packet loss per link based on the conditions of the environment, where the channel is not ideal.

4.2 MAC Layer

MAC layer is designed under the Carrier Sense Multiple Access with Collision Avoidance (CSMA/CA) mechanism [12], established by IEEE 802.15.4/Zigbee standard which takes into account a channel evaluation algorithm to prevent collisions, called clear channel assessment (CCA). Moreover, at this layer we can graduate the radio coverage for nodes and thus, variation of the transmission and receiving power.

4.3 Network Layer

In communication networks, there are routing protocols classified into two groups: proactive routing protocols and reactive routing protocols [13, 14]. When nodes are under a reactive protocol they ask for a route only when it is needed. This involves high latency for the first packet and some independence among routes. The implementation of this layer also enables analysis of node spatial distribution in a uniform and non-uniform way and analysis of traffic load distribution of balancing links.

4.4 Functions in the Simulator

Figure 4 present a scheme showing relationships among the main functions of the simulator. First of all, the connectivity matrix of nodes describes nodes that are connected. Therefore, traffic packets begin. This is where each node receives a packet, opens it, processes it and takes a decision. This decision can be found in its routing table and send the packet or simply forward it. Meanwhile, nodes are consuming energy, and we can see statistics when needed.

The *startUp* function turns on generically all nodes or one that has been turned off. It can turn on them in a uniformly random way or in a particular distribution. The *channelMonitor* function gets the input time variable in which the node will listen to the channel to see if a delay is needed or not. The *CSMACA algorithm* function execute the CSMA/CA algorithm, with respect to the decision-making loop. The *eventSignal* function classifies the type of events to be processed in the network. This function has subfunctions processing to redirect each of the events. It gives flexibility and organization. The *Generator* function generate packets with respect to the type of packet needed by the node. The *receivePacket* is part of three separate functions which together receive and process a packet at a node: receiving, opening and processing. This function determines the time when the packet arrives and gets the source from which came the packet. The *openPacket* function takes the packet time and it opens the packet in the current node to establish what the source and destination of the packet are. The *process* function processes the packet according to the type. There are a number of functions associated with processing of every single type of packets on the network. The *updateTable* function updates the routing tables of the nodes. The function fills the fields to know all the possible routes to the

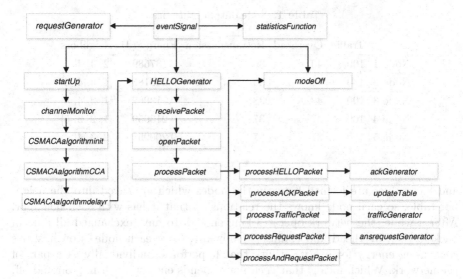

Fig. 4. Main functions in the CML-WSN simulator.

destination that were learned. Here there are parameters for each routing protocol such as flags for valid routes, complete routes or quality of each path. The *modeOff* function allows a node turns off and it cannot send or receive packets and immediately its routing table is cleaned. Finally, *statisticsFunction* function can be called at any time of simulation time. Here there are the statistics of network processes. It can have local statistics (by node) or global statistics (over the entire network). Packet statistics, collisions, energy pattern, and so on are obtained.

5 Results and Discussion

A simple WSN of 5 nodes was implemented to demonstrate how the network simulator operates. The physical modeling of the channel was done obtaining a certain percentage of the packets loss on each link. In the beginning, each node is turned on randomly. Each node starts discovering the network by sending HELLO packets. Then, when a node listens to a HELLO packet, it replies with an ACK packet. When a node receives an ACK packet, it records the node that sent it into the neighbors table which causes the establishment of a link and a possible active route. Thus, when the exchange of HELLO and ACK packets ends, the nodes can start sending regular traffic packets to the required destinations.

For this particular example, the network was designed to follow the hierarchical routing protocol [15] where there is a sink node or base station which becomes the unique destination for all the nodes in the network. Then, the nodes establish parent-child relationships according to the rules of the routing protocol

Table 1. Node output statistics.

	Traffic	Overhead	Retransmission	Energy (J)	Neighbors
Node 1	100	40	30	0.137689	[2, 3, 4]
Node 2	100	49	39	0.270185	[1, 3, 4, 5]
Node 3	100	48	38	0.213067	[1, 2, 4, 5]
Node 4	100	47	37	0.213059	[1, 2, 3, 5]
Node 5	100	37	27	0.200958	[2, 3, 4]

and hierarchies are formed between the nodes which are saved into the neighbor table, so each node knows the relationship that it has with each neighbor. After a while, the network operates long enough to have exchanged all kind of packets (i.e., overhead and traffic). Meanwhile, since each node is on it starts consuming energy for every activity that it performs individually as a part of the network. Which means that each node spends energy in turning on and off, switching, listening to the channel using the algorithm CSMA/CA, transmitting and receiving packets and using the microprocessor.

After completing the simulation, the program outputs a series of files which contain relevant statistics about the process. Table 1 present the Node information at the end of the simulation. It consists of information of traffic packets, overhead (i.e., data packets used by protocols), retransmission and energy generated by each node. Also, the neighbors of nodes are provided as information of the connectivity of the network.

The general stats are presented in Table 2. It includes a global information of the packets (e.g., traffic, overhead, packet loss, retransmission) and also global information about the energy utilized for the network.

For more details on the application of the CML-WSN simulator, the reader can be referred to [16], where the CML-WSN was compared to a real 100-Nodes WSN, with satisfactory results.

Table 2. General output statistics

Packets		Energy (J)	
Traffic	500	Start	0.000001
Overhead	221	MCU	0.28125
Lost by collision	114	Switching	0.002921
Lost by interference	64	Transmission	0.6022275
Retransmission	171	CSMA/CA	0.008829
Dropped	6	Shutdown	0.000007
		Receiving	0.139677
		Total	1.03496

6   Conclusions and Future Work

The Internet of Things comes from the evolution of telecommunications and information technologies. Therefore, to push its potential it is important to improve and understand better the infrastructure that makes it possible. A fundamental part of it are the WSNs, which allow the communication of sensors to gather intel of their surroundings. They collaborate as a team not only to collect data but to process it as information. To comprehend and design better networks, different simulators have been created to date (e.g., NS-2 [7], TOSSIM [10] and OPNET [8]).

Unfortunately, these simulators usually have a restricted number of models for each layer, and in many cases they are not realistic models, i.e. the physical layer using free space model which is certainly a good approach for some basic analysis but it may differ from real data collected from deployed networks. Besides, such simulators do not allow the user to add functionality to them. These constraints have as a consequence that the information and statistics only focus on particular areas which make it harder to acquire a global overview of the results.

For that reason, a network simulator, called Configurable Multi-Layer WSN (CML-WSN) simulator, was designed and developed to be able to implement different routing protocols, propose improvements, analyze performance parameters and apply optimized parameters related to WSNs. The CML-WSN simulator is capable of working on the Physical, MAC and Network layers, which allows the user to collect more information about each node and a comprehensive overview of the network. The simulator outputs a set of .txt files which enables the user to read quickly the results and to export it to other software to generate charts. The next step is to add a user-centered designed Graphic User Interface to the simulator that improves the interaction during the setup and results. Furthermore, adding the possibility of designing the network graphically and obtaining the information either raw or as a set of predefined charts. Lastly, aiding the user to make smarter decisions on how to build a WSN by understanding how the design and each sensor affects it.

References

1. Luo, H., Liu, Y., Das, S.K.: Routing correlated data in wireless sensor networks: a survey. IEEE Netw. **21**(6), 40–47 (2007)
2. Kulkarni, N., Prasad, R., H.C.N.G.: Performance evaluation of AODV, DSDV & DSR for quasi random deployment of sensor nodes in wireless sensor networks. In: International Conference on Devices and Communications (2011)
3. Korkalainen, M., Sallinen, M., Krkkinen, N., Tukeva, P.: Survey of wireless sensor networks simulation tools for demanding applications. In: International Conference on Networking and Services, pp. 102–106, April 2009
4. Yu, F., Jain, R.: A survey of wireless sensor network simulation tools. Washington University in St. Louis, Department of Science and Engineering (2011)
5. Musznicki, B., Zwierzykowski, P.: Survey of simulators for wireless sensor networks. Int. J. Grid Distrib. Comput. **5**(3), 23–50 (2012)

6. Nayyar, A., Singh, R.: A comprehensive review of simulation tools for wireless sensor networks (WSNs). J. Wirel. Netw. Commun. **5**(1), 19–47 (2015)
7. McCanne, S., Floyd, S.: The LBNL network simulator (1997). http://www.isi.edu/nsnam
8. Korkalainen, M., Sallinen, M.: A survey of RF-propagation simulation tools for wireless sensor networks. In: International Conference on Sensor Technologies and Applications, pp. 342–347, July 2010
9. Cavin, D., Sasson, Y., Schiper, A.: On the accuracy of MANET simulators. In: ACM International Workshop on Principles of Mobile Computing, pp. 38–43, October 2002
10. Mora-Merchan, J., Larios, D., Barbancho, J., Molina, F., Sevillano, J., Leon, C.: mTOSSIM: a simulator that estimates battery lifetime in wireless sensor networks. Simul. Model. Pract. Theory **31**, 39–51 (2013)
11. Shakshukia, E., Malikb, H., Sheltamic, T.: A comparative study on simulation vs. real time deployment in wireless sensor networks. J. Syst. Softw. **84**, 45–54 (2011)
12. LAN/MAN Standards Committee: Part 15.4: Wireless Medium Access Control (MAC) and Physical Layer (PHY) Specifications for Low-Rate Wireless Personal Area Networks (WPANs). IEEE Computer Society (2006)
13. The IETF website (2003). http://www.ietf.org/rfc/rfc3561.txt
14. The IETF website (2007). http://www.ietf.org/rfc/rfc4728.txt
15. Del-Valle-Soto, C., Mex-Perera, C., Olmedo, O., Orozco-Lugo, A., Galván-Tejada, G., Lara, M.: An efficient multi-parent hierarchical routing protocol for WSNs. In: Wireless Telecommunications Symposium (WTS), 1–8 April 2014 (2014)
16. Del-Valle-Soto, C., Mex-Perera, C., Olmedo, O., Orozco-Lugo, A., Galván-Tejada, G., Lara, M.: On the MAC/Network/Energy performance evaluation of wireless sensor networks: contrasting MPH, AODV, DSR and ZTR routing protocols. Sensors J. **14**, 22811–22847 (2014)

Conceptual Model for the Explanation of the Phenomenon of Radical Innovation in the Disruption of the Internet of Things, on Scales of Smart Objects, Homes and Cities

David Soasti Bareta[✉] and Gerardo Muñiz

Instituto Tecnológico y de Estudios Superiores de Monterrey,
64849 Monterrey, NL, Mexico
dsoasti@gmail.com, gerardo.muniz@itesm.mx

Abstract. The Internet of Things is an emerging, mainly technology driven, field, seen as a radical modifier of the semantic relationships between people, objects and cities. Based on the empirical study of various products and systems within the Internet of Things environment, a conceptual model is proposed to explain the phenomenon of Design (Meaning) Driven Innovation and its particular variables, where the radical innovations, make sense in society. It is argued that the variables: Social Willingness to Change, Network of Visionaries, Technology and Meanings are four actors for the construction of new and radical meanings in products.

Keywords: Internet of Things · Innovation · Design driven innovation · Conceptual · Model

1 Introduction

The Internet of Things has the potential to profoundly change society. Gartner predicts that by 2020, 25 billion objects will include connectivity capabilities [1].

Currently, products are being developed in the Internet of Things under three approaches: Technology as the main axis [2]; User Centered Design [3]; the third approach proposes a paradigm shift based on the hidden possibilities of a technology [4,5]. The Internet of Things requires a non-user-centered model to reach its disruptive potential, with an approach that challenges the established paradigms and proposes value from a sociological perspective. Thus, the aim of this paper is to propose a conceptual model that explains the phenomenon of radical innovation in the disruption of the Internet of Things.

2 Theoretical Framework

Design-Driven Innovation states that *technological epiphanies* occur at the meeting point of breakthrough technologies and breakthrough meanings. This proposes a radical approach to innovation which does not give people an incremental interpretation of what they are already familiar with, but proposes different,

© ICST Institute for Computer Sciences, Social Informatics and Telecommunications Engineering 2017
E. Sucar et al. (Eds.): AFI 2016, LNICST 179, pp. 103–108, 2017.
DOI: 10.1007/978-3-319-49622-1_12

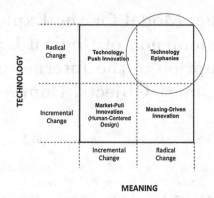

Fig. 1. Conceptual model of radical and incremental innovation [6].

novel and unexpected meanings [6] that end up imposing the new paradigm. The model proposed by Verganti connects the two dimensions of innovation: technology and meaning [7], with the drivers: technology, design and users (see Fig. 1). Thus the model defines four types of innovations: **Market-led Innovations.** The objective is to meet users needs (User Centered Design) [7]. **Technology driven innovations.** They integrate functionality and technology, and come from radical changes in technology without changing the meaning of the product [7]. **Meaning Modification.** These innovations begin by understanding the subtle and tacit dynamics in the socio-cultural models, and result in radically new meanings and languages, often involving a change in the socio-cultural systems [7]. **Technological Epiphanies.** They bring a radical change in the meaning enabled by the emergence of new technologies or by the use of existing technologies in completely new contexts [8].

3   Methodology

A review and analysis of IoT products was carried out. It followed an analytical - deductive process considering: a smartWatch chronology summary, analysis of existing products, identification of potential variables, statement of hypothesis, proposed models, Selecting the most appropriate model, description of the proposed variables, and finally model validation.

3.1   Description of the Proposed Variables

3.1.1   Social Willingness to Change
This variable includes five criteria that build Disruptive innovation: *Exploring the Benefits of Quantification of Time:* Technology plays the role of controlling tasks that do not require human supervision, thus contributes transcendentally to important tasks, perceived and unperceived. *Exploring Transcendence:* It refers to all the radical innovations that improve life in terms

of time, vitality and health quality [9], that allows people to be recognized as part of an elite, and as such follow their habits and behaviors [10]. *Exploring Connections in the Sociocultural Context:* **Subjective Norm:** This refers to a perceived social pressure for making, or not, a decision influenced by the opinions of higher influences or peers [11,12]. **Image:** It is defined as the extent to which the use of an innovation is perceived as improving ones status in a society [13]. **Compatibility:** It is based on emotional, symbolic and aesthetic factors. *Social compatibility* concerns the willingness to be different and independent [10]. *Aesthetic compatibility* refers to the idea of the visual impact that affect the aesthetic response of people; that is a visual display connecting parts in a meaningful way [14]. **Personal Innovativeness:** This is defined as the propensity of certain individuals for taking risks [15] as part of his personality. *Exploring the new symbolic values and interaction patterns:* **Narcissism:** Reflects the material conditions of life in a society in which the social level depends more on consumption than on production [16,17]. **Hedonism:** Achieving a real presence in the world, and enjoying the existence jubilantly: to smell better, to taste and hear better and to consider passions and instincts as friends [18,19]. *Exploring calm in the face of uncertainty:* It refers to the will of society to minimize the uncertainty caused by a radical innovation as it appears in a particular social environment.

3.1.2   Network of Visionaries

It is responsible for visualizing future scenarios to use, and for proposing new *Cultural Prototypes*, that are a medium which encodes and reveals new visions and interpretations of a company. It is described as cultural because, it refers to a new meaning or new language [6]. *Personal Attitude Towards Technology:* The Social Constructivism of Technology is an inherently social process, where non-technical elements play a decisive role in its genesis and consolidation [20]. *The Will to Transcend:* It is the personality characteristic of a visionary to move toward new ways to face reality and everyday life; the desire to offer products based on technology, as a new and seductive approach to changing the world. *Personal Innovativeness:* It refers to the willingness to take risks and accept them as a personality characteristic of the Visionary, not as a consumer, but as social and technological researcher. *Skills and Knowledge:* It is a professional team with experts such as: Engineers and IT experts, Sociologists, Semioticians, Interdisciplinary Designers, Artists.

3.1.3   Technology

It addresses the quantification of people and their activities. The characterization of this variable implies: **Perception:** The sensors convert those physical aspects of reality into digital numeric arguments. **Connectivity:** Connectivity allows access to the network and compatibility [21]. **Intelligence:** The merging of computing and algorithms produce a new generation of smart product experience, where Big Data, Data analytics, Data Management are the way that technology proposes new ways to create value. **Expression:** Allows interaction between people and the tangible world. This characteristic includes interfaces and user experience [21].

3.1.4 Meanings

The Meaning variables are stated as follows (see Fig. 2): *Innovative Culture of the Firm:* Characterized by the ability of the firm to provide adequate space for the proposal of new concepts, new opportunities and exploring future scenarios yet to be designed. *Technology Integration:* The role of technology integration is to act as a facilitator for the realization of the proposed radical design innovation, by applying a technology process of social constructivism. *Seductive Power:* It refers to the ability of the network, to deliver new ideas and dissemination of different cultural prototypes generated by the proposed design discourse of the firm [6]. *Value:* It refers to the perception of people on the radically innovative design proposal, it includes the four criteria below: *Perceived usefulness:* Seeks to explain the short-term consequences. Is the design product perceived as helpful? [15]; *Ease of use:* The evaluation of the extent to which interaction with a technology system is free from mental effort [15]. *Novelty:* It has the role of imposing an induced interest in the new meaning of the proposal [6] *Socio-cultural assessment of the new Meaning:* At the *social level*, this raises the concept of behavioral belief: Does my social group value this new proposal? [6,15]. At the *individual level*, the concept of normative belief arises: How much does my person improve, socially speaking, when I use the product or service? [6,15].

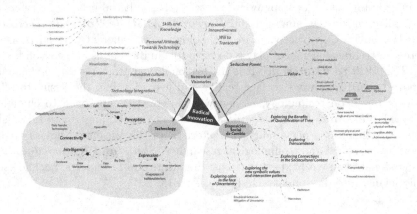

Fig. 2. Model C, described in detail.

4   Results and Discussion

The model was validated by a network of twelve visionaries. The summary of their views: *Network of Visionaries* was understood as the source of value in the proposed model since its not user centered. **Technology** was understood as the muscle that builds the proposed Innovation. **Meanings** are seen as novel paradigms, where the proposal of innovation is offered through the seductive power of the visionaries. **Social Willingness to Change**, its an element to leverage innovation proposals as a means of support for connecting with people. Respondents agreed with the potential of art to explore new paths, new expressions that generate novel paradigms involving new meanings.

4.1 Conclusions

The adoption of radically innovative proposals in the Internet of Things aims to improve such values as the extension of life with quality, improved social and self-image, novelty, ease of use and perceived usefulness. This applies to the three scales of application considered in this work.

Diversity in the Network of Visionaries is essential for building design discourse, and a diversity of views generates greater and better results and possibilities of interpretation of the design discourse.

Personal user needs are not meant to be satisfied as such, they have a paradigmatic basis, but this kind of innovations are proposals made by firms that integrate a high level of innovation, and that challenge the established paradigm, while creating a new niche where the firm can enjoy a level of control around monopoly, at least for a while.

References

1. Velosa, A., Hines, J., Hung, L., Perkins, E., Satish, R.: Predicts 2015: The Internet of Things (2015)
2. Atzori, L., Iera, A., Morabito, G.: From smart objects: the next evolutionary step of the internet of things. IEEE Commun. Mag. **52**, 97–105 (2014)
3. Cordoba Rubino, S., Hazemberg, W., Huisman, M.: The value and meaning of meta products (2010)
4. Verganti, R.: Design-Driven Innovation Changing the Rules of Competition by Radically Innovating What Things Mean. Harvard Bussiness Press, Boston (2009)
5. Utterback, J.M.: Design-Inspired Innovation. World Scientific Publishing Company, Hackensack (2006)
6. Verganti, R.: Design Driven Innovation: An Introduction. In: Design-driven innovation changing the rules of competition by radically innovating what things mean. Harvard Business Press, Boston (2009)
7. Norman, D.A., Verganti, R.: Incremental and radical innovation: design research vs technology and meaning change. Des. Issues **30**, 78–96 (2013)
8. Verganti, R.: How companies can systematically create innovations that customers don't even know they want (2011)
9. Rose, D.: Enchanted objects design, human desire, and the Internet of Things. Kirkus Rev. **82**, 69 (2014)
10. Cappetta, R., Cillo, P., Ponti, A.: Convergent designs in fine fashion: an evolutionary model for stylistic innovation. Res. Policy **35**, 1273–1290 (2006)

11. Taylor, S., Todd, P.: Assessing IT usage: the role of prior experience. MIS Q. **19**, 561–570 (1995)
12. Taylor, S., Todd, P.A.: Understanding information technology usage: a test of competing models. Inf. Syst. Res. **6**, 144–176 (1995)
13. Moore, G.C., Benbasat, I.: Development of an instrument to measure the perceptions of adopting an information technology innovation. Inf. Syst. Res. **2**, 192–222 (1991)
14. Veryzer, R.W., Hutchinson, J.W.: The influence of unity and prototypicality on aesthetic responses to new product designs. J. Consum. Res. **24**, 374–394 (1998)
15. Agarwal, R., Prasad, J.: A conceptual and operational definition of personal innovativeness in the domain of information technology. Inf. Syst. Res. **9**, 204–215 (1998)
16. Castro, S.J.: En teora, es arte: una introduccin a la esttica, San Esteban (2005)
17. Trechera Herrera, J.L.: Revista Envo - El narcisismo: epidemia de nuestro tiempo. http://www.envio.org.ni/articulo/243
18. Hekkert, P.: Design aesthetics: principles of pleasure in design. Psychol. Sci. **48**, 157–172 (2006)
19. https://es.wikipedia.org/w/index.php?title=Hedonismo&oldid=88087286
20. Lpez Cerezo, J.A.: Ciencia, Tecnologa y Sociedad: el estado de la cuestin en Europa y Estados Unidos (1998). http://www.rieoei.org/oeivirt/rie18a02.htm
21. Internet of Things: Six Key Characteristics—DesignMind. http://designmind. frogdesign.com/2014/08/internet-things-six-key-characteristics/

MAIoT - An IoT Architecture with Reasoning and Dialogue Capability

Juan Carlos Nieves[1]([✉]), Daniel Andrade[2], and Esteban Guerrero[1]

[1] Department of Computing Science, Umeå University, 901 87 Umeå, Sweden
`{jcnieves,esteban}@cs.umu.se`
[2] Instituto Tecnológico Superior de Xalapa, 910-96 Xalapa, Veracruz, Mexico
`daniel.andrade.sd@gmail.com`

Abstract. This paper describes MAIoT, a Multiagent-based Architecture which aims to coordinate Internet of Things (IoT) devices. MAIoT is distinguished by its capabilities for allowing dialogues between IoT devices. To support theses dialogue capabilities, the IoT devices are wrapped into rational agents with reasoning and dialogue capabilities.

Keywords: Internet of Things · Multiagent systems · Rational agents · Dialogues

1 Introduction

The information technology (IT) industry and IT research communities have been working in the development of Internet of Thing (IoT) platforms in order to improve our daily life. For instance, IoT platforms have been developed in order to build up the so called *smart homes* which aim to improve the experiences of their inhabitants [7].

To achieve "smart" IoT capabilities, different open challenges have been identified [1,3,5]. Among them, we can point out: a.- *intelligence distribution*: interpretation of dispersed sensor-data and reasoning about it; b.-*standardization*: adoption of industrial standards; and c.- *flexibility*: "Plug & Play" smart objects deployed in environments. In this regard, *establishing dialogues* among smart devices and anticipate needs of a user are major challenges [7]. Against this background, we present here a Multiagent Architecture for Internet of Things (MAIoT) which aims to coordinate and provide IoT services. In this architecture, we follow a *dialogue-based* approach based on rational agents in order to coordinate IoT services. In these settings, *inquiry dialogues* aim to agree or disagree services supported by IoT devices. To conduct dialogues between IoT devices which are wrapped into rational agents, we follow an argumentation-based approach, introduced by [6], which supports collaborative decision making processes in the settings of the so called *agreement rules*.

© ICST Institute for Computer Sciences, Social Informatics and Telecommunications Engineering 2017
E. Sucar et al. (Eds.): AFI 2016, LNICST 179, pp. 109–113, 2017.
DOI: 10.1007/978-3-319-49622-1_13

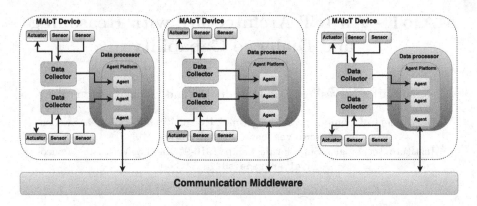

Fig. 1. Physical diagram of MAIoT architecture.

2 MAIoT Architecture

In this section, we describe our multiagent architecture for IoT devices. The MAIoT architecture hosts IoT devices in terms of the so called MAIoT devices. A MAIoT device is composed by three modules: *a data processor*, *a data collector* and *an agent platform*. The data processor hosts an agent platform and is connected to other data processors, each one with its own agent platform, through *a communication middleware*.

The data collector is controlled by one agent, see Fig. 1, and is integrated with sensors and actuators. The data collector has as aim both to perceive data from the environment through sensors and to send this data to the agent.

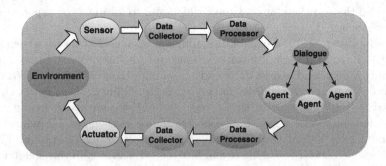

Fig. 2. Data workflow diagram of the MAIoT architecture.

The agents hosted by MAIoT devices exchange information with other agents hosted by different MAIoT devices through dialogues and provide services through their actuators. The agents take part of inquiry dialogues in order to agree IoT services which are defined according to user preferences and needs. Inquiry dialogues, among other types of dialogues, were defined by [8] in order to collaboratively build new knowledge. In our architecture, agents take part in the negotiation (an inquiry dialogue) of a topic in which the agents do not know if a given topic is true or false; hence, they require the collaboration of other agents, see Fig. 2.

To formalize our dialogue system, we follow the dialogue style introduced by [2,6], in which three types of moves are allowed: *open*, *assert* and *close*. In an open move, an agent starts a new dialogue with a given topic. In an assert move, an agent assert arguments related to a given topic; and in a close move an agent wants to finish the current dialogue; however, if another agent does not agree, this dialogue will not be closed and will still open.

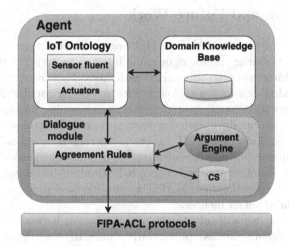

Fig. 3. Internal architecture of a MAIoT agent.

As Fig. 3 shows, agents are composed by three modules: an IoT ontology, a dialogue module and a domain knowledge base. In the **IoT ontology module**, information from sensors is interpreted in terms of the **Semantic Sensor Network Ontology**[1], and stored in the **Domain Knowledge base module**. In the **Dialogue module**, agents read messages from other agents through *FIPA ACL protocols*, and perform a decision-making process inquiring their own agreement rules and their **Domain knowledge bases**. Then, a decision about to execute of services, by means of actuators, is taken.

3   Ongoing Project

MAIoT devices are being used in an agent-based assistive architecture for computer-supported assessment: UmU-Act project [4].

---

[1] https://www.w3.org/2005/Incubator/ssn/ssnx/ssn.

The architecture integrates a generic core ontology based on medical and health terminologies with the IoT ontology in order to reason and share information among IoT agents. A MAIoT architecture has been implemented by considering three agents: *context*, *activity* and *coach* agents. This architecture is intended to track and evaluate human activity in a home-care environment. UmU-Act architecture considers MAIoT devices deployed in a Raspberry Pi[2] platform using Java Agent DEvelopment Framework (JADE)[3] framework, and Arduino[4] platform for capturing and managing of sensor data.

We will describe details of use cases and an evaluation of the MAIoT architecture in an oncoming extended version of this paper.

4   Conclusion and Future Work

In this paper, we introduce MAIoT, a Multi-agent Architecture for the Internet of Things with reasoning and dialogue capabilities. The major characteristics of the MAIoT architecture are summarized as follows: 1.- *Reasoning and dialogue capabilities*: MAIoT agents are endowed with reasoning capabilities by considering an argumentation-based approach. Internal reasoning processes of MAIoT agents combines a domain knowledge base and an IoT ontology; 2.- *IoT orientation*: interoperation of MAIoT agents is warranted by considering an IoT ontology. Interoperability and decentralization of smart devices can be achieved by considering a dialogue approach using IoT standard-based communications. 3.- *Flexibility and generalization*: MAIoT agents can be deployed as Plug & Play standard-complaint smart devices.

As future work, we will investigate the interaction between MAIoT agents and human agents (individuals), particularly aiming to support the improvement of individual's situations and quality of life [4].

References

1. Atzori, L., Iera, A., Morabito, G.: The internet of things: a survey. Comput. Netw. **54**(15), 2787–2805 (2010)
2. Black, E., Hunter, A.: An inquiry dialogue system. Auton. Agents Multi-agent Syst. **19**(2), 173–209 (2009)
3. Gubbi, J., Buyya, R., Marusic, S., Palaniswami, M.: Internet of things (iot): a vision, architectural elements, and future directions. Future Gener. Comput. Syst. **29**(7), 1645–1660 (2013)
4. Lindgren, H., Baskar, J., Guerrero, E., Nieves, J.C., Nilsson, I., Yan, C.: Computer-supported assessment for tailoring assistive technology. In: Proceedings of the 6th International Conference on Digital Health Conference, DH, Montréal, QC, Canada, 11–13 April, pp. 1–10 (2016)
5. Miorandi, D., Sicari, S., Pellegrini, F., Chlamtac, I.: Internet of things: vision, applications and research challenges. Ad Hoc Netw. **10**(7), 1497–1516 (2012)

---

[2] https://www.raspberrypi.org/.
[3] http://jade.tilab.com/.
[4] https://www.arduino.cc/.

6. Nieves, J.C., Lindgren, H.: Deliberative argumentation for service provision in smart environments. In: Bulling, N. (ed.) EUMAS 2014. LNCS, vol. 8953, pp. 388–397. Springer, Heidelberg (2015). doi:10.1007/978-3-319-17130-2_27
7. Pretz, K.: Laying the foundation for smarter homes - building smarter homes. Inst. **39**(4), 4–5 (2015)
8. Walton, D.N.: The New Dialectic: Conversational Contexts of Argument. University of Toronto Press, London (1998)

FI-eHealth 2016

An Internet System to Self-monitoring and Assess Feeding in Young Mexicans

Miguel Murguía-Romero[1,3]([✉]), Bernardo Serrano-Estrada[2],
Itzell A. Gallardo-Ortíz[1,3], J. Rafael Jiménez-Flores[3],
and Rafael Villalobos-Molina[1,3]

[1] Uniad de Biomedicina, FES Iztacala,
Universidad Nacional Autónoma de México,
Ave. de los Barrios 1, Los Reyes Iztacala,
54090 Tlalnepantla, Estado de México, Mexico
miguelmurguia@ciencias.unam.mx
[2] SERES Sistemas Especializados, Mexico City, Mexico
[3] Carrera de Médico Cirujano, FES Iztacala,
Universidad Nacional Autónoma de México,
Ave. de los Barrios 1, Los Reyes Iztacala,
54090 Tlalnepantla, Estado de México, Mexico

Abstract. Obesity and metabolic syndrome pave the way to type 2
diabetes and cardiovascular disease. Obesity and metabolic syndrome
prevalence are high (39% and 13%, respectively) in young Mexican population where feeding habits are one of the main factors leading to these
maladies. So, a plausible strategy to address the problem is to suggest
young to review and control their feeding habits. We present an internet
system to register, self-monitoring, and assess feeding habits for young
Mexican to review and control them. This system is organized in eight
questionnaires, one of them about food frequencies. Also anthropometrics data such as weight, height, waist and hip circumference are registered to assess and follow-up weight condition, through body mass
index, and waist/hip ratio. The user could generate a pdf report that
automatically summarizes all the data captured in the questionnaires
in two pages. A follow up charts of some parameters are also available for monthly data collection once the user fills the system. More
than 2,000 young students have used this system since 2013 and is open
universally (www.misalud.abacoac.org) to all young people wanting to
self-monitoring her/his feeding habits, and obtaining general health recommendations.

Keywords: Nutrition · Mexican young · Obesity · Weight control ·
Metabolic syndrome

1 Introduction

It is known that obesity is a worldwide epidemic [1,2], and that this health problem not only affects adults, but also young and even children. In this regard,

© ICST Institute for Computer Sciences, Social Informatics and Telecommunications Engineering 2017
E. Sucar et al. (Eds.): AFI 2016, LNICST 179, pp. 117–127, 2017.
DOI: 10.1007/978-3-319-49622-1_14

Mexico is among the countries with high obesity prevalence [3], and among young Mexican (17–24 years old) obesity is also a problem: it was estimated that 39% of young Mexicans are pre-obese or obese (body mass index >25) [4]. Our research group (GMISARA: Multidisciplinary Research Group on Health and Academic Performance; www.gmisara.abacoac.org) has been investigated the physical health of first grade undergraduate students of Mexico City at the Facultad de Estudios Superiores Iztacala of UNAM, mainly focused on metabolic disorders such as metabolic syndrome and its components (obesity, blood pressure, levels of blood glucose, triglycerides, HDL cholesterol, insulin resistance, among others parameters).

2   Metabolic Syndrome and Obesity Among Young Mexican

Mexican young present a metabolic syndrome prevalence of 13.4% [5], disaggregating by its components and by sex, the prevalences are: low HDL-cholesterol (55% women; 29% men), high waist circumference (49%; 28%; central obesity is the second parameter with highest prevalence), high triglycerides (15%; 22%), high blood glucose (7%; 13%), and high blood pressure (6%; 19%). Only 29% of the young have none parameter altered, thus 70% present one or more alterations of the metabolic syndrome. Insulin resistance among young Mexican has been estimated that ranged from 14% up to 30% depending on the sex and region [6].

The high values of obesity, metabolic syndrome and alterations of its components show that young Mexican are prone to develop, in one or two decades, type 2 diabetes and cardiovascular disease, as can be heart attack and atherosclerosis, among others diseases [7].

3   Promoting Health Among Young

As part of our research protocol, university students are invited to participate in an evaluation of its physical health annually, where blood samples and anthropometrics are taken by the physicians of the team. The project has two main objectives: (a) conduct scientific research on metabolic syndrome, and (b) to promote the physical health among students. Since year 2008, our research group has evaluated near to 7,000 university students, making blood and urine laboratory analysis [8]. Since year 2012 we implemented an internet system to collect medical history previous to the blood sample, we then gave to the students a report evaluating its physical health, including some general recommendations [9]. The Internet system presented here is an evolution version of such version, given that the process for recording medical history represents an opportunity to give the participant some general recommendations on her/his feeding habits and weight condition, among other issues.

The MiSalud internet system takes the advantage to make recommendations on self-reporting anthropometrics data and feeding habits to all young that want to use the system, and not only to those that decide to participate in a more deeply study where blood and urine samples are needed.

Fig. 1. MiSalud system showing the 'Food frequency' questionnaire.

4   Internet System for Self-monitoring

The system is organized in eight questionnaires (Table 1; www.misalud.abacoac. org), and the interface is based on a selectable list and ratio-buttons (Fig. 1). The user should register in the system to assign a password; in the register section the user specifies his/her name, birthdate, gender, among other general information. One of the questionnaires is about eating habits, where the user specifies the frequency of food consumption and portions (Figs. 1 and 2).

The system presents to the user the next sections, each one corresponding to one questionnaire:

– Register (*Datos de registro*).- Name, email, birthday, password, address, sex, phone, school registration number.
– Data set (*Muestra*).- Update questionnaires or select the data set (monthly).
– Anthropometrics measures (*Datos antropométricos*).- User self-measures of weight, height, waist circumference, and hip circumference.
– Family history (*Antecedentes heredo-familiares*).- Diseases of user, mother, father, and mothers and fathers grandmother and grandfather.
– Food and beverages (*Alimentos y Bebidas*).- Eating habits. Frequency, portion and type of food eating by the users.
– Physical activity (*Actividad física*).- Type, frequency and time of physical activity.

Table 1. Sections of the health report.

Section	Data	Content
Heading	Title, date, registration number	Includes the date (month) of data capture, and date of report generation
General data	Name, email, gender, age	Update questionnaires or select the data set (monthly)
Anthropometrics	Weight, Height, Waist circumference, Hip circumference	User self-measures of weight, height, waist circumference, and hip circumference
Weight Assessment	Body Mass Index	Classify BMI into one of the WHO classes: Underweight, Normal weight, Overweight, Obese.
	Waist Circumference	Classify into Normal or Altered, depending on cut off point for Latin American (<80 cm women; text-less90 cm men)
	Waist/Hip ratio	Classify into Normal or Altered, depending on cut off point (<0.85 women; <0.90 men)
Physical activity assessment	Hours of exercise at week	Classify into Insufficient exercise, Adequate exercise, or Null exercise
Feeding Assessment	Fast food intake	Classify into Low or null consumption or High consumption
	Sweetened beverages	Classify into Low or null consumption or High consumption
	Fruits intake	Classify into Low or null consumption or Adequate consumption
	Vegetables intake	Classify into Low or null consumption or Adequate consumption
Footnote	Disclaimer and warning	Paragraph that warns that the reports is designed for young Mexicans

- Birthplace (*Lugar de nacimiento*).- Birthplace (Country, State, Municipality or County) of user, mother, father, and mothers and fathers grandmother and grandfather.
- Life habits (*Hábitos y estilo de vida*).- Whether the user works or not, has access to a computer/internet at home, has access to internet in her/his mobile phone, daily time dedicated to social networks, number of sleep hours.

   The foods are classified in ten groups to facilitate user to find them, and taking into account Mexican food guides [10].

5   The Health Report

Once the user fill all questionnaires, she/he has access to generate an automatic report with weight valuation (body mass index, waist circumference, and waist/hip ratio) and general recommendation on her/his feeding habits, and

Lista de alimentos agregados

Grupo de alimentos	Alimentos	Porción	Número de porción	Frecuencia	Editar	Borrar
HUEVO	HUEVO SOLO	PIEZA	1 PORCION	DIARIO (7 DIAS A LA SEMANA)		
BEBIDAS	JUGO DE FRUTAS NATURAL	250 ml (VASO CHICO)	1 PORCION	DIARIO (7 DIAS A LA SEMANA)		
BEBIDAS	CAFE	< 250 ml	3 PORCIONES	DIARIO (7 DIAS A LA SEMANA)		
BEBIDAS	AGUA NATURAL	600 ml (BOTELLA)	1 PORCION	6 DIAS A LA SEMANA		
BEBIDAS	ATOLE	250 ml (VASO CHICO)	1 PORCION	1 VEZ AL MES		
BEBIDAS	LECHE ENTERA	250 ml (VASO CHICO)	1 PORCION	4 DIAS A LA SEMANA		
BEBIDAS	CERVEZA	350 ml (VASO MEDIANO, LATA)	1 PORCION	2 DIAS A LA SEMANA		
BEBIDAS	VINO TINTO	250 ml (VASO CHICO)	1 PORCION	4 DIAS A LA SEMANA		
BEBIDAS	AGUA DE FRUTAS NATURAL	250 ml (VASO CHICO)	1 PORCION	1 DIA A LA SEMANA		
ANTOJITOS	TAMAL	PIEZA	2 PORCIONES	1 DIA A LA SEMANA		
CARNE BLANCA	PESCADO	PIEZA O FILETE	1 PORCION	1 DIA A LA SEMANA		
CARNE BLANCA	MARISCOS	VASO CHICO	1 PORCION	1 VEZ AL MES		
CARNE ROJA	RES	BISTEK GRANDE (> 100 gr)	1 PORCION	2 DIAS A LA SEMANA		

Fig. 2. List sample of foods added by the user in the 'Food frequency' questionnaire (Fig. 1).

hours of exercise at week (Fig. 3). The report has eight main sections (Table 1). The Feeding Assessment summarizes the frequency of consumption (Figs. 1 and 2) registered in the Food and beverages questionnaire. The recommendation are grouped in four subsections: Fast food intake, Sweetened beverages, Fruits intake, and Vegetables intake, because these four issues are among the main causes of a bad nutrition in young. We hypothesized that if the young are alerted in these points, they could be more conscious on the food they are consuming, and hence, on one hand, to improve their diets, and on the other and, to persist on their good habits.

One of the tables of the database contains the criteria to classify whether or not the frequency of each type of meal is adequate (Table 1). The system groups all the meals of the same type and then sum frequencies to obtain a final and general frequency of consumption. Based on this frequency the system gives a general recommendation, v.gr. acceptable frequency for vegetables seven days a week or higher.

Some statistical on these four points, based on users of the last year (Table 2), reveals that they are really key point to improve the feeding habits of young Mexican. Less than half of young drink daily natural water (40.4% women; 33.7% men), and not all young drink it at least once a week (58.6%; 56.8%); also less than half of young eat vegetables at least three times a week (44.7%; 33.7%); fish is not very popular among young (16.5%; 17.8%).

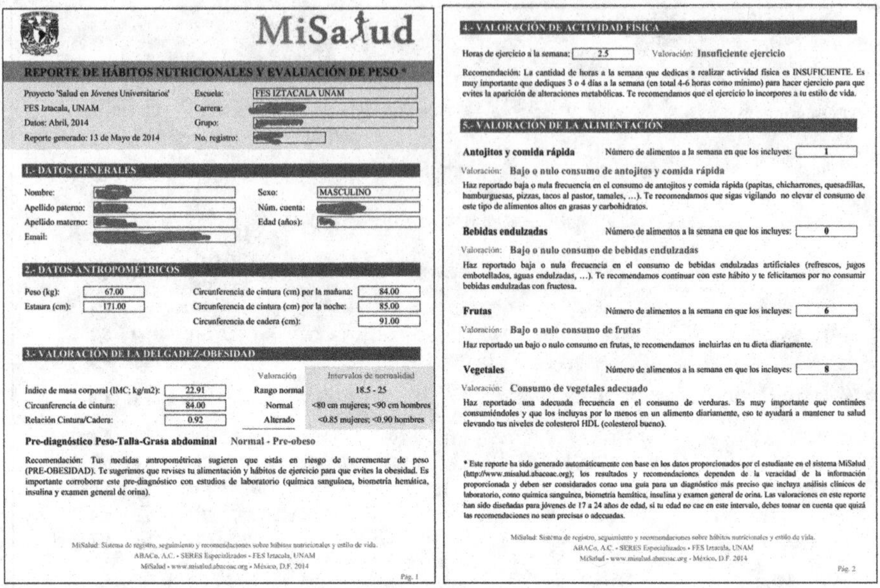

Fig. 3. Eating habits report. (A) Front page: Anthropometrics and weight evaluation and general recommendations; (B) Back page: Physical activity and eating evaluation and general recommendations.

The internet system has a double function: as a tool for self-monitoring on feeding habits, giving general recommendation, and as a research tool collecting massive data of young population. Additional to the health report, the system provides a follow-up charts (Fig. 4) that allows to the user self-monitoring her/his weight condition and feeding habits, among others.

6 Users of the System

Up to date, 2057 users have been registered in the system; as it is open to be used universally, so many university students used it. Here we only report statistics of user participating in the project "Physical health assessment" in years 2013 and 2015, where an integral assessment was performed to each student including clinical analyses of blood and urine, blood pressure, and anthropometrics, that is, 1,335 students participating in the project. All of them were invited to fill up the questionnaires in MiSalud; 77.7% (1,037) of them did it. We classified the registers in 'reliable' and 'not reliable', according to the number of food that the user chose to add to the consuming list: at least one beverage, and at least eight different kinds of meals, resulting in 449 registers of users marked as 'reliable', that are the base of the statistics of feeding habit reported here.

Table 2. Some statistics of the users of MiSalud system.

Frequency		Natural water	Sweetened drink	Fruits	Vegetables	Fish
Women (%)						
Dailly		159 (40.4)	16 (4.1)	48 (12.2)	22 (5.6)	-
6 days a week		20 (5.1)	1 (0.3)	23 (5.8)	17 (4.3)	-
5 days a week		23 (5.8)	20 (5.1)	67 (17)	22 (5.6)	1 (0.3)
4 days a week		12 (3)	9 (2.3)	38 (9.6)	48 (12.2)	1 (0.3)
3 days a week		13 (3.3)	21 (5.3)	48 (12.2)	67 (17)	3 (0.8)
2 days a week		4 (1)	28 (7.1)	37 (9.4)	39 (9.9)	10 (2.5)
1 day a week		-	11 (2.8)	10 (2.5)	15 (3.8)	29 (7.4)
1 day a month		-	5 (1.3)	1 (0.3)	4 (1)	15 (3.8)
1 day every 2 momnths		-	1 (0.3)	-	-	6 (1.5)
TOTAL women	394	231	112	272	234	65
(%)	(100)	(58.6)	(28.4)	(69)	(59.4)	(16.5)
Men (%)						
Dailly		57 (33.7)	3 (1.8)	12 (7.1)	6 (3.6)	-
6 days a week		10 (5.9)	1 (0.6)	7 (4.1)	4 (2.4)	-
5 days a week		19 (11.2)	10 (5.9)	27 (16)	13 (7.7)	-
4 days a week		6 (3.6)	15 (8.9)	13 (7.7)	11 (6.5)	-
3 days a week		2 (1.2)	11 (6.5)	24 (14.2)	23 (13.6)	1 (0.6)
2 days a week		2 (1.2)	10 (5.9)	14 (8.3)	17 (10.1)	6 (3.6)
1 day a week		-	9 (5.3)	7 (4.1)	6 (3.6)	16 (9.5)
1 day a month		-	1 (0.6)	1 (0.6)	-	7 (4.1)
1 day every 2 months		-	-	1 (0.6)	-	-
TOTAL men	169	96	60	106	80	30
(%)	(100)	(56.8)	(35.5)	(62.7)	(47.3)	(17.8)

7   Related Works

There are several internet systems to register and monitoring nutrition, one of them was developed by the Public Health School of the University of São Paulo for data collection, assessment and monitoring of the health and nutritional status of students by means of a structured 24–h recall method [11], the "NutriSim: System of health and nutrition monitoring - nutrition of school children".

A group of nutritional researches in Murcia, Spain, have developed the system GRUNUMUR a tool for human nutrition studies, including three types of questionnaires for dietary habits: 24 h recall, 7–days dietary record and Food Frequency Questionnaire, that also give reports of recommendations to young users, mainly university students [12].

Jung et al. developed the DES: Diet Evaluation System, a web based dietary survey program for Korean population, based on 24–h recall methodology [13], that gives recommendations on the total amount of nutrients given a list of food frequencies with their respective portions. The system contains a list of 4,222 common Korean foods each with information on 17 nutrients, so the system can calculate the total amount of nutrients intake for a given diet.

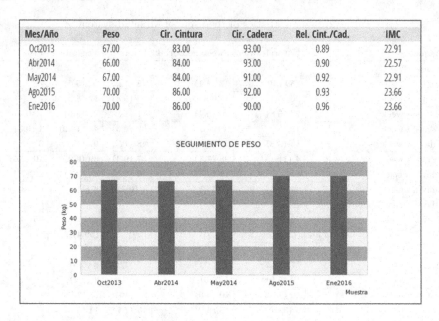

Mes/Año	Peso	Cir. Cintura	Cir. Cadera	Rel. Cint./Cad.	IMC
Oct2013	67.00	83.00	93.00	0.89	22.91
Abr2014	66.00	84.00	93.00	0.90	22.57
May2014	67.00	84.00	91.00	0.92	22.91
Ago2015	70.00	86.00	92.00	0.93	23.66
Ene2016	70.00	86.00	90.00	0.96	23.66

Fig. 4. 'Results' interface of MiSalud Internet system, showing the follow-up graphs of Weight, and the related measures table.

Our goal was not to build a system to calculate nutrient amounts for the diet of the user, instead, to detect general pattern identified as good or bad feeding habits, and give general recommendations to both, encourage to continuing with good habits, as is to daily include vegetables in the diet, and to alert on bad habits, as is to drink with high frequency high sweetened beverages.

8   System Evaluation

Several aspects can be evaluated of a system, one of them is the usability, and other is the effectiveness to modify positively feeding habits.

Furer et al. reported an evaluation on usability of a system to monitoring nutrition of school children by 17 Information technology professionals by means of a "Questionnaire for System Usability", containing 30 questions divided into six sections: easy to learn, easy to remember, error control, efficiency, efficacy, and satisfaction [11].

An evaluation on feeding habits improvement after an intervention in under-graduate students of US, using an online course system; components included e-mail messages, posted information, and behavior checklists with tailored feed-back, showed a low efficacy [14]. Based on the cognitive theory, eight variables were evaluated: (1) Social cognitive theory variables, (2) Positive outcome expec-tations, (3) Negative outcome expectations, (4) Self-efficacy for low-fat dairy intake, (5) Self-efficacy for total dairy intake, (6) Self-regulation, (7) Social sup-port for total dairy (family), and (8) Social support for total dairy (friends).

They found that the intervention was effective in modifying only two cognitive theory constructs: Self-efficacy for total dairy intake and Self-regulation, but did not improve the remaining six constructs measured.

Jung *et al.* performed an evaluation of a web based dietary survey program in Korean population, based on 24–h recall methodology [13]. The success rate was 63% (1–18 y) and 68% (19–49 y), i.e., the number of successful interviews out of all interviews, and was improved up to 92% and 78%, respectively, after include more devises. The average time of interviews was 14 min, and the daily nutrient intake calculated with the system was comparable to that calculated from national dietary survey. We have not evaluated the success interview of our system yet, but as it can be accessed by several types of devices, including cell phone, we will take advantage of its ubiquity to increase success on its use.

MiSalud has the double purpose of (a) register the feeding habits as survey to public health assessment, and (b) to give feedback to users on their feeding habits on monthly basis (Table 3). The success rate is 77.7%, i.e. of 1,335 students participating in the project (and who attended to our laboratory for a physical health evaluation, including anthropometrics and blood and urine laboratory analysis), 1,037 registered in the web page and filled the questionnaires. We classified the registers in 'reliable' and 'not reliable', according to the number of food that the user chose to add to the consuming list: at least one beverage, and at least eight different kinds of meals, resulting in 449 registers of users mark as 'reliable', that represent 43.3% of success.

To assess the usability perception we included the question: 'How easy is to use the system?' The percentages of answers obtained were: 1.4% Difficult, 14.9% Somehow difficult, 38.8% Easy, 44.9% Very easy. The percentages were similar if we included only of reliable users: 1.0%, 13.6%, 40.8%, and 44.7%, respectively.

To assess the perception of user on how useful is the system to improve their feeding habits we included the question: 'How important for improve your feeding habits the system is? ' The percentages of answers obtained were: 0.3% Bad, 6.7% Somehow good, 53.8% Good, and 39.1% Very good.

9   Discussion

The Internet provide the opportunity to distribute massively tools for health care, particularly here we presented a tool for self-monitoring of feeding habits and weight condition. The MiSalud system is universally available to all young that want to use it. This kind of system could help to address the obesity epidemic, particularly in Mexico, a country where the pre-obese and obese prevalence among young is one of the highest in the world.

No assessment has been made on the putative positive impact on the feeding habits of users. It is possible to obtain a statistical report on the frequent users, and compare them against users that have accessed only once, inviting them to a second assess.

The system is designed specifically for young Mexican, and thus, the food catalogue is constrained to foods mainly found in Mexico City area, and the

Table 3. Database table for recommendation report. The ranges reffer to number of days a week that the participant includes the meal: MIN (inclusive), and MAX (less than).

Group	Frequency: days a week MIN–MAX	Diagnostic_Text
Excercise	0–0	Do not do exercise
Excercise	1–3.5	Insufficient exercising
Excercise	3.5–8	Adequate excercising
Excercise	8–100	More than 8 h a week of exercising
Snacks	0–3	Low or zero consumption of snacks and fast food
Snacks	3–100	High consumption of snacks or fast food
Sweetened_beverages	0–3	Low or zero consumption of sweetened beverages
Sweetened_beverages	3–100	High consumption of snacks and fast food
Fruits	0–7	Low or zero consumption of fruits
Fruits	7–14	Adequate intake of fruits
Fruits	14–100	High consumption of fruit
Vegetables	0–0	Zero consumption of vegetables
Vegetables	1–7	Low consumption of vegetables
Vegetables	7–100	Suitable vegetable consumption

interface is in Spanish language, thus, adaptations are required if it is wanted its use for young of other regions.

10   Conclusions

MiSalud system is an internet system to assess health, mainly on feeding habits and weight condition available universally in internet (www.misalud.abacoac.org). More than 2,000 university young have been used the system obtaining the health report with general recommendations, and having access to the follow-up charts.

Nevertheless, the system is designed specifically for young Mexican, adaptations to other populations are possible, via replacing database catalogues, and translate the interface messages to other languages.

Acknowledgments. We thanks to all young participants using MiSalud system, their cooperation and interest in their health are centrals in this project. This project was supported in part by DGAPA, UNAM: grants PAPIME-PE207516, and PAPIIT-IN219915.

References

1. Low, S., Chin, M.C.: Deurenberg-Yap M: review on epidemic of obesity. Ann. Acad. Med. Singap. **38**, 57–59 (2009)
2. Seidell, J.C.: Obesity, insulin resistance and diabetes: a worldwide epidemic. Br. J. Nutr. **83**, S6–S8 (2000)
3. Barquera, S., Campos-Nonato, I., Hernández-Barrera, L., Pedroza-Tobías, A., Rivera-Dommarco, J.A.: Prevalencia de obesidad en adultos mexicanos (in English), ENSANUT 2012. Salud Pública de México **55**, S151–S151 (2013). In Spanish
4. Murguía-Romero, M., Jiménez-Flores, R., Molina, V., Méndez-Cruz, A.R.: Estimating the geographic distribution of the Metabolic Syndrome prevalence in young Mexicans. Geospatial Health **6**(3), 43–50 (2012)
5. Murguía-Romero, M., Jiménez-Flores, J.R., Sigrist-Flores, S.C., Tapia-Pancardo, D.C., Ramos-Jiménez, A., Méndez-Cruz, A.R., Villalobos-Molina, R.: Prevalence of metabolic syndrome in young Mexicans: a sensitivity analysis on its components. Nutr. Hosp. **32**(1), 189–195 (2015)
6. Villalobos-Molina, R., Jiménez -Flores, J.R., Mendez-Cruz, A.R., Sigrist-Flores, C.S., Murguía-Romero, M., Tapia-Pancardo, D.C., Esparza-Romero, J., Ramos-Jiménez, A., Urquidez-Romero, R.: Resistencia a la Insulina y Síndrome Metabólico en Jóvenes Universitarios de dos Regiones de México. Revista de la Conferencia Científica Anual Sobre Síndrome Metabólico **2**(1) (2015)
7. Ford, E.S., Schulze, M.B., Pischon, T., Bergmann, M.M., Joost, H.G., Boeing, H.: Metabolic syndrome and risk of incident diabetes: findings from the European Prospective Investigation into Cancer and Nutrition-Potsdam Study. Cardiovascular Diabetology **7**(35) (2008)
8. Murguía-Romero, M., Méndez-Cruz, R., Villalobos-Molina, R., Rodríguez-Soriano, N.Y., González-Dalhaus, E., Jiménez-Flores, R.: Knowledge-based system for diagnosis of metabolic alterations in undergraduate students. In: Sidorov, G., Hernández Aguirre, A., Reyes García, C.A. (eds.) MICAI 2010. LNCS (LNAI), vol. 6437, pp. 467–476. Springer, Heidelberg (2010). doi:10.1007/978-3-642-16761-4_41
9. Murguía, M., Serrano, B., Jiménez, R., Villalobos, R.: Sistema en Internet para el registro de antecedentes clínicos y hábitos de alimentación para el estudio del síndrome metabólico. Revista de la Conferencia Científica Anual Sobre Síndrome Metabólico. Congreso 2014. **1**(1) 53 Cd. de México, 15–16 de Agosto, 2014
10. Pérez-Lizaur, A.B., Palacios-González, B., Castro Becerra, A.L.: Sistema Mexicano de Alimentos Equivalentes. 3rd edn. Fomento de Nutrición y Salud, A.C. 108 p. (2008)
11. Ferri Ruggeri, B.F., Voci, S.M., Borges, C.A., Slater, B.: Assessment of the usability of a nutritional epidemiology computerized system. Rev. Bras. Epidemiol. **16**(4), 966–975 (2013)
12. Perez-Llamas, F., Garaulet, M., Torralba, C, Zamora, S.: Desarrollo de una versión actualizada de una aplicación informática para investigación y práctica en nutrición humana (GRUNUMUR 2.0). Nutr. Hosp. **27**(5), 1576–1582 (2012)
13. Jung, H.J., Lee, S.E., Kim, D., Noh, H.: Improvement in the technological feasibility of a web-based dietary survey system in local settings. Asia Pac. J. Clin. Nutr. **24**(2), 308–315 (2015)
14. Poddar, K.H., Hosig, K.W., Anderson, E.S., Nickols-Richardson, S.M., Duncan, S.E.: Improves self-efficacy and self-regulation related to increased dairy intake in college students. J. Am. Diet. Assoc. **110**, 1723–1727 (2010)

A Conversational Agent for Use in the Identification of Rare Diseases

Ana Olivia Caballero Lambert[1]([✉]), Cesar Horacio Torres Montañez[2],
Monica Bueno Martinez[2], and Marcelo Funes-Gallanzi[3]

[1] Universidad Iberoamericana, León, Guanajuato, Mexico
ana.caballero@leon.uia.mx
[2] Natura Xalli, Tepic, Nayarit, Mexico
{cesar.torres,monica.bueno}@naturaxalli.com
[3] AVNTK, S.C., Guadalajara, Jalisco, Mexico
mfg@avntk.com

Abstract. This paper presents work in progress on implementing a conversational agent, Dr. Rachael, in the form of a virtual caregiver, for use in helping to identify rare diseases. The rationale for the system is grounded in the fact that rare disorders by their very nature are difficult to diagnose unless the caregiver or doctor is familiar with a wide range of these conditions. The conversational agent uses unstructured free-flowing natural language together with a large database of rare disorders, and is easily updatable by human caregivers without any technical expertise. Matching of users' comments with database entries is performed using a general cognition engine; which is able to understand natural language regardless of specific wording or grammar. In this paper we give a comprehensive background to and an overview of the system, with a focus on aspects pertaining to natural language processing and user interaction. The system is currently only implemented for English.

Keywords: General cognition engines · Artificial cognition systems · Diagnosis · Rare diseases

1 Introduction

Rare diseases pose a large challenge to society, and gravely affect the lives of many children. Approximately 75 % of rare diseases affect children and 30 % of rare disease patients die before the age of 5. There are approximately 7,000 rare diseases identified. A rare disease is a life-threatening or chronically debilitating condition. A disease is defined as rare in Mexico when there is one sufferer per 2000 inhabitants (or nearly 10 million people currently), in Europe when fewer than 5 in 10,000 people are affected, and in the US when fewer than 200,000 people are affected. Almost 5 % of the world's population are living with a rare disease [1]. The longer it takes to diagnose a rare disease, the more physicians the patient needs to see. 40 % of rare disease patients are misdiagnosed at least once. For people with a rare disease, the mean average length of time from symptom onset to accurate diagnosis is approximately 4.8 years [2]. People with a rare disease may experience low quality

© ICST Institute for Computer Sciences, Social Informatics and Telecommunications Engineering 2017
E. Sucar et al. (Eds.): AFI 2016, LNICST 179, pp. 128–139, 2017.
DOI: 10.1007/978-3-319-49622-1_15

of life and high levels of disability. This difficult journey to diagnosis and care can increase medical, economic and social burdens [3]. Rare diseases often hide behind common symptoms of other more common illnesses, making the diagnosis extremely challenging and often leading to mis-diagnosis. Despite progress made in this area, there remains a need to better understand the obstacles patients and caregivers within the rare disease community face in obtaining a correct and timely diagnosis. The path to improve diagnosis can only be helped by all stakeholders joining together to find solutions to help ensure accurate diagnosis of rare diseases at an early stage. An accurate diagnosis may be the first step to improving the care for those living with a rare disease and their families. In more than 50 % of cases it is those living with a rare disease, or their families, who ultimately manage to discover the correct diagnosis of the patient and inform the doctor. There are resources such as http:// www.ncbi.nlm.nih.gov/pubmed/ & http://rarediseases.org/for-patients-and-families/information-resources/rare-disease-information/ but these are not easy to use, they list conditions alphabetically and assume the user has a relatively high level of scientific knowledge that normally lay people do not possess.

There is a need therefore for a user-friendly tool to help families or caregivers find the correct diagnosis for a patient at an early stage, without limitations of time, a specific doctors' knowledge or any preconceptions. We are committed to helping raise awareness of rare diseases, including the diagnostic challenges, and to implementing initiatives to support an improved diagnosis journey. One such initiative is to make available a conversational agent, initially provided with knowledge of about 1,000 diseases, specifically targeted at rare diseases patients and their families. Our aim is that the system could form a part of the tools available to doctors in the future. In this paper we give an overview of the "Dr. Rachael" system, its rationale, design and implementation. The next section gives a background to and a rationale for the system. We then describe the conversational agent and the user interaction in Sects. 3 and 4. Following this, in Sect. 5 we describe the characteristics of the domain and the users, which lead to the choice of a general cognition engine to do the matching of users' comments with the available knowledge, which described in Sect. 6. We then describe the structure of the database, the interface for updating this knowledge base, and some sample interactions in Sect. 7. Finally, in Sect. 8, we present some conclusions and suggestions for future work.

2   Background and Rationale

Patients with rare diseases form a rather heterogeneous group with respect to their thoughts and questions regarding their disorder; especially in the early stages. Anecdotal clinical experience indicates that patients tend to ask the same kinds of questions using similar language for a given disorder. The aim of Dr. Rachael is to be able to interact in an easy-going non-structured way for as long as is necessary in order to provide likely leads for the condition affecting a patient, at times when a human caregiver is not available. Dr. Rachael is a conversational agent powered by a general cognition engine, embodied as a virtual caregiver, accessible through a web interface. Comments and questions are posed to the system using written natural language. By providing an embodiment of a conversational agent, the hope is to support a more natural feeling dialogue, finding likely leads and to promote users' trust in the answers. In addition, it is hoped that such a system will be user-friendly and easy-going in providing suggestions and advice, lessening the focus on the patient's problems.

The reader might raise concerns regarding the use of a conversational agent in helping to find a likely diagnosis for patients whose condition could be long-term and life-threatening. The rationale for the use of Dr. Rachael is that research by the patient or his family, who are prepared to put in the time and reading necessary, is often the way the correct diagnosis to rare diseases is reached and any means that can be devised to shorten the time to reach the correct diagnosis should be tried. The scientific basis for this rationale is discussed in detail in [4]. By focusing on providing answers to questions related to the likely disorder, based on scientific facts and expressed in a professional, yet comprehensible, encouraging, motivating and empathetic language, the hope is that the system will help in disrupting the worries and thoughts of the patients. There are of course potential problems with Internet based treatments and diagnostics tools. For example, Internet access might be a limiting factor [5]. However, for instance a survey shows that 95 % of the Swedish population in the age group of 15-24 year olds, have access to the Internet in their homes, and that 86 % use the Internet on a daily basis [6], the statistics being quite similar throughout the developed world. Furthermore, it should be noted that the aim of leveraging a virtual caregiver is not to replace human caregivers. Instead, one should view these as complementary parts of the long and often fraught diagnosis process for rare diseases. More generally, Internet-based treatments have previously been used successfully for example in the treatment of agoraphobia [7] and ADHD [8]. These naturally focused on the psychological aspects of the disorders and were based on Cognitive Behavioral Therapy and working memory training, respectively. The present work is not directly inspired by this previous work, since the nature of the disorders are very different.

3   Conversational Agent

While one should not take for granted that the use of a conversational agent will benefit all information system applications, there are some associated properties that make them especially beneficial to this specific application. As discussed earlier, patients with rare diseases find it hard to obtain the correct diagnosis in a reasonable period of time, and often need to do some research on their own while not having much technical or scientific knowledge.

Numerous studies have shown that these aspects are not currently being addressed effectively. For example, some ideas present in the system can be conveyed more directly, by use of facial expressions and body gestures, than is possible with text alone. Studies have also shown that by using friendly small talk, verbal and non-verbal expression of emotion and expressions of expertise, empathy and trust can be conveyed [9]. Furthermore, by using relaxed knowledgeable artificial characters a sense of confidence, which can have motivational effects, can be conveyed [10]. Dr. Rachael is capable of holding a normal conversation discussing a range of topics, as well as having a large amount of knowledge about symptoms of more than 1,000 rare diseases; while body movement, speech generation and recognition are currently being implemented.

4   User Interaction

Although we make use of a conversational agent, the primary communication channel used in the system is written text. Users interact with Dr. Rachael by posing questions using natural language entered using a standard text-field, see Fig. 1. If a comment is made by the user, Dr. Rachael will make a suitable related comment, based on a association of ideas very much as a person would. If a posed question has a high similarity with a question in the database, the answer is presented directly to the user by Dr. Rachael. If no such question is found, the closest available general comment is given.

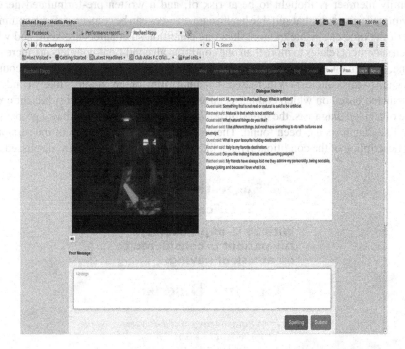

Fig. 1. Screen-shot of Dr. Rachael answering the question: "Do you like making friends and influencing people?"

Thus, a conversation can range from discussing general concepts to replying to specific questions, as shown by the following example:

Rachael said: Hi, my name is Rachael Repp. If You were a spy what would your alias be?
Guest said: I would like to be called Superman.
Rachael said: I would like to be remembered as a good person.
Guest said: Are you good or just want to convince me you are nice?

Rachael said: I am just a girl who knows what she wants.
Guest said: I often have a stomach ache.
Rachael said: You are a collective of every experience you have had in your life.
Guest said: I have lost weight recently.
Rachael said: Weight loss is common in people with Crohn's disease.
Guest said: I sometimes have constipation, pain and swelling in the stomach.
Rachael said: When Crohn's disease causes intestinal obstruction, the symptoms may include pain, constipation, swelling of the abdomen, and/or vomiting.
Guest said: What is it called when you get an infection by the bacteria that are in the intestines?
Rachael said: The name is septicemia.

After each session, the user is provided with the most likely condition that the user or family member is thought to be at risk of, and a written pre-formulated general description is given, so that suitable health care services can be contacted. Each comment most of the time can relate to more than one condition so counters are kept, and when a given statement relates to more than one condition all conditions counters are increased by one. If a given statement is related to only one condition, then only the counter associated to this condition is increased. The final rating of the patient's likely condition is calculated based on which counter is largest, and where there is not sufficient confidence of a given diagnosis, the three top conditions are displayed, yielding a probability that a like diagnosis has been found. The user can also see, at the end of the session, a short description of the condition(s) most likely to apply to the symptoms discussed, see

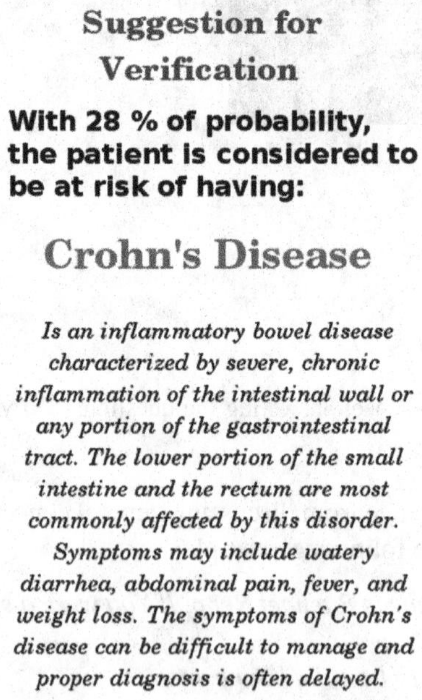

Suggestion for
Verification

With 28 % of probability, the patient is considered to be at risk of having:

Crohn's Disease

Is an inflammatory bowel disease characterized by severe, chronic inflammation of the intestinal wall or any portion of the gastrointestinal tract. The lower portion of the small intestine and the rectum are most commonly affected by this disorder. Symptoms may include watery diarrhea, abdominal pain, fever, and weight loss. The symptoms of Crohn's disease can be difficult to manage and proper diagnosis is often delayed.

Fig. 2. Screen-shot of the "Suggestion for verification" showing a brief text giving a condition the patient is considered to be at risk of.

Fig. 2. This feature allows the patient or the family to get a firm suggestion even if the session lasts a long time or is even completed over many sittings, hopefully helping in the right direction towards a suitable diagnosis. This kind of feedback is an integral part of the method on which Dr. Rachael is based, which has been previously applied by our group to the diagnosis of eating disorders and personality tests.

5   Domain Characteristics

A number of characteristics of the domain and the patient group, in combination with the rather small scale of the project so far, has influenced the choices made in designing the system. First of all, the domain which the system needs to cover is too broad for the system to cover using limited resources. Secondly, since the system may be employed in a real-world situation either by doctors, patients or their families, users with no technical training should be able to quickly expand the knowledge base using only natural language, in case the system lacks coverage of a certain sub-domain. It follows that the knowledge base in principle should consist of a set of concise information field together with more or less frequently asked questions and answers to these questions.

Matching users questions to this database on the surface looks like a standard information retrieval (IR) task. However, the domain and task at hand differs from those considered in traditional IR in a number of ways:

- Large data set – the number of answers is quite large and apply in many cases to more than one condition (currently about 100 out of 1,200 considered in the first stage of testing).
- Short description – each condition is described by its symptoms, some questions and answers and a short description, so quite a few words (on average about 300)
- Narrow sub-domains – several descriptions relate to distinct conditions, although many details apply to more than one condition so there is a large amount of overlapping.
- Stressed, fatigued users – patients or carers often find it hard to concentrate for a long period of time, and so might need to come back many times and perhaps benefit from some light entertainment!

Traditional IR methods, using a traditional bag-of-words (BoW) representation or latent semantic indexing (LSI) [11] for instance, work well on large data sets, with longer documents, however they often place a high burden on the users to have a lot of knowledge, both of IT and the specific field, and sift through search result sets in order to find what they are looking for. In the case of patients with rare diseases, we want to keep session results down to a minimum, preferably delivering the correct diagnosis in answer to a conversation directly if a sufficiently high probability of disease identification has been achieved, or at least to keep details through a database, user code and password for the user to come again. Due to the wide variation in educational level and vocabularies, the system must handle morphological variation and possess a considerable vocabulary. The system should also be able to handle spelling errors gracefully, since the users are often to some degree fatigued spelling errors are to be expected.

Furthermore, since the users interact with the system in English, both grammar and vocabulary can vary widely so natural language processing must be handled appropriately. These issues are not as important when many long documents are drawn from a large domain, and when there is no limit on search result size, since the probability of a certain morphological form, or spelling variation, occurring at least somewhere in at least some relevant document is high.

6   General Cognition Engine

As previously discussed, standard IR methods are not suited to the present task. Instead we need a representation and similarity measure that handles morphological variation, spelling errors, and compound words.

In order to facilitate interaction, we firstly acquire information by converting all text to a simplified version using Basic English implemented in a proprietary tool called "Simplish" capable of understanding standard English of 100,000 words. We then create a multidimensional ideogram to represent each sentence, similar to the logic used in creating Chinese symbols, and store these in the memory of the general cognition engine in such a way that two sentences having the same meaning, regardless of vocabulary or grammar, result in ideograms of similar shape and position in the memory space. Details of this method are beyond the scope of this article and will be the subject of a related publication in the near future. Memory retrieval is achieved using a nearest-neighbor search of ideograms in 12 dimensions. We have therefore enabled the computer to "understand" what the user says, moving artificial intelligence from "pattern matching" strategies to "concept matching".

Possibly the most fundamental aspect of cognition is memory, which is itself broken down into three distinct tasks: acquisition, storage and retrieval; bearing in mind that it is well-established that order helps memory. Knowledge and experience are most easily transferred through language and at the root of the concept of language lies the very definition of a word. For centuries words like "virtue" have defied an exact generally-accepted definition, though this is a subtle complex term. However, as first noted by Wittgenstein (1953) even simple words like "dog" or "game" can be equally challenging. His suggestion was that there exists a "family resemblance" which allows us to identify a particular instance as a member of a group such as a "dog". Using the idea of meaning being defined in terms of a word's relationship to others is attractive but involves deriving a matrix of word relations that implies many more entries than the average number of neurons in a human brain, if a standard vocabulary is used. This fact leads us to two conclusions: first, that it is likely that basic-level categorization is in fact used by the brain, and second that it would therefore be useful to find a way to represent a full vocabulary in terms of a reduced vocabulary, that can act as a proxy for this set of basic-level categorizations. The conversion of text into a reduced-vocabulary form is achieved by *Simplish*, a proprietary tool that converts standard English into a reduced-vocabulary version of 1,000 words - 850 basic words, 50 international words and 100 specialised words – said reduced vocabulary being employed as a proxy for a set of basic-level categorizations. This representation therefore yields an effective means of knowledge acquisition. A reduced-vocabulary also has the advantage of reducing ambiguity as a by-product of the translation process.

Using a reduced-vocabulary representation of knowledge, where words have been associated to each other, enables the mapping of language, through the use of standard multivariate techniques, to a low-dimensionality space where a multidimensional ideogram (a graphic symbol that represents an idea or concept) can be produced as an illustrative point in this subspace, as might be represented in the brain (using variables such as coordinates x, y, z, potential, neurotransmitter, frequency, phase, etc.). The low-dimensionality ideogram is the storage medium. These ideograms will be similar even if different words or grammar are used, because their form and position is given by the relationship of a semantic unit to all other members of the basic-level categorization.

The result of this strategy is to establish a means to map semantic similarity into spatial and shape proximity, i.e. the distance between two points (concepts), or between all points in more complex shapes such as those due to ideograms, is a measure of how similar their meanings are. Spatial proximity can be used to yield a means for information retrieval for a given query, via the association of ideas as a human does, implemented here through the application of nearest-neighbour search algorithms for instance, a method that is well-known in the art, either to a single point or to sets of points describing an ideogram. This strategy enables concepts to be mapped either as part of a data-driven step or concept-driven strategy for contextual information needed in problem-solving. We can plot and step along an evolving path and come across both types of information if relevant.

This approach enables us to merge equivalent concepts, do summaries, order data, find relevant contextual data easily, identify sentences having similar meaning, do true abduction (as originally proposed by C. S. Peirce) on knowledge, and implement a means to identify metaphors. It basically places knowledge in a position and shape depending on meaning and so requires no prior training to understand any given topic, hence the term "general cognition engine". Note that no pattern-matching method, ontology, topic map, or prior training of any kind is used. Current work is centered on deduction using the STUDENT world-algebra algorithm [12] combined with the E-theorem prover from the Technical University Munich [13], while decision-making is achieved through a Bayes decision tree obtained automatically directly from the text. We have implemented two prize-winning (http://www.innovation-council.org.uk/2014-awards/) applications: a simple summary generator available in www.simplish.org and a conversational agent available at www.rachaelrepp.org that is being developed for competing for the Loebner Prize and on which Dr. Rachael is based. The system uses a single-processor implementation for the ANN, which is fast enough given the database size, but current work centers on implementing a fully parallelized version using the FLANN library [14] since as the size of the database increases this will be needed.

7   Knowledge, Comments, Questions and Answers

As described above, the knowledge base of the system consists of a knowledge base containing symptoms, a description and some questions and answers for each condition, formulated in natural language. Each comment or answer can be linked to several different conditions and counters are kept for each. Comments and answers are assigned to one or more conditions. Responses are further assigned a mood, which is currently used to control the body language and facial expressions of Dr. Rachael. In order to collect data and involve the users early on in the design of the system, a small-scale pilot study was performed, covering only 150 conditions. The experiment resulted in an initial database of symptoms, descriptions, questions and answers, which were mostly based on the NORD database and have subsequently been refined for our purposes. It also gave valuable information on the characteristics of the language use by the patients, the degree of spelling errors and other aspects of language variation.

An important point worthy of mention is that not all rare diseases are difficult to diagnose, such as Fibrodysplasia Ossificans Progressiva or Tourette's. A sub-group of particular interest is that made up of conditions which are rare *and* difficult to diagnose, mostly because they are easily confused with more common conditions. It is this latter group upon which we have concentrated our attention.

A web-based "editor interface" aid in the expansion of the database is currently in progress. Using this interface, a human caregiver can add, remove and update symptoms, descriptions, questions and answers, add alternative formulations to an answer, and browse and search comments/questions posed to the system that were left unanswered.

While the database is necessary for the conversational agent, it could also be potentially useful in providing human caregivers with a common ground, so that patients are not given conflicting answers when asking different caregivers the same question. It could also potentially be useful in highlighting mildly frequently asked questions and topics, allowing the human caregivers to better prepare for these questions.

8   Conclusions and Future Work

In this paper we presented some early results of a conversational agent being used to aid in the identification of 150 rare diseases, based on one of the few available conversational agents able to "understand" natural language effectively. An initial study and some trials shows that there is indeed a need for this kind of system among patients with rare diseases, and suggests that the current system fulfills the demands of these patients satisfactorily. Currently, data is being collected to raise the number of diseases covered up to 1,200, the results of trials will then be used to determine the final refinement steps of the implementation and possible improvements to all aspects of the system. We have high hopes on the utility of the final system, which is to be finished later this year.

Although the current system is well received by medical practitioners, patients and family members, it is important to point out that it is an "informational" tool and there is yet no evidence that the system is an effective tool to help identify rare diseases. This can only be proved by conducting a randomized controlled trial in a clinical setting prior to it being regarded as a "diagnostic tool" for any disease. The system was developed on a small budget, using mostly our own proprietary software, some open source software and standard web technology throughout, showing that it is indeed possible to build usable systems in this domain as a small scale research project with limited funding.

Currently, the system is only implemented for English, but the natural language processing modules are in principle language agnostic. Of course there are still much room for improvement, both to the dialogue and interaction aspects and to the natural language processing aspects of the system. We are happy to receive comments and suggestions for further improvements from the participants of this symposium, and will look eagerly towards any offers of collaboration in this project.

Appendix: Crohn's Disease

General Discussion

Crohn's disease is an inflammatory bowel disease characterized by severe, chronic inflammation of the intestinal wall or any portion of the gastrointestinal tract. The lower portion of the small intestine and the rectum are most commonly affected by this disorder. Symptoms may include watery diarrhea, abdominal pain, fever, and weight loss. The symptoms of Crohn's disease can be difficult to manage and proper diagnosis is often delayed. The exact cause of Crohn's disease is unknown[1].

Signs & Symptoms

Crohn's disease typically affects the lower portion of the small intestine and/or the colon, especially the right colon. Occasionally, inflammation may occur in the middle and lower portions of the small intestine. In some cases, there is inflammation of the membranes that line the mouth, the esophagus, and/or stomach. The symptoms of Crohn's disease may begin abruptly or appear slowly over a long period of time. Symptoms that may develop over time include nausea, vomiting, fever, night sweats, loss of appetite, a general feeling of weakness, waves of abdominal pain and discomfort, diarrhea and/or bleeding. Weight loss is common in Crohn's disease.

Acute attacks of Crohn's disease may cause fever, elevated white blood cell counts, and/or severe pain in the lower right abdomen. These symptoms are frequently confused with appendicitis. Crohn's disease may cause lesions in the intestinal wall and the surrounding lymph nodes. Abscesses may occur before the appearance of other symptoms. Grooves on the inner surface of the intestines may also occur. These may feel like a solid mass in the abdomen and when the mucosal lining of the intestines becomes thickened, it may feel like cobblestones. Deep open abscesses, scarring, and some degree of intestinal obstruction may occur as a result of chronic inflammation of the intestine. In some cases, fistulas and abscesses may create an opening through the intestinal wall and result in infection by the bacteria that occur naturally in the intestines. Massive, abnormal enlargement of the colon is a serious complication of Crohn's disease and may result in intestinal bleeding into the abdomen and septicemia.

When Crohn's disease causes intestinal obstruction, the symptoms may include pain, constipation, swelling of the abdomen, and/or vomiting. This may be due to the

---

[1] Source for the material: http://rarediseases.org/rare-diseases/crohns-disease/ .

accumulation of fluid in the intestines or thickening of the muscosal layers of the intestinal walls. Inflammation and obstruction may occur together and can impair digestion and the absorption of food and may lead to malnutrition. Crohn's disease rarely occurs in children, and is characterized by failure to thrive, fever, and/or abnormally low levels of circulating red blood cells. Children may also experience joint pain and stiffness. Growth and sexual development are often delayed. Initially, children with Crohn's disease may not experience diarrhea or abdominal pain. People with Crohn's disease may have anemia, abnormally low levels of albumin in the blood, abnormally high white blood cell counts, and/or a deficiency of vitamin B-12. Other laboratory findings may include abnormally low blood levels of sodium, potassium, calcium, and/or magnesium. Individuals with Crohn's disease may also have symptoms that are not related to intestinal dysfunction. These may include joint pain, or skin and eye problems. A fatty like substance may accumulate in various parts of the body. Blood circulation may be impaired by abnormally thick blood, dehydration, and/or lack of movement or exercise. In some cases, arthritis may occur resulting in swollen and painful joints. In rare cases of Crohn's disease, liver function may be impaired. In some cases, affected individuals may experience diminished bone mass resulting in thinning and weakness of the bones.

References

1. Aronson, J.: Rare diseases and orphan drugs. Br. J. Clin. Pharmacol. **61**(3), 243–244 (2006). http://www.ncbi.nlm.nih.gov/pmc/articles/PMC1885017/
2. Engel, P.A., et al.: Physician and patient perceptions regarding physician training in rare diseases: the need for stronger educational initiatives for physicians. J. Rare Disord. **1**(2) 2013. http://www.journalofraredisorders.com/pub/IssuePDFs/Engel.pdf
3. Rare Diseases UK. Key Statistics from the RDUK Report 'Experiences of Rare Diseases: An Insight from Patients and Families'. http://raredisease.org.uk/index.htm
4. Rare Disease Impact Report: Insights from patients and the medical community, Shire, April 2013. http://www.geneticalliance.org.uk/docs/e-update/rare-disease-impact-report.pdf
5. Carlbring, P., Andersson, G.: Internet and psychological treatment. How well can they be combined? Comput. Hum. Behav. **22**(3), 545–553 (2006)
6. Nordicom-Sveriges Internetbarometer 2007. MedieNotiser 2/2008. ISSN 1101–4539 (2008)
7. Carlbring, P.: Panic! Its Prevalence, Diagnosis and Treatment via the Internet. Doctoral thesis, Department of Psychology, Uppsala University (2004)
8. Klingberg, T., Forssberg, H., Westerberg, H.: Training of working memory in children with ADHD. J. Clin. Exp. Neuropsychol. **24**(6), 781–791 (2002)
9. de Rosis, F., Cavalluzi, A., Mazotta, I., Novielli, N.: Can embodied conversational agents induce empathy in users? In: AISB'05 Virtual Characters Symposium (2005)
10. Berry, D., Butler, L., de Rosis, F., Laaksolahti, J., Pelachaud, C., Steedman, M.: Final evaluation report, the Magister project. January (2004)
11. Dumais, S.T., Furnas, G.S., Landauer, T.K., Deerwester, S.C.: Using latent semantic analysis to improve information retrieval. In: Proceedings of CHI 1988: Conference on Human Factors in Computing, pp. 281–285 (1988)
12. Bobrow, D.G.: Natural Language Input for a computer problem solving System. Ph.D Thesis, MIT (1964)

13. Schulz, S.: System description: E 1.8. In: McMillan, K., Middeldorp, A., Voronkov, A. (eds.) LPAR 2013. LNCS, vol. 8312, pp. 735–743. Springer, Heidelberg (2013). doi: 10.1007/978-3-642-45221-5_49

14. Muja, M., Lowe, D.G.: Scalable nearest neighbor algorithms for high dimensional data. IEEE Trans. Pattern Anal. Mach. Intell. **36**(11), 2227–2240 (2014)

15. Wittgenstein, L.: Philosophical Investigations. Blackwell, Oxford (1953). (G.E.M. Anscombe, trans.)

Using Intermediate Models and Knowledge Learning to Improve Stress Prediction

Alban Maxhuni[1], Pablo Hernandez-Leal[2], Eduardo F. Morales[2(✉)],
L. Enrique Sucar[2], Venet Osmani[3],
Angelica Muńoz-Meléndez[2], and Oscar Mayora[3]

[1] DISI, University of Trento, Via Sommarive 9 Povo, 38123 Trento, Italy
`maxhuni@disi.unitn.it`
[2] INAOE-Instituto Nacional de Astrofísica,
Óptica y Electrónica, Sta. María Tonantzintla, Puebla, Mexico
`{pablohl,emorales,esucar,munoz}@inaoep.mx`
[3] CREATE-NET, Via Alla Cascata 56/D Povo, 38123 Trento, Italy
`{vosmani,omayora}@create-net.org`

Abstract. Motor activity in physical and psychological stress exposure
has been studied almost exclusively with self-assessment questionnaires
and from reports that derive from human observer, such as verbal rating and simple descriptive scales. However, these methods are limited in
objectively quantifying typical behaviour of stress. We propose to use
accelerometer data from smartphones to objectively quantify stress levels. Used data was collected in real-world setting, from 29 employees in
two different organisations over 5 weeks. To improve classification performance we propose to use *intermediate models*. These intermediate
models represent the mood state of a person which is used to build the
final stress prediction model. In particular, we obtained an accuracy of
78.2 % to classify stress levels.

Keywords: Motor activity · Stress prediction · Smartphones

1 Introduction

OVER the last decades there has been rising concern worldwide about the growth
and negative impact of work-related stress. The prevalence of stress-related illnesses such as burnout has increased dramatically in the European Union (EU)
[1,2]. Recent studies show that stress is ranked as a second most common work-
related health problem across the members of the EU. In the Fourth European
Working Conditions Survey conducted in 2015, 22 % of workers from the EU
have reported the impact of work-related stress [2]. Furthermore, a high prevalence of stress has also been reported in USA, where 55 % of employees have
reported increased workload having a significant impact on physical and mental
health [3]. Recent studies show that individuals with high-stress were accompanied by physical and psycho-social complaints and decreased work-control [4].

© ICST Institute for Computer Sciences, Social Informatics and Telecommunications Engineering 2017
E. Sucar et al. (Eds.): AFI 2016, LNICST 179, pp. 140–151, 2017.
DOI: 10.1007/978-3-319-49622-1_16

To date, current approaches for measuring stress rely mostly on self-reported questionnaires [1]. This presents an issue for effective measurements, due to subjectivity factors. For example, employees might be more predisposed to report information in their favour or in the favour of their organisation, rather than reporting their true health state. To overcome these issues, smartphones are becoming suitable means to carry out these kinds of studies, due to their availability, rich set of embedded sensors and their capacity to be unobtrusive for the subjects [5–8].

Motor activity-related behaviour (i.e. body hyperactivity, trembling, uncontrollable movement, hand movement) has shown association with perceived stress [9]. In the context of our study, the following research questions are put forth:

- Is there a relationship between motor activity features that can be automatically extracted from a accelerometer sensor embedded on smart phones and the self-reported stress levels?
- Is it possible to improve stress detection by incorporating intermediate, *hidden*, variables related to the subjects' mood, before building the final model for predicting stress?

The present work tries to answer both these research questions by comparing standard stress measurement questionnaires and motor activity behaviour during phone conversations.

We performed an experimental analysis using real world data. While, we have previously reported on the use of accelerometer data to estimate stress levels [5], this study differs from that work in two important aspects:

- The use semi-supervised learning to complete the models for subjects with missing data.
- The induction of *intermediate models* to predict mood variables, which are incorporated in the final model in order to improve the accuracy of the predictions.

Our results show that using standard supervised models we achieved an accuracy of $\approx 65\%$. This measure is increased to $\approx 69\%$ when using the semi-supervised methods and to $\approx 71\%$ when using *intermediate models*. Finally, combining semi-supervised learning and intermediate models we achieve an accuracy of $\approx 78.2\%$; a notable improvement over the initial score.

The rest of this paper is organized as follows. Section 2 reviews related work on stress detection based on current technology. The study methodology, data acquisition, and feature extraction are presented in Sect. 3. The proposed approach of intermediate models is presented in Sect. 4 and experiments are presented in Sect. 5. Finally, the conclusions of the study are presented in Sect. 6.

2   Related Work

Several methods have tried to infer stress based on physiological signals, such as heart-rate variability, blood pressure, body temperatures and respiration [10, 11]. However, the use of physiological sensors has some limitations:

- sensors may have a large size to cover many signal types [10],
- sensors (e.g., skin conductance sensor) limit the movement of the subjects [11]
- sensors increase the discomfort [12] since they need to be carried all the time.

The miniaturization of wearable sensors has made it possible to include them in smartphones. Recently, there is interest in inferring stress using those sensors, since they are a personal and common accessory among people. A summary of the works aiming at stress detection are described in Table 1. The work in [13] proposed a method for detecting stress based on speech analysis and the variation of speech articulation using smartphones. The authors have reported a predictive accuracy of stress of 81 % and 76 % for indoor and outdoor environments, respectively, using the vocal production of 14 subjects. However, in real-life activities this approach may lead to misinterpretation of speech and therefore of emotion.

In order to infer relationship dynamics of people and behaviour changes in daily activities, smartphones have been suggested as a promising candidate to obtain user's context. Research work using smartphones for long-term stress monitoring has collected many types of contextual data (e.g., physical activities, social activities and locations) that could help in inferring stress from behaviour changes. In this line, "MoodScope"[14] is a self tracking system to help users manage their mood. The system detects user's mood from smartphones usage data, such as email messages, calls and SMS logs, application usage, web browsing histories and location changes. The authors reported an initial 66 % accuracy of subjects' daily mood, improving to 93 % after two months of training.

In another relevant work, Bauer and Lukowicz [15] aimed at recognizing stress from 7 students before and after an exam period. The assumption is that students are likely to be under stress during the exam sessions. They acquired data from smartphones (location, social proximity through Bluetooth, phone calls and SMS logs) reporting an average accuracy of 53 % during the exam session. In [16] the authors monitored 18 subjects for a period of 5 days. In addition to smartphone features they included a wrist sensor. In order to recognize stress levels, the authors applied correlation analysis and reached a 75 % accuracy using machine learning techniques to classify stress moments.

Similarly, Muaremi et al. [17] measured smartphone mobility data (phonecalls, SMS, location and physical activity) and wearable Heart Rate Variability (HRV) sensor data to classify perceived stress. The authors emphasize the importance of recording human voice as a potential source for non-intrusive stress detection. The authors at [16] propose to infer work-relevant stress events using an external hardware (i.e., HRV) and sensor measurements obtained from smartphones. Furthermore, in [18] the authors used context information from the environment, such as weather condition, social proximity obtained by Bluetooth scanning, call logs, SMS logs, and self-reported surveys about personality traits to predict stress events.

As presented in Table 1, recent studies have explored the potential of physiological signals for measuring stress related signs from sensor data (e.g., Gal-

Table 1. Main related works in Stress Detection showing the features and details.

Study	Items measured	Controlled/ Uncontrolled Setting	Obtrusiveness Level
Kim et al.[19]	Heart Rate Variability (HRV)	controlled	High
Lu et al.[13]	Smartphone (Speech analysis)	Both	High
Bauer et al.[15]	Smartphone (Location, bluetooth, phone-call and SMS)	Uncontrolled	Medium
textbf Likamwa et al.[14]	Smartphone (E-mails, Call and SMS logs, application usage, web browsing histories and location changes)	Unknown	High
Sano et al.[16]	Wrist sensors and Smartphone (Phone usage duration, phone calls and SMS logs)	Uncontrolled	Medium
Muaremi et al.[17]	HRV and Smartphone (Phone- and SMS logs, Location, Audio Stress Response)	Uncontrolled	High
Bogomolov et al.[18]	Smartphone (Call logs, SMS, bluetooth and weather)	Uncontrolled	Medium

vanic Skin Response (GSR), Electro-Cardiogram (ECG)) and smartphone sensors (e.g., location, audio recording). However, there are several concerns about using physiological sensors, basically due to their obtrusiveness. In contrast, we explore the potential of using a single sensor with the aim of detecting perceived stress levels. We choose to use accelerometer sensor due to their advantages (non-visual and non-auditory) and thus mitigate privacy concerns [20,21].

2.1 Motor Activity Monitoring

Currently, the clinicians assess motor activity in laboratory settings. Studies measuring level of motor activity in psychological stress have typically used traditional monitoring with paper and pencil diaries, and questionnaires [22].

Monitoring motor activity during sleep may be measured by actigraphs [23] (using piezoelectric accelerometer). However, little is known if data captured from an actigraph could provide motor activity characteristics in perceived stress level in working environments.

Smartphones are a good candidate for monitoring motor activity behaviour patterns in daily activities. Information from smart phones enables easier monitoring and tracking of people than traditional methods, as most people already carry a smartphone so no additional sensors are required. Another benefit of using this technology is that other information (such as phone calls, location, use of social networks) can be obtained and included. In this paper, we collect data from accelerometers during phone calls to infer motor activity changes in working employees.

144 A. Maxhuni et al.

3 Data Preparation

This section presents how the data was collected and the feature extraction process.

3.1 Data Collection

In this research work, we focus on analysing accelerometer raw data during phone conversation, where we are sure that the subjects are holding their smartphones. This type of measurement has the advantage of their availability and unobtrusiveness. We believe that analysing data collected from accelerometer readings during the phone conversations provide adequate information for classifying the perceived stress that can be also used to show the trajectory of perceived stress (e.g., low-to-high, high-to-low) in working environments.

The second type of data includes subjective information related to subjects' perceived stress, job-demands and mood states. We developed a questionnaire in a smart phone application to assess psychological variables related to work stress. The questionnaire is clinically validated to capture users perceived stress and mood states of the employees at work. Three times a day the questionnaires appeared automatically (9am -at the beginning of the work, 2pm -around noon, and 5pm -before leaving workplace). The questionnaire was derived from the POMS (Profile of Mood State) scale [24] which has two dimensions related to affect of mood states, including, "Positive Affect" (PA) (e.g., Cheerful, Energetic, Friendly) and "Negative Affect" (NA) (e.g., Tensed, Anxious, Sad, Angry) and the rest measures disengagement from work, where questions were presented in mixed order. Each question has five response alternatives, ranging from 1 (absolutely agree) to 5 (absolutely disagree). The answers were stored on the mobile device and constituted part of the analysis. For the purpose of our analyses, the score distribution has been segmented into three regions, which in our case correspond to three ordinal classes: ("low" or "poor"), when score < 3; ("moderate" or "fair"), when score $= 3$; and ("high" or "sufficient"), when score > 3.

For this study, we analysed the information from 29 subjects[1] in their work environments, with data collected during their phone conversation and self-reported stress. In total, we obtained 7189 phone calls, however, we have only 5767 labeled instances or 80.22 % useful data of the total phonecalls.

Table 2 shows the number of times that are associated with each stress level ("high", "moderate", and "low"). Results show that half of the time the user perceived some level of stress and that during stress-less days the subjects have a higher amount of phone calls.

---

[1] One of the subjects had very few phone calls recorded during the trial and was removed from the study.

Table 2. Number of Phone-Calls by perceived Stress Level (SL).

	Nr.Phone Calls	High SL	Moderate SL	Low SL
Incoming:	1696 (100%)	355 (20.9%)	511 (30.1%)	**830 (48.9%)**
Outgoing:	2912 (100%)	547 (18.7%)	839 (28.8%)	**1526 (52.4%)**
Missing:	1159 (100%)	220 (18.9%)	405 (34.9%)	**534 (46.1%)**
Total instances:	5767	1122	1755	**2890**
%	100%	19.46%	30.43%	**50.11%**

3.2 Feature Extraction

From the raw accelerometer data a total of 30 features (10×3 - for all Minimum, Maximum and Mean) from the frequency domain were extracted (as shown in Table 3). Feature extraction was performed on non-overlapping fixed length windows of 128 samples (25.6 seconds each). We used Fast Fourier Transform (FFT) and discrete Fourier Transform (DFT) to investigate the strength of motor activity signals during phone conversations[2]. Since we aim at understanding motor activity behaviour around the phone conversation, we keep the following accelerometer segments:

- One minute before the phone conversation,
- The reading from the entire duration of the phone call.
- One minute after the conversation ended.

Table 3. Frequency domain features used in the study, where the lower row means that we extracted the minimum, maximum and mean values for all the frequency domain features.

Frequency Domain	
FFT Sum Energy	FFT Mean Energy
FFT Std.Dev. Energy	Peak Power
Peak with DFT Bin	Peak Magnitude
Entropy	DFT Energy
Frequency Domain Entropy	Frequency Domain with DFT
For all: **Min, Max, Mean**	

Figure 1 depicts the data collection, feature extraction (intensity of phone handling during phone conversation by computing features from frequency domain) and prediction process presented in this work.

---

[2] Phone conversations with less than 10 seconds were discarded in our dataset.

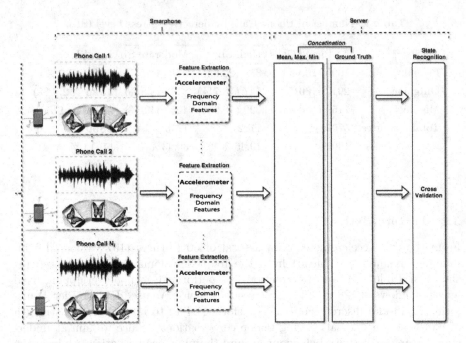

Fig. 1. Proposed approach: data collection, feature extraction and prediction for classifying stress at work of employees.

4   Stress Modelling Using Intermediate Models

In this section we describe the proposed approach that combines intermediate models and semi-supervised learning for estimating stress levels based on smart phones.

4.1   Intermediate Models

The information provided by the users through the questionnaires is useful, however, it is a tedious task for each user. In this research we propose to predict the mood variables associated to the questionnaires using the data from the smartphone to alleviate the user from this burden. Then, we use the predicted mood variables with the rest of the data from the smartphones to predict the stress levels. We call the models that predict the mood variables from the questionnaire *intermediate models* as their are used as input for the final predictive model. Although the use of additional variables, such as latent variables, have been previously used in the literature, we are not aware of research that aims at building an intermediate model that can then be used as input for the final model. Figure 2 illustrates the procedure for building the intermediate models. We train a classifier to predict the information from the questionnaires using the features extracted from the smartphone (feature extraction and Q_1' in the figure, to create a model – intermediate model – that can predict the variables

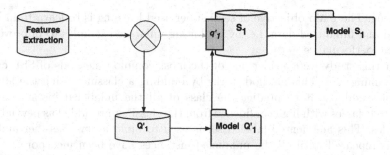

Fig. 2. Intermediate Models. Based on the accelerometer data from the smart phones, 30 frequency domain features are extracted. These are used to build the intermediate models for the mood variables, Q_1; and the model for stress, S_1. In the prediction stage both models are combine via a weighted linear combination to predict the stress level.

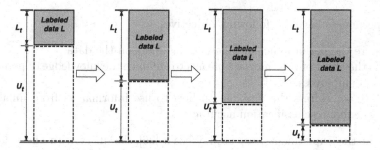

Fig. 3. Semi-Supervised Learning Method (SSL), where L represents labeled instance, U unlabeled instances, and t number of iterations, $L = L_t \cup U_t$

of the questionnaire). We then use the information from the smarphones and the predicted values from the intermediate model (q'_1 in the figure) to create model that can predict the level of stress.

In this study, we used six variables derived from NA and PA (3 per each mood affect) to build 6 intermediate models. We train each classifier separately using each the self-reported questionnaires derived from the 'Positive Mood Affect (PA)' and the 'Negative Mood Affect (NA)'.

In the prediction stage, the intermediate models use the information from the smartphones to predict a weighted set of mood variables based on the accuracy of each model. Then all the data from the smartphones and the mood variables are used as input for the final stress model.

4.2 Semi-supervised Learning

In real applications missing labeled instances are a common issue and the standard supervised approaches ignore the unlabeled instances. But this information, even when it is not complete, can be helpful and should not be discarded. Semi-supervised learning (SSL) [25] has been suggested as a method aiming to address

148   A. Maxhuni et al.

this issue. The main objective of semi-supervised learning is to learn from both labeled and unlabeled data, i.e. by exploiting unlabeled samples to improve the learning performance.

For this study we consider one of the most common methods of SSL called Self-Training [25]. This method works by building a classifier using the labeled examples and use it to predict the class of all the unlabeled instances. The predicted classes with high confidence from the classifier are added as new labeled examples. This augmented labeled set is used to build a new classifier and the cycle is repeated until all the unlabeled instances have been incorporated into the training set or until there is no more examples in the unlabeled set with high confidence (see Fig. 3).

5   Experiments

Our experiments have the following objectives:

- Compare the performance of different classifiers on the data.
- Assess the effect of *intermediate models* to enhance the knowledge of perceived stress in employees.
- Use SSL to address the problem on how to use information from unlabeled data to enhance classification accuracy.

For all the experiments, we used Weka's [26] classifiers with their default parameters. We build a model for each subject and performed a 10-fold cross validation for all the experiments; we report the global accuracy, precision, recall and f-score values. Table 4 show the results using different classifiers. In the first experiment we compare the performance of the classifiers using a supervised and a semi-supervised learning (SSL) algorithms. In the second experiment we analyse the impact of using the intermediate models, with and without SSL.

In our data set, more than 27.6 % of the phone conversation did not have an associated stress level (the user did not answer the questionnaire). To address this issue, we used the Self-Training Method described above. We followed a simple approach where we divided the data into ten folds, where the training data was used to classify the unlabeled data (as shown in Fig. 3), as threshold for the confidence we used $\geq$ 80 % for the highest classified value. Then we used all the classified data with the original training set to produce an extended training set. As can be seen from the results adding information from generated from SSL and intermediate models improves the results in terms of accuracy, precision, recall and F-measure for all the classifiers, in some cases as for C4.5 the improvement is nearly 10 %.

By incorporating the intermediate models, a further improvement is obtained in both cases, with and without SSL. As it can be observed in Table 4, the best results are obtained by combining SSL and the intermediate models, and in particular with the random forest classifier.

Table 4. Comparison in terms of accuracy, precision, recall and F-measure of supervised learning (Sup), semi-supervised learning (SSL) and using intermediate models (IM) with different classifiers for predicting perceived stress.

Algorithm		Sup (%)	SSL (%)	Sup+IM (%)	SSL+IM (%)
C4.5	**Accuracy:**	59.24	68.66	67.51	**77.24**
	(±SD)	(±15.40)	(±15.53)	(±15.21)	(±16.80)
	Precision:	58.43	68.12	66.20	**74.43**
	Recall:	59.23	69.07	67.51	**74.66**
	F-Measure:	58.68	68.72	66.47	**73.81**
Random	**Accuracy:**	65.50	69.21	71.68	**78.20**
Forest	(±SD)	(±12.72)	(±12.91)	(±12.98)	(±12.00)
	Precision:	61.49	65.76	68.15	**73.09**
	Recall:	65.50	69.21	71.49	**75.45**
	F-Measure:	61.71	65.56	68.58	**72.74**
AdaBoost.M1	**Accuracy:**	61.88	63.51	66.51	**75.18**
	(±SD)	(±17.21)	(±15.57)	(±16.40)	(±16.76)
	Precision:	54.19	54.91	59.82	**65.14**
	Recall:	61.88	63.51	**64.29**	56.33
	F-Measure:	56.24	56.91	**59.95**	57.36
SVM	**Accuracy:**	60.59	61.70	68.70	**77.11**
	(±SD)	(±16.81)	(±16.53)	(±15.84)	(±15.84)
	Precision:	48.29	52.96	63.42	**69.03**
	Recall:	60.59	61.71	66.60	**72.67**
	F-Measure:	51.91	54.09	63.62	**68.89**
Bagging	**Accuracy:**	64.67	69.48	68.70	**77.11**
	(±SD)	(±15.15)	(±13.62)	(±15.80)	(±15.84)
	Precision:	58.46	64.85	63.24	**68.80**
	Recall:	64.67	**69.47**	66.42	68.13
	F-Measure:	60.26	65.56	63.36	**67.67**

6   Conclusions

In this paper we presented a study of how to classify the perceived stress of employees from accelerometer data extracted from smart phones during phone conversations. We used real data from employees during 8 working weeks on unconstrained conditions. We extracted several features to analyse the motor activity-related behaviour from different users. To deal with unlabeled data we propose the use of semi-supervised learning techniques. Additionally, we developed a novel approach to incorporate unobserved variables, *intermediate models*.

We experimentally evaluated the impact of using SSL, intermediate models and both of them, using different base classifiers. The proposed approach for creating intermediate models has been shown to increase the prediction of the stress level of the users using the data derived from motor activity; from 61.5 % using the standard supervised methods to $\geq$78 % after applying intermediate models and SSL.

A future work we would like to analyse in more depth the models obtained from each person in order to obtain clusters of people who behave similarly; this could help to build prediction models for new users with few data.

References

1. Näätänen, P., Kiuru, V.: Bergen burnout indicator 15, Edita (2003)
2. European foundation for the improvement of living and working conditions, Fourth European Working conditions Survey. http://www.eurofound.europa.eu/ewco/surveys/EWCS2005/index.htm
3. Stress in america, American Psychological Association. http://apa.org/news/press/releases/stress/index.aspx?tab=2
4. Milczarek, M., Rial-González, E., Schneider, E.: OSH [Occupational safety, health] in figures: stress at work-facts and figures, Office for Official Publications of the European Communities (2009)
5. Ceja, E., Osmani, V., Mayora, O.: Automatic stress detection in working environments from smartphones' accelerometer data: A first step. Biomed. Health Inf. IEEE J. 1, 99 (2015)
6. Ferdous, R., Osmani, V., Marquez, J.B., Mayora, O.: Investigating correlation between verbal interactions, perceived stress. In: 37th Annual International Conference of the IEEE Engineering in Medicine and Biology Society (EMBC), IEEE, Milano (2015)
7. Hernandez-Leal, P., Maxhuni, A., Sucar, L.E., Osmani, V., Morales, E.F., Mayora, O.: Stress modelling using transfer learning in presence of scarce data. In: Ambient Intelligence for Health, Springer International Publishing, Puerto Varas, Chile, pp. 224–236 (2015)
8. Osmani, V., Ferdous, R., Mayora, O.: Smartphone app. usage as a predictor of perceived stress levels at workplace. In: 9th International Conference on Pervasive Computing Technologies for Healthcare, IEEE (2015)
9. Morgan III., C.A., Hazlett, G., Wang, S., Richardson Jr., E.G., Schnurr, P., Southwick, S.M.: Symptoms of dissociation in humans experiencing acute, uncontrollable stress: a prospective investigation. Am. J. Psychiatry
10. Bakker, J., Pechenizkiy, M., Sidorova, N.: What's your current stress level? detection of stress patterns from gsr sensor data. In: IEEE 11th International Conference on Data Mining Workshops (ICDMW), pp. 573–580 (2011)
11. Roh, T., Bong, K., Hong, S., Cho, H., Yoo, H.-J.: Wearable mental-health monitoring platform with independent component analysis, nonlinear chaotic analysis. In: Annual International Conference of the IEEE Engineering in Medicine and Biology Society (EMBC), IEEE, pp. 4541–4544 (2012)
12. Wijsman, J., Grundlehner, B., Liu, H., Hermens, H., Penders, J.: Towards mental stress detection using wearable physiological sensors. In: Engineering in Medicine and Biology Society, EMBC, Annual International Conference of the IEEE, pp. 1798–1801. IEEE (2011)

13. Lu, H., Frauendorfer, D., Rabbi, M., Mast, M.S., Chittaranjan, G.T., Campbell, A.T., Gatica-Perez, D., Choudhury, T.: Stresssense: Detecting stress in unconstrained acoustic environments using smartphones. In: Proceedings of the ACM Conference on Ubiquitous Computing, pp. 351–360 (2012)
14. LiKamWa, R., Liu, Y., Lane, N.D., Zhong, L.: Moodscope: building a mood sensor from smartphone usage patterns. In: Proceeding of the 11th Annual International Conference on Mobile Systems, Applications, and Services, pp. 389–402. ACM (2013)
15. Bauer, G., Lukowicz, P.: Can smartphones detect stress-related changes in the behaviour of individuals? In: IEEE International Conference on Pervasive Computing and Communications Workshops (PERCOM Workshops), pp. 423–426 (2012)
16. Sano, A., Picard, R.W.: Stress recognition using wearable sensors, mobile phones. In: Humaine Association Conference on Affective Computing and Intelligent Interaction (ACII), pp. 671–676 (2013)
17. Muaremi, A., Arnrich, B., Tröster, G.: Towards measuring stress with smartphones and wearable devices during workday and sleep. BioNanoSci. **3**(2), 172–183 (2013)
18. Bogomolov, A., Lepri, B., Ferron, M., Pianesi, F., Pentland, A.S.: Daily stress recognition from mobile phone data, weather conditions, individual traits. In: Proceedings of the ACM International Conference on Multimedia, pp. 477–486. ACM (2014)
19. Kim, D., Seo, Y., Cho, J., Cho, C.-H.: Detection of subjects with higher self-reporting stress scores using heart rate variability patterns during the day. In: 30th Annual International Conference of the IEEE Engineering in Medicine and Biology Society, EMBS, pp. 682–685. IEEE (2008)
20. Matic, A., Osmani, V., Mayora-Ibarra, O.: Analysis of social interactions through mobile phones. Mobile Networks Appl. **17**(6), 808–819 (2012)
21. Matic, A., Osmani, V., Mayora, O.: Speech activity detection using accelerometer. In: Annual International Conference of the IEEE Engineering in Medicine and Biology Society (EMBC), pp. 2112–2115 (2012)
22. Prasad, M., Wahlqvist, P., Shikiar, R., Shih, Y.-C.T.: A review of self-report instruments measuring health-related work productivity. Pharmacoeconomics **22**(4), 225–244 (2004)
23. Mezick, E.J., Matthews, K.A., Hall, M., Kamarck, T.W., Buysse, D.J., Owens, J.F., Reis, S.E.: Intra-individual variability in sleep duration and fragmentation: associations with stress. Psychoneuroendocrinology **34**(9), 1346–1354 (2009)
24. McNair, D.M., Lorr, M., Droppleman, L.F.: Profile of mood states, Univ (1971)
25. Zhu, X.: Semi-supervised learning literature survey
26. Hall, M., Frank, E., Holmes, G., Pfahringer, B., Reutemann, P., Witten, I.H.: The weka data mining software: an update. ACM SIGKDD Explor. Newsl. **11**(1), 10–18 (2009)

Sensor Abstracted Extremity Representation for Automatic Fugl-Meyer Assessment

Patrick Heyer[1]([✉]), Felipe Orihuela-Espina[1], Luis R. Castrejón[2],
Jorge Hernández-Franco[3], and Luis Enrique Sucar[1]

[1] Instituto Nacional de Astrofísica, Óptica y Electrónica (INAOE), Puebla, Mexico
patrickhey@prodigy.net.mx
[2] Hospital Universitario de la Benemérita Universidad Autónoma de Puebla
(HU-BUAP), Puebla, Mexico
[3] Instituto Nacional de Neurología y Neurocirugía (INNN), Mexico City, Mexico

Abstract. Given its virtually algorithmic process, the Fugl-Meyer
Assessment (FMA) of motor recovery is prone to automatization reducing subjectivity, alleviating therapists' burden and collaterally reducing costs. Several attempts have been recently reported to achieve such
automatization of the FMA. However, a cost-effective solution matching expert criteria is still unfulfilled, perhaps because these attempts
are sensor-specific representation of the limb or have thus far rely on
a trial and error strategy for building the underpinning computational
model. Here, we propose a sensor abstracted representation. In particular, we improve previously reported results in the automatization of
FMA by classifying a manifold embedded representation capitalizing on
quaternions, and explore a wider range of classifiers. By enhancing the
modeling, overall classification accuracy is boosted to 87% (mean: 82%
± 4.53:) well over the maximum reported in literature thus far 51.03%
(mean: 48.72 ± std: 2.10). The improved model brings automatic FMA
closer to practical usage with implications for rehabilitation programs
both in ward and at home.

Keywords: Automatic motor dexterity assessment · Gesture classification · Gesture representation · Sensor independent representation ·
Automatic Fugl-Meyer

1 Introduction

The economic burden of motor rehabilitation programs for patients with motor
disability due to stroke or traumatic brain injury among others to public health
systems as well as families is untenable [8]. Obvious measures to contain those
costs include reducing the continuous demand of expert supervision during the
rehabilitation therapy sessions. Robotic rehabilitation [12], virtual rehabilitation [1] and telerehabilitation [2] are among a new generation of rehabilitation
therapeutic modalities which, with current status, already can match classical

© ICST Institute for Computer Sciences, Social Informatics and Telecommunications Engineering 2017
E. Sucar et al. (Eds.): AFI 2016, LNICST 179, pp. 152–163, 2017.
DOI: 10.1007/978-3-319-49622-1_17

occupational therapy (moderate [3]) success on motor recovery, but which alleviate the need for continuous supervision. Moreover, the later two can easily be delivered at patient's home further reducing costs without compromising the recovery with still margin for improvement.

Whether in ward or at home, these innovative therapeutic alternatives still rely on an expert for something as routinary as the assessment of motor recovery using a clinically validated scale such as the Fugl-Meyer Assessment (FMA) [4]. Since the FMA is applied routinely to monitor patient progress and its application is almost algorithmic, it is no surprise that several attempts have been made to automatize the assessment procedure [6]. The automatization of the FMA can free therapist time, reduce any remainings of subjective appreciation [5], and also afford the aforementioned therapeutic alternatives even greater independence and wider home applicability. Ultimately, automatic assessment of the patient motor recovery may proved to be the enabling element for home based rehabilitation.

Despite the obvious interest to have an automatized version of the FMA, having a definitive solution sufficiently reliable that can help the clinicians remains unsolved. Even though we have suggested above that the assessment procedure proceeds almost algorithmically, matching the human expert criterion with a cost-effective solution is challenging. Differences in sensing strategies i.e. selection of the appropriate sensors, and their positioning in the assessment stage whether on-body or off-body, differences in signal processing and analysis strategies, and small variations in clinical application of the assessment among experts are likely candidates to explain this current mild success of the computational models developed for the task.

If the above hypothesized candidacies are preventing higher success of the computational models, then it is likely that the combination of (a) developing a body mechanics representation weakly dependent on the sensing strategy and (b) optimizing the subsequent modeling decisions shall boost the accuracy and success rates of the automatic assessment model. Focusing only on the upper limb, our contribution here is a new abstract representation of the arm mechanics that reduces the commonly tight dependency of the representation on the acquiring sensor. This is achieved by projecting different sensing configurations to a common space capitalizing on quaternions. Then, the classification stage is flexibilized by testing a wide number of combinations between processing and decision making stages. Preliminary results of this research (only 6 patients and only 2 classification models) have been published in [22].

2   Related Work

Given the obvious benefits of having an automated version of the motor assessment procedures, it is unsurprising that a number of solutions have been proposed in the literature across different clinical scales e.g. the Arm Motor Ability Test (AMAT) [9], the Wolf Motor Function Test (WMFT) [10,19], the Chedoke-McMaster Hand Stage [11], and of course the Fugl-Meyer score [6,7]. These solutions either use expensive sensing geometries or their classification rate is still far from satisfying. Moreover, although those methods with expensive sensing setup have managed to obtain good results in controlled settings but they tend to have an obtrusive factor in the sensor arrangement that makes them unfit for the very purpose they were developed!. Additionally, these methods also use the data from the sensors directly as features for their evaluation which makes the solution sensor specific. Finally, several solutions for assessment of motor dexterity following impairment have been further suggested with unobtrusive low-cost sensing geometries e.g. [18,20], but since they do not rely on clinical standard scales they are naturally of limited interest. In summary, a cost-efficient solution capable of matching expert evaluation on clinically validated schemes is still elusive.

3   Methods

3.1   Experiment Setup

Following consent, 9 patients with motor impairment from different origin underwent FMA agreed to participate from two hospitals in Mexico; Hospital Universitario de la Benemérita Universidad Autónoma de Puebla (HU-BUAP) and Hospital General Sur de Puebla (HGSP). The patients present different types of neurological damage including: stroke, and traumatic brain injury, but all require FMA as part of their rehabilitation process. Blinded pictures of the hospital sessions at both hospitals are shown in Fig. 1. The participants where monitored during the assessment performed by a trained clinician whilst their upper limb kinematics were concurrently being monitored using two sensing geometries (Fig. 1); (a) two Inertial Measuring Units (IMU) -one within an *ad-hoc* controller of a virtual rehabilitation platform developed previously by our group [13] and (b) one Microsoft Kinect[TM]. Additionally, the experimental session was video recorded for visual inspection purposes. Table 1 summarises the 10 items of the Fugl-Meyer score for the upper limb.

To compensate for this small sample size[1] additional data was further collected from 15 healthy volunteers recruited among the faculty and students of the Instituto Nacional de Astrofísica, Óptica y Electrónica (INAOE) in Mexico executing the Fugl-Meyer exercises using the same setup and protocol as used in the clinical data capture. The healthy volunteers carried out five repetitions of the exercises defined in the upper extremity subsection of the FMA, simulating all three levels of motor dexterity (at their own interpretation after a brief description by the experimenter). Data was segmented in a bespoken software develop by our group was used to separate the samples corresponding to each of the five repetitions, giving us a total of 750 synthetic samples (10 FMA exercises × 5 repetitions × 15 subjects) for each of the 3 levels of FMA in addition to the 60 samples obtained from patients.

---

[1] We are currently in the process of collecting further clinical data.

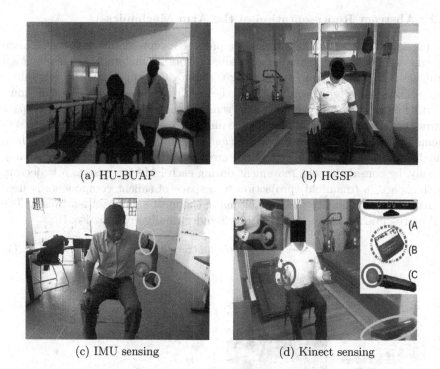

(a) HU-BUAP   (b) HGSP

(c) IMU sensing   (d) Kinect sensing

Fig. 1. Experimental setup and sensing geometry. (a-b) Sessions of motor assessment of patients at the two participating hospitals. (c) The placement of IMU's *yellow*, and color tracking reference *Blue*. (d) Location of the arm joints and relationship as established by the Kinect sensor. (Color figure online)

Table 1. The 10 items Fugl-Meyer subscale for the upper limb. Upon execution, each different exercise is scored 0 (no movement), 1 (clearly impaired movement) or 2 (normal or close to normal movement).

Exercise	Description
1	Move hand from knee to same side ear
2	Move hand from knee to opposite side knee
3	Move hand from knee to lumbar spine
4	Raise hand from knee to 90° (pointing at horizon)
5	With elbow touching body rotate hand
6	Raise hand from knee to 90° sideways
7	Raise hand from pointing at horizon to straight up
8	With elbow touching body flex and extend hand
9	With elbow touching body rotate hand clockwise
10	Move hand from knee to nose five times as fast as possible

3.2   Abstract Representation of the Arm Mechanics

To partially address our hypothesis, we propose a representation R that is non-specific across a family of motion amenable sensors[2] to maintain the classification problem independent from the sensing technologies available at the rehabilitation centers. This representation R is the result of a composition of functions. First, transforming each sample of the sensors' output S to an orientation space represented by quaternions f where the dimensions are dictated by the limb segments upper arm (*brachium*), forearm (*antebrachium*) and hand (*manus*). Then, the dimensional differences in variance are nullified using some normalization g. Finally, by considering the movement during each FMA exercise as a trajectory in the space, a (manifold) projection to a space of salient components is used to reduce dimensionality while maintaining the most significant features h. The full representation is illustrated in Fig. 2 and formally given by Eq. 1:

$$R = h \circ g \circ f(S) \tag{1}$$

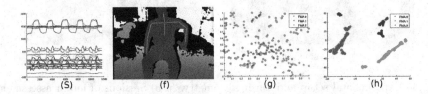

Fig. 2. Plot of the data during the different stages of composition. (S) Sensor data acquired by either, (f) Limb segment orientation (illustrative), (g) Normalized data from different FMA scores, (h) Projection of salient components using t-SNE.

The next subsections detail the last two transformations.

Normalization. To nullify dimensional variance one of three different normalization schemes where used, namely: classical *normalization* to a unitary range, *regularization*, and *quaternion* normalization. The first two consist in scaling the data to avoid overfitting when training machine learning algorithms. The third is avoids floating-point precession errors that will cause a quaternion not to have a unit length The particular choice of each of these possible transformations lead to different representations, all sharing their detachment of the sensing geometry.

Feature Extraction; Projection to Salient Component Space. A large number of manifold embedding approaches (and its corollary dimensionality

---

[2] Full abstraction from the sensing geometry is beyond the scope of this work. For instance, we do not aim at being capable of achieving our goal of automatic motor assessment from say thermal sensors.

reduction application) exist, ranging from the classical Principal Component Analysis (PCA) to the sophisticated Isomap. For a review of the topic, the reader is directed to [21]. They all involve two steps; whether implicit or explicit; (1) imposing a distance function defining the topology of the space, and (2) projecting to a "different" space, often with less dimensionality, either by choosing a different view, i.e. a different coordinate set, and/or removing those dimension of less interest[3]. Previously we have also explore the rotational effect of PCA [22]. Here, considering the dynamics of the exercises that we aim to decode we opted for a projection with t-distributed stochastic neighbor embedding (t-SNE) [14]. t-SNE is a nonlinear probabilistic embedding which favours a similarity definition that abstracts the dynamics of the process as opposed to alternatives with a similarity purely based on the manifold shape e.g. Isomap or Locally Linear Embedding, as exemplified by its impressive separation of the handwriting MNIST dataset in the original publication. Specifically, t-SNE models each high-dimensional object into a (normally) two or three dimensional point Fig. 3 by converting the ambient Euclidean distances between datapoints into conditional probabilities representing similarities among objects as per Eq. 2.

$$dist(x_i, x_j) = p_{x_i, x_j} = \frac{exp(-||x_i - x_j||^2/2\sigma_i^2)}{\sum_{k \neq j} exp(-||x_i - x_k||^2/2\sigma_i^2)} \quad (2)$$

where $x \in X$ are the datapoints and σ_i is the variance of the Gaussian that is centered on datapoint x_i.

The projection itself minimizes the sum of Kullback-Leibler divergences over all datapoints using gradient descent.

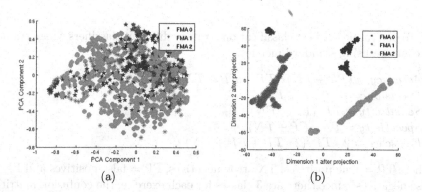

(a)   (b)

Fig. 3. Visual comparison of two different projection techniques showing clear advantage for using t-SNE in this particular domain. In both cases, the example corresponds to data from exercise seven from the FMA, and the colors index the labelled assessment score in that particular exercise. (a) First two salient dimensions using PCA. There is no evident separability among the different classes. (b) First two salient dimensions using t-SNE. The high separability among different classes is self-evident.

---

[3] The definition of what is an interesting view of the dataset correspond to the domain demands.

3.3   Classification

Given the representation achieved with Eq. 1, the assessment itself consists in labeling the observation with a score 0, 1 or 3 according to the Fugl-Meyer scale. This is addressed here as a classical supervised classification problem. The classification model partitions the space into subregions each one assigned a class label. Figure 4 illustrates several partitioning possibilities. The problem is then not so much to build a particular model, but to choose the best classifier in some sense, often in terms of their capacity for generalization.

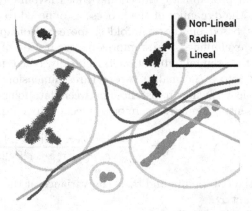

Fig. 4. Different separation possibilities for the same representation. Although the depicted possibilities are all correct, they differ in their capacity to generalize.

To determine the best classification strategy different classifiers where trained to compare using standard metrics:

– $Accuracy = (TP + TN)/(TP + FP + TN + FN)$
– $Precision = TP/(TP + FP)$
– $Sensitivity = TP/(TP + FN)$
– $Specificity = TN/(FP + TN)$
– $F - score = 2 * TP/(2 * TP + FP + FN)$

Where TP = true positives, TN=true negatives, FP = false positives and FN = false negatives. Since there are 3 classes for each exercise, the confusion matrices are summarized to the binary hit or miss labeling. For presenting the results, the different metrics are later averaged across all ten FMA exercises.

Validation was attempted by means of classical cross-folding experimental replication. A total of 2400 (= $2 \times 3 \times 4 \times 10 \times 10$) classification exercises were carried out using;

– 2 sensing geometries (IMU-based or Kinect-based),
– 3 different normalization methods (see section on normalization above),

- 4 different classifiers; Naive Bayes classifier [15], Random Forest (RF) [16], and Support vector machines (SVM) [17] using linear and radial function based kernels,
- 10 FMA exercises (see Table 1), and
- 10 fold repetition for cross-folding based assessment of internal (reproducibility) and external (generalizability) validity.

ANOVA at 5% significance was used to determine statistical significance. Mann-Whitnney-U pairwise comparisons when ANOVA detected significant differences in at least one treatment.

A leave one out classification comparison was made comparing results of classifying healthy participants and patients using a mixed training set and classifying all exercises for one participant at a time.

4   Results

Table 2 summarizes the classification rates across the different metrics. The specific combination of quaternion normalization and SVM with radial basis function kernel sistematically affords the higher means (assumed to be associated to generalizability) and lower standard deviations (std) (assumed to be associated to reproducibility).

Figure 2 shows the average classification rates among the different classifiers using quaternion normalization with three different sensing setups, exhibiting similar results independent of the sensing technique used as hypothesized (Fig. 5).

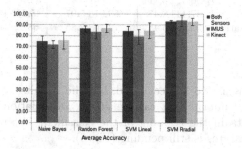

Fig. 5. Average classification for the different sensing setups. Three possible data inflow combinations are shown: Using both IMU's and Kinect data, using only the data from the IMU's, and that only of the Kinect sensor. (mean ± std)

The effect of including data from healthy participants is dissected in Table 3. Understandably higher rates of classification are found for healthy subjects. This is not to be misunderstood as inflated rates. Although it is tempting to quickly argue that only data from patient should be accounted for, that is true only for the evaluation, but not for the training. In other words, only classification of

Table 2. Summary of classification rates achieved by the different approaches. In all cases mean ± std is indicated. Top most results are highlighted in gray.

Accuracy				
	{Naive Bayes}	{Random Forest}	{SVM lineal}	{SVM radial}
Normalization	76.96±9.32	79.43±6.29	63.81±12.54	71.05±5.23
Regularization	71.02±8.56	73.43±5.98	69.26±11.03	80.23±5.62
Quaternion Normalization	74.48±5.23	86.49±2.74	84.18±4.62	93.12±1.09
Precision				
	{Naive Bayes}	{Random Forest}	{SVM lineal}	{SVM radial}
Normalization	69.05±8.34	72.18±7.30	54.20±12.61	62.07±4.96
Regularization	62.12±8.25	64.97±5.71	60.17±11.00	73.15±5.25
Quaternion Normalization	66.01±4.89	81.04±3.29	78.25±4.83	90.19±0.87
Sensitivity				
	{Naive Bayes}	{Random Forest}	{SVM lineal}	{SVM radial}
Normalization	69.13±9.67	72.15±6.31	54.32±12.56	62.15±4.60
Regularization	62.06±9.01	64.85±6.68	60.27±12.05	73.14±5.76
Quaternion Normalization	66.04±5.01	80.96±2.64	78.05±5.33	90.01±1.32
Specificity				
	{Naive Bayes}	{Random Forest}	{SVM lineal}	{SVM radial}
Normalization	81.67±8.43	83.78±6.92	70.24±12.49	76.59±5.12
Regularization	76.50±8.31	78.64±6.74	75.08±11.87	84.44±6.03
Quaternion Normalization	79.55±4.75	89.48±3.15	87.69±4.72	94.75±0.61
F-score				
	{Naive Bayes}	{Random Forest}	{SVM lineal}	{SVM radial}
Normalization	68.96±8.58	71.96±7.25	54.04±12.33	62.08±6.03
Regularization	61.82±8.53	64.80±5.62	60.04±11.76	73.00±5.33
Quaternion Normalization	66.02±5.92	80.78±2.34	78.00±4.67	90.06±0.45
AUC				
	{Naive Bayes}	{Random Forest}	{SVM lineal}	{SVM radial}
Normalization	56.42±8.71	60.46±6.83	38.17±12.74	0.476±7.09
Regularization	47.43±8.47	50.91±5.97	45.20±11.58	61.75±5.84
Quaternion Normalization	52.57±5.45	72.46±2.85	68.42±4.86	85.32±0.31

patient observations has to be accounted, but the training of the model should benefit of whatever information can be given. Dissociation of the benefit of including these data in the training of the classifiers, but not counting them in the classification rates is still pending (Fig. 6).

5   Discussion and Conclusions

The proposed representation affords high classification rates[4] regardless of the classifier and without depending on a specific sensing technology. The representation benefits from the so called quaternion normalization. Its low dependency on the sensing geometry, suggested by the small differences in classification across the tested geometries, suggests that the approach proposed facilitates its use in

---

[4] Previously reported values were well below these figures.

Table 3. Classification rates by type of participant. Dissociation of the effect in the classification rates due to the participant status.

Exercise	Patients	Healthy	Patients and Healthy
1	45.09 ± 7.89	95.75 ± 0.92	93.19 ± 2.66
2	44.84 ± 8.65	95.64 ± 1.92	92.65 ± 0.8
3	42.17 ± 3.41	98.83 ± 2.6	95.74 ± 0.34
4	45.39 ± 9.78	95.25 ± 0.26	93.11 ± 2.66
5	42.47 ± 2.63	96.34 ± 1.79	94.15 ± 1.52
6	39.14 ± 10.46	96.49 ± 2.99	93.19 ± 2.85
7	49.18 ± 8.9	95.61 ± 0.62	92.63 ± 2.43
8	45.93 ± 3.39	94.2 ± 0.96	92.05 ± 2.54
9	33.68 ± 3.48	94.81 ± 1.5	92.17 ± 2.36
10	50.36 ± 5.48	96.17 ± 0	92.43 ± 2.01

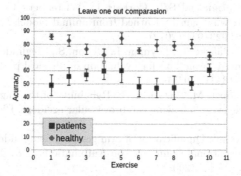

Fig. 6. Average classification for every exercise using leave one out classification results are shown as mean ± std. *The similarity of the classification seems to be directly related to the level in the recovery hierarchy, during rehabilitation some movements are recovered sooner than others in a predefined sequence, further analysis is required.*

different rehabilitation settings including those where non-intrusive assessment is required.

The incorporation of data from healthy participants, unfortunately limits the generalization of these findings. Our previous results suggests these data may be easier to classify than patient data [22], and thus the classification rates may look like higher than they might have look shall only data from patient may have been used. In this sense, we consider that to get a stronger validation of our solution a bigger dataset only from patients data is necessary.

Although the present effort has enhanced the classification by exploring several possible combinations, this is still open to mathematical optimization. We are currently working to achieve optimal modeling by means of full model selection techniques.

Apart from the use of the proposed method for upper extremity assessment our proposal should be suitable for other kinds of movement analysis the possibilities being currently being discussed are directly related to the FMA scale using whole body information. Other areas could be gait analysis and evaluation of Parkinson syndrome tremors.

Acknowledgment. The leading author has received a scholarship No. 339981 from CONACYT.

References

1. Adamovich, S.V., Fluet, G.G., Tunik, E., Merians, A.S.: Sensorimotor training in virtual reality: a review. NeuroRehabilitation **25**, 29 (2009)
2. Reinkensmeyer, D.J., Pang, C.T., Nessler, J.A., Painter, C.C.: Web-based telerehabilitation for the upper extremity after stroke. IEEE Trans. Neural Syst. Rehabil. Eng. **10**, 102–108 (2002)
3. Krakauer, J.W., Carmichael, S.T., Corbett, D., Wittenberg, G.F.: Getting neurorehabilitation right: what can be learned from animal models? Neurorehabilitation Neural Repair **26**, 923–931 (2012)
4. Fugl-Meyer, A.R., Jääskö, L., Leyman, I., Olsson, S., Steglind, S.: The post-stroke hemiplegic patient. 1. a method for evaluation of physical performance. Scand. J. Rehabil. Med. **7**, 13–31 (1975)
5. Duncan, P.W., Propst, M., Nelson, S.G.: Reliability of the Fugl-Meyer assessment of sensorimotor recovery following cerebrovascular accident. Phys. Ther. **63**, 1606–1610 (1983)
6. Quintana, G.E., et al.: Qualification of arm gestures using hidden markov models. In: 8th IEEE International Conference on Automatic Face & Gesture Recognition, FG 2008, pp. 1–6. IEEE (2008)
7. Hou, W.-H., Shih, C.-L., Chou, Y.-T., Sheu, C.-F., Lin, J.-H., Wu, H.-C., Hsueh, I.-P., Hsieh, C.-L.: Development of a computerized adaptive testing system of the Fugl-Meyer motor scale in stroke patients. Arch. Phys. Med. Rehabil. **93**, 1014–1020 (2012)
8. Ma, V.Y., Chan, L., Carruthers, K.J.: The incidence, prevalence, costs and impact on disability of common conditions requiring rehabilitation in the US: stroke, spinal cord injury, traumatic brain injury, multiple sclerosis, osteoarthritis, rheumatoid arthritis, limb loss, and back pain. Arch. Phy. Med. Rehabil. **95**(5), 986–995.e1 (2014)
9. Allin, S., Ramanan, D.: Assessment of post-stroke functioning using machine vision. In: MVA2007 IAPR Conference on Machine Vision Applications, 16-18 May, Tokyo, Japan, pp. 8–18 (2007)
10. Virgilio, F.B., Cruz, V.T., Ribeiro, D.D., Cunha, J.P.: Towards a movement quantification system capable of automatic evaluation of upper limb motor function after neurological injury. In: 2011 Annual International Conference of the IEEE Engineering in Medicine and Biology Society, EMBC, pp. 5456–5460. IEEE (2011)
11. Hester, T., Hughes, R., Sherrill, D.M., Knorr, B., Akay, M., Stein, J., Bonato, P.: Using wearable sensors to measure motor abilities following stroke. In: International Workshop on Wearable and Implantable Body Sensor Networks, BSN 2006, p. 4. IEEE (2006)

12. Balasubramanian, S., Wei, R., Perez, M., Shepard, B., Koeneman, J., Koeneman, E., He, J.: RUPERT: an exoskeleton robot for assisting rehabilitation of arm functions. In: Virtual Rehabilitation, 163–167. IEEE (2008)
13. Sucar, L.E., Orihuela-Espina, F., Velazquez, R.L., Reinkensmeyer, D.J., Leder, R., Hernández Franco, J.: Gesture therapy: an upper limb virtual reality-based motor rehabilitation platform. IEEE Trans. Neural Syst. Rehabil. Eng. **22**(3), 634–643 (2014)
14. der Maaten, V.L., Hinton, G.: Visualizing data using t-SNE. J. Mach. Learn. Res. **9**, 2579–2605 (2008)
15. Murphy, K.P.: Naive Bayes classifiers. University of British Columbia (2006)
16. Svetnik, V., Liaw, A., Tong, C., Culberson, J.C., Sheridan, R.P., Feuston, B.P.: Random forest: a classification and regression tool for compound classification and QSAR modeling. J. Chem. Inf. Comput. Sci. **43**, 1947–1958 (2003)
17. Hearst, M.A., Dumais, S.T., Osman, E., Platt, J., Scholkopf, B.: Support vector machines. IEEE Intell. Syst. Appl. **13**, 18–28 (1998)
18. Olesh, E.V., Yakovenko, S., Gritsenko, V.: Automated assessment of upper extremity movement impairment due to stroke. PLoS ONE **9**(8), e104487 (2014)
19. Wade, E., Parnandi, A.R., Matarić, M.J.: Automated administration of the Wolf Motor Function test for post-stroke assessment. In: 4th International Conference on Pervasive Computing Technologies for Healthcare (PervasiveHealth), Munich, Germany, pp. 1–7 (2010)
20. Hondori, H.M., Ling, S.-F.: A method for measuring human arm's mechanical impedance for assessment of motor rehabilitation. In: 3rd International Convention on Rehabilitation Engineering & Assistive Technology (i-CREATe 2009), Singapore, p. 4 (2009)
21. Carreira-Perpiñán, M.A.: A review of dimension reduction techniques University of Sheffield, University of Sheffield, Technical report, CS-96-09 (1997)
22. Heyer, P., Felipe, O.-E., Castrejón, L.R., Hernández-Franco, J., Sucar, L.E.: Sensor adequacy and arm movement encoding for automatic assessment of motor dexterity for virtual rehabilitation. Accepted at 9th World Congress for NeuroRehabilitation

FINE 2016

A Platform for Creating Augmented Reality Content by End Users

Fernando Vera[✉], J. Alfredo Sánchez, and Ofelia Cervantes

Laboratory of Interactive and Cooperative Technologies,
Universidad de las Américas Puebla, Puebla, Mexico
{fernando.verapo,alfredo.sanchez,ofelia.cervantes}@udlap.mx

Abstract. We present work in progress towards the development of a platform for the creation of augmented reality (AR) content by the end user. Based upon a review of existing AR authoring tools and scenarios we have envisioned in the context of smart cities, we have developed SituAR, an architecture for a platform in which the user is able to create AR content using multimedia elements. Our emphasis is on making augmented reality easier to put together and to empower users to become authors in AR scenarios. We also include social media elements for users to share, rank, and comment the content created in order to add new information and to facilitate interaction. This paper discusses the architecture of SituAR and its potential.

Keywords: Augmented reality · Authoring tools · User-generated content

1 Introduction

This paper presents progress on a novel platform for the creation of in-situ augmented reality (AR) content by the end user. SituAR is a platform devised to create AR annotations via mobile devices in the context of smart cities.

AR technology is an important field of study with huge potential for expanding contexts of use, as it adds information to the physical world and is defining new ways for users to interact with their surroundings. The main objective of augmented reality is to take advantage of available devices to enhance user experience. AR has been used successfully in areas such as games, learning environments, and so-called points of interest (POI's) in smart cities. Still, there is ample room for empowering users so they not only view but also create AR content.

1.1 Augmented Reality Content Creation

Authoring tools for AR have been created both in commercial and research contexts. For example, the Designer's Augmented Reality Toolkit (DART) is a well-known authoring solution that extends the functionality for augmented reality in 3D modelling platforms, such as Google SketchUp and Autodesk's 3D Studio Max. Another software library for building AR applications is ARToolKit, which uses video tracking

© ICST Institute for Computer Sciences, Social Informatics and Telecommunications Engineering 2017
E. Sucar et al. (Eds.): AFI 2016, LNICST 179, pp. 167–171, 2017.
DOI: 10.1007/978-3-319-49622-1_18

capabilities that calculate the camera position and orientation relative to physical markers in real time. Today, both AR applications and their contents are mostly created by system developers; users who interact with these applications are mere viewers of information. For new content, users must wait for updates. Some desktop applications already allow users without programming skills to create augmented reality content. For example, some web applications for creating augmented reality through markers provide toolbars or widgets for attaching photos, URLs, videos and other multimedia content. However, this interaction takes place on the desktop, not at the spot in which the enriched content is relevant.

1.2   Transmedia Storytelling

In order to engage users in the creation of added-value quality content, we propose transmedia storytelling, which is a new way of telling stories across multiple platforms and creating an immersive experience for the viewer. The purpose of transmedia storytelling not only is to reach a wider audience by expanding the target market, but to expand the narrative itself [10]. In transmedia storytelling, engagement with each successive media heightens the audience's understanding, enjoyment and affection for the story [11]. Coordinated storytelling across multiple platforms offers users a new, more compelling perspective of the involved characters [6], with interaction and collaboration of the audience [11].

2   Related Work

Our approach to AR aims to enhance points of interest (POIs) for smart cities. In this context, one of the main issues has been how to use tags to represent information. In [2] floating labels using GPS coordinates are described as one of the most frequently used techniques. Geolocation and markers can be combined: The former uses the mobile device's GPS whereas the latter identifies a space that displays content in real time [8]. The use of these markers is supported by platforms such as Wikitude, Layar, Junaio, Vuforia and ARtoolkit, which are useful to prototype augmented reality [9]. Even though AR-oriented devices, such as Google Glasses and Hololens, have become available, mobile devices such as smartphones and tablets are still more popular tools to experiment with AR applications [4].

Langlotz et al. introduce the concept of Augmented Reality 2.0, which refers to a trend of making users content creators and not only consumers, one of the main characteristics of the Web 2.0 [7, 12]. FitzGerald proposes user generated content (UGC) for location-based learning [3]. Commercial AR applications related to POIs such as Layar, Here City Lens, Yelp Monocle, and Wikitude [1], allow users to view information related to POIs and to upload images or create comments, but users cannot create annotations while visiting POIs. Thus, users are not able to create stories in-situ either.

Annotation is a technique that associates information with places, objects or people. Hansen created a taxonomy for all kinds of system annotations [5]. He described four main challenges for ubiquitous annotation: Anchoring, which describes the linkage between physical entities and information; structure, which describes the object's relationships; presentation, which describes the type of information that is presented and especially how it is presented in relation to the physical entities; and editing, which describes how the annotation is edited or authored. These concepts are important for the design we present next.

3 SituAR Conceptual Design

The conceptual design of SituAR, our platform for in-situ creation of AR content is illustrated in Fig. 1. SituAR has four main interaction modules: Multimedia, social media, 3D tools and maps. The user is able to create multimedia annotations such as text, pictures, videos and audio. All the augmented reality elements created can receive comments, ratings and can be shared. SituAR allows the user to create 3D geometric shapes and perform actions such as moving, rotating, scaling, and copying elements to paste them into the environment. Another feature is freehand drawing, through which people can create multiple shapes. Mapping real-world objects also has been considered. The user can take a panoramic picture and create its 3D model. In addition to available default 3D models, an online community allows designers to upload their models and share them with the SituAR community. Users can see their private annotations on a map as well as the public annotations made by other users. Collaborative tags allow users to search specific information and filter their results by using tags, dates and selecting the type of the multimedia element.

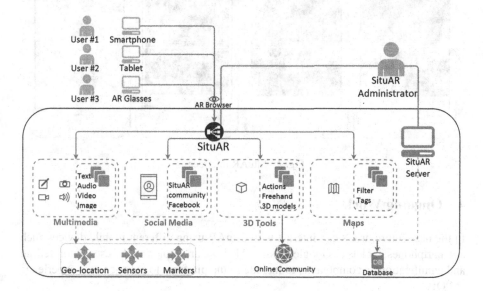

Fig. 1. SituAR conceptual design

SituAR uses a client/server architecture. The data generated by SituAR will allow users to explore the city and interact in a ubiquitous computing environment.

Furthermore, users can tell stories using the 3D models, text, audio, pictures and videos. They can share their experience by locating multimedia elements in the context. This information can be seen in the SituAR community. Also, it can be shared in social media services such as Facebook and Twitter. In order to deploy augmented reality, an AR browser is also included in SituAR. Moreover, the use of AR markers, geo-location and sensors such as RFID are proposed.

Figure 2 presents some interfaces that have been prototyped to illustrate SituAR's main functions. The main interface displays the available options: Creating and visualizing annotations, viewing a map and expanding nearby annotations. The prototype has five multimedia elements: audio, video, image, 3D models and text. New elements can be uploaded and placed in the real world. The 3D model option allows the user to create geometric shapes in a real environment. Another feature is the default 3D models which designers share them through an online community. The goal of this platform is to enrich the content of SituAR. A relevant component of our platform is "AR Maps", which allows users to visualize all the content published by the end user. This feature has filters in order to make specific search. Interfaces are based on the conceptual design and will be evaluated with potential users in order to validate SituAR.

Fig. 2. SituAR interfaces.

4   Ongoing Work

In the near future, users can interact with SituAR using different mobile devices such as smartphones, tablets or Google glasses. Also, we are exploring the use of storytelling and gamification as components to include in the platform to enhance user experience at POIs.

References

1. Agarwal, A., Sharma, N.K., Gupta, P., Saxena, P., Pal, R.K., Mehrotra, S., Wadhwa, M.: Mobile application development with augmented reality. Int. J. Comput. Sci. Eng. **2**, 20–25 (2014)
2. Choi, J., Jang, B., Kim, G.J.: Organizing and presenting geospatial tags in location-based augmented reality. Pers. Ubiquit. Comput. **15**(6), 641–647 (2011)
3. FitzGerald, E.: Creating user-generated content for location-based learning: an authoring framework. J. Comput. Assist. Learn. **28**(3), 195–207 (2012)
4. Gervautz, M., Schmalstieg, D.: Anywhere interfaces using handheld augmented reality. Computer **45**, 26–31 (2012)
5. Hansen., F.A.: Ubiquitous annotation systems. In: Proceedings of Seventh Conference on Hypertext and Hypermedia, HYPERTEXT 2006, p. 121. ACM Press, New York (2006)
6. Jenkins, H.: Transmedia Storytelling and Entertainment: An annotated syllabus in Continuum: Journal of Media & Cultural Studies. Commun. Mass Media Complete, EBSCOhost, Viewed **26**, 943–958 (2014)
7. Langlotz, T., Mooslechner, S., Zollmann, S., Degendorfer, C., Reitmayr, G., Schmalstieg, D.: Sketching up the world: in situ authoring for mobile augmented reality. Pers. Ubiquit. Comput. **16**(6), 623–630 (2012)
8. Madden, L.: Professional augmented reality browsers for smartphones: programming for junaio, layar and wikitude. John Wiley & Sons (2011)
9. Mullen, T.: Prototyping augmented reality. John Wiley & Sons (2011)
10. Phillips, A.: A creator's guide to transmedia storytelling: How to captivate and engage gradaudiences across multiple platforms. McGraw Hill Professional (2012)
11. Pratten, R.: Transmedia Storytelling: Getting Started. Workbook Project (2012)
12. Schmalstieg, D., Langlotz, T., Billinghurst, M.: Augmented Reality 2.0. In: Virtual Realities, pp. 13–37. Springer Vienna (2011)

Strategic Learning Meta-model (SLM): Architecture of the Regulation Model (RM) Based on the Cloud Computing

Rafaela Blanca Silva-López[1], Oscar Herrera-Alcántara[1(✉)], and Jalil Fallad-Chávez[2]

[1] Universidad Autónoma Metropolitana, Av. San Pablo No. 180, Col. Reynosa Tamaulipas,
02200 Delegación Azcapotzalco, Distrito Federal, Mexico
{rbsl,oha}@correo.azc.uam.mx

[2] Universidad de Guadalajara, Centro Universitario de la Costa Sur, Circuito Escolar Ciudad
Universitaria, 04510 Guadalajara, Jalisco, Mexico
jfallad@cucsur.udg.mx

Abstract. In this work we present the architecture of the Regulation Model (RM) as a third layer of the Strategic Learning Meta-model (SLM). The SLM conforms a personalized virtual learning environment that consists of three layers: *The Intelligent Layer* that includes a virtual learning environment, *The Infrastructure Layer* based on the Cloud Computing, and *The Regulation Model*. The RM is based on the Ned Herman's Whole Brain Theory that divides the brain into four quadrants associated to thinking styles. The RM considers six components: (i) The teacher; (ii) The learner or student; (iii) The process facilitator; (iv) The emotional facilitator; (v) The didactic material; and (vi) The learning activities. Our experiments implement the RM and consider five test cases. The experimental results show an improvement in the final scoring of *creative*, *logic* and *process* thinking styles of undergraduate students.

Keywords: Regulation Model · Personalized virtual learning environment · Cloud computing · Strategic learning · Virtual learning environment

1 Introduction

In the context of Virtual Learning Environments (VLE), the integration of a Regulation Model (RM) is relevant once it facilitates the feedback mechanism and the learning monitoring of students. This is based on the hypothesis that the involvement of the dominant thinking style of each student in the RM facilitates the development of personalized activities and allows to define a relationship between the students and the teacher, and opens the possibility to develop cognitive abilities of the students to promote the *strategic learning*.

In this paper we present the architecture of the Regulation Model (RM) as a third layer of the Strategic Learning Meta-model (SLM). The SLM conforms a personalized virtual learning environment that consists of three layers: *the intelligent layer* that includes a virtual learning environment, *the infrastructure layer* based on Cloud

E. Sucar et al. (Eds.): AFI 2016, LNICST 179, pp. 172–184, 2017.
DOI: 10.1007/978-3-319-49622-1_19

Computing, and *the regulation model*. The RM is based on the Ned Herman's Whole Brain Theory, where the brain is divided into four quadrants (thinking styles). The RM considers six components: (i) The teacher; (ii) The learner or student; (iii) The process facilitator; (iv) The emotional facilitator; (v) The didactic material; and (vi) The learning activities. Our experiments implement the RM and consider five test cases with undergraduate students enrolled in language programming courses. The experimental results show an improvement in the final scoring of creative, logic and process thinking styles of undergraduate students.

The paper is organized as follows: In Sect. 2 we present a conceptual framework that support the development of SLM, in Sect. 3 we present our methodology that considers the design of the architecture for the Regulation Model as the top layer of the SLM. In Sect. 5 we present cases of study that describe the implementation of the RM in language programming courses for undergraduate students. In Sect. 6 we present experimental results, and finally, in Sect. 7 we present our conclusions and comment about future work.

2 Conceptual Framework

In recent years, the research on didactic models have become an important factor for the success of online courses. For example, Mödritscher, et al. [1] applied *learning curves* to measure the error rates when the users interact with educational adaptive systems, and their results show that the learning error rates follow a Power Law Distribution. The use of learning curves to evaluate the teaching model is valuable because of the feedback given to teachers and educational content generators for online courses. Authors such as Mödritscher, et al. [1]; Mizoguchi, et al. [2]; Salaheddin Odeh, Qaraeen [3]; Tedman, et al. [4] and Samarakou, et al. [5], have focused their researches on issues associated with the assessment of teaching models [1] and have proposed methods and techniques to evaluate e-Learning environments [3].

2.1 The Conceptualization of the Learning Assessment

Knowles et al., identify learning as: (a) product, the final result of a learning experience; (b) process, composed by all the events that it happens on learning experience in the course; and finally, (c) function, that enhances critical aspects such as motivation, retention and transfer that generates behavioral changes in human learning [6]. Furthermore, the learning is also conceptualized as the participation in activities that allow sharing knowledge. Peñalosa [7] proposed the Theory of Situated Action and the Theory of Situated Cognition focused on the subject participation to achieve learning.

Also, Peñalosa [7] makes a comparison between the three learning conceptualizations that he calls metaphors: (1) acquisition, (2) construction, and (3) participation. Peñalosa, concludes that the acquisition is *objectivist*, where the student has a passive role. On the other hand, the metaphor of the construction is *constructivist*, *psychogenetic* and *cognitive*; where the student plays an active role and in this case Peñalosa interprets the knowledge as the result of an interaction. The metaphor of the *participation* has a social and constructivist orientation where the student is active and is involved in cultural practices also it assumes socialization processes, mediation, and cultural activities.

Peñalosa believes that learning is an *appropriation of the knowledge* that gives place to the interaction between students (subjects) and the didactic material (objects) of interest that is adapted to their needs [7].

2.2 Paradigm Shift in Learning Assessment

Some authors such as Lafourcade, Carreño, De Miguel-Diaz and Diaz-Barriga [8] agree that the evaluation is a stage of the educational process that aims to evaluate student's achievements systematically. Ryan et al. [8] introduces a *student self-regulation*, where he or she becomes aware of his or her learning.

In one hand, according to Hoffmann [9], the whole process should seek the student's observation individually, to analyze and understand his learning and thinking styles. Additionally to get data and to define strategies to foster their learning. This approach makes clear how important is the personalization in order to improve the learning process.

On the other hand, when the evaluation comes from online learning it requires a sensible strategy and a valid performance evaluation.

Peñalosa recommend three phases in the learning evaluation: (a) the initial evaluation, at the beginning of the course to know the knowledge level and the abilities of the students; (b) the formative evaluation, along the docent activity, and for large and continuous periods, and (c) the final evaluation, at the end of the course. The importance of the continuous evaluation of the learning resides in the feedback given to the student [10].

Peñalosa presents a classification of the kind of evaluations for online education: (a) automatic evaluation, evaluation when concluding; (b) elaborative, where the student generate a deliverable product, and (c) collaborative, where the student is evaluated from the collaborative work. Besides, this assessment considers that the interactivity plays a fundamental role for the student feedback to produce a scaffolding effect in the student's performance [10].

2.3 Mediator Evaluation

From the Hoffmann's point of view, the mediator evaluation process seeks to observe students individually in order to analyze and to understand their learning differences. Its objective is to define strategies that may improve students' learning [9].

Therefore, the evaluation is a process that involves three stages: *to observe, to analyze and to offer* better opportunities for the student. When the teacher understands the learning and thinking techniques of their students, he or she modifies his o her pedagogical behavior, so the students may increase intellectually their outcomes.

The principles of the mediator evaluation are: (a) The ethical principle of valuing students' differences: *all the students always learn*; (b) The pedagogical principle of the teaching-researching action: *the students learn in a better way with good learning opportunities;* and (c) The dialectic principles of temporariness and complementary: significant learnings becomes lifelong learning [9].

2.4 Neuroscience Whole Brain Theory

The regulation model is based on the *Neuroscience Whole Brain Theory* proposed by Ned Herrmann. This author presents the integration of Sperry's brain hemispheres, and the MacLean' triune brain theories. Herrmann proposes that the brain is conceptually divided into four quadrants that determines dominant thinking styles.

Ned Herrmann, presents the problem of the cerebral dominance based on two theories, the *Cerebral Hemispherical Theory* of Sperry and the *Triune Brain Theory* of MacLean, as well as his own experimental results with biological feedback equipment (bio-feedback) and electroencephalography [11].

Herrmann builds a metaphorical model of the brain by proposing its division into four quadrants: two upper cortical quadrants and two lower limbic quadrants. Each quadrant is associated to a particular style of thinking, creating and learning. Each thinking process might be described in terms of preferences or quadrant dominance.

The whole brain model considers the diversity of all possible preferences and behaviors as the response to several learning situations, both individual and organizational, and determines the problem solving and the decision making strategies. Hence, the quadrants depend of genetic predispositions, and are modelled by the social learning and the cultural influence, so the individuals develop their preferences throughout life.

One of the most important aspects of the Herrmann's model is the proposition that the creative process requires a full activation of the brain. All its potential must be activated as a set of multiple interactions, and all forms of information processing are possible and they are associated to genetic predispositions basis, the environment and the culture [12].

The model identifies how the individuals perceive, learn, solve a problem and make decisions. Each of the cerebral quadrants have different functions, as is shown in Table 1.

Table 1. Characteristics of cerebral quadrants.

Cerebral quadrant	Location	Characteristics
A	Left upper lobule	Logical thinking style: analytic, mathematic, based on concrete facts, qualitative and critic, and focused on the reasoning
B	Left lower lobule	Process thinking style: A controlled, organized, sequential, detailed, and process oriented
C	Right lower lobule	Relational thinking style: emotional and sensorial (musical), symbolic, from interpersonal to spiritual
D	Right upper lobule	Creative thinking style: Theoretical, conceptual, holistic and global. Integrates, synthetize, artistic, spatial, visual, metaphoric, and creative

2.5 Strategic Learning Metamodel

In this section, we propose an architecture of the reactive layer of the Strategic Learning Metamodel (SLM) [13]. SLM integrates the principles of the Mediator Evaluation, the learning activities customization, the assessment, the supervised and personalized attention, as well as the collaborative work in the learning communities that aims to provide the reinforcement of abilities for the workgroup, the leadership and the trading, among others. The SLM optimizes the physical and human resources from an institution, through the reduction of the desertion and aiming to increase the students scoring. In Fig. 1, we show the meta-model that includes the infrastructure layer, the intelligent layer and the reactive layer.

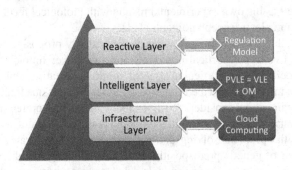

Fig. 1. Strategic Learning Metamodel (SLM)

The infrastructure layer is based on the cloud computing [14]; the Personalized Virtual Learning Environment (PVLE = VLE + OM) that merges a Virtual Learning Environment (VLE) with the customization of learning activities supported by an ontological model [15] (OM); and the Regulation Model that is focused in the assessment, monitoring, feedback and motivation of the students.

In Fig. 2, we show the general architecture that includes the technological aspects and the psycho-pedagogical approach of the SLM [13]. Also, in Fig. 2, we identify the VLE component supported by: the LMS (Sakai), the Application Server (Tomcat), and the virtualization infrastructure (VmWare).

The LMS requires an Application Server that uses a database (PostgreSQL, MySQL), a framework (Hibernate) for Object-Resource mapping, a Business Logic Server (Spring), a Model-View-Controller (Struts) and the file storage system that depends of the operating system.

Also, in Fig. 2, we identify the inference motor (ontologies) and the virtualization infrastructure. The inference motor includes the Apache web server, and the Protégé framework. Both, the application server and the inference motor are supported by the virtualization infrastructure.

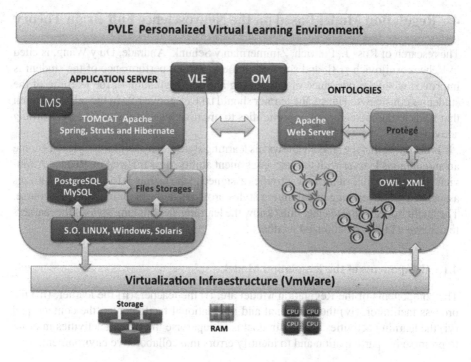

Fig. 2. Architecture of the Strategic Learning Metamodel.

3 Methodology

Our methodology considers: The empirical referent, the design of the architecture of the
regulation model, and the design of the ontology for activity recommendation.

The *empirical referent* describes the context of the learning environment that, in this
case, corresponds to Structured Programming courses for undergraduate students of the
Metropolitan Autonomous University at Azcapotzalco, Mexico.

The design of the architecture of the Regulation Model (RM) is inspired by the Ned
Herman Whole Brain Theory and considers the next components: (i) the teacher, (ii) the
learner, (iii) the process facilitator, (iv) the emotional and motivational facilitator, (v)
the content, and (vi) the learning activities. The RM corresponds to the top layer of the
SLM and because of its relevance is described in Sect. 4.

The ontology is a recommendation system associated to learning activities that uses
the Graphical Ontology Design Methodology (GODeM) [16], and the notation of *Onto
Design Graphics (ODG)* [17]. We apply the ontological model for learning activities
customization for specific courses.

As a first stage the *concept-proof* is developed without learning activities customization.

As a second stage, the customization of the learning activities is developed and the
theoretical concepts are applied.

Finally, the results of the first stage are compared with the results of the second stage.

4   Regulation Model Based on the Neuroscience Full Brain Theory

The research of Ross J., Pintrich, Zimmerman y Schunk, Andrade, Du y Wang, is cited in Rebeca Anijovich [18], and shows that the academic performance of the student is improved when the relevance of monitoring and self-regulation of the learning of the student is considered. Hence, the learner should take an active role in the self-regulation that leads to the increment of opportunities to improve his performance of the learning activities.

Is desirable that the student knows his learning style and his thinking style to become an autonomous learner with the self-assessment ability, as is referred by Rebeca Anijovich [19]. Hence, one of the first activities assigned to the learner is to answer the quizzes associated to the learning and thinking styles provided at the beginning of each course. The facilitators and the teacher must know the learning and thinking style of the learners to achieve a higher customized feedback.

4.1   Components of the Regulation Model

The components of the Regulation Model are: (i) the teacher, (ii) the learner, (iii) the process facilitator, (iv) the emotional and motivational facilitator, v) the content, and (vi) the learning activities. The main goal is to supervise the student activities in order to promote his participation and to identify errors in a collaborative environment.

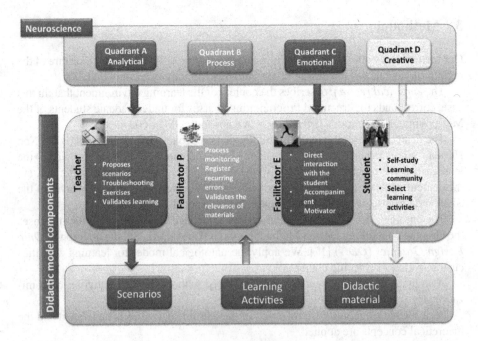

Fig. 3. Regulation Model.

In the RM, each component is associated with a cerebral quadrant as is described by the whole brain theory. The teacher is associated with quadrant A (analytic), whereas the learner is associated with quadrant D (creative), the emotional facilitator is associated with quadrant C (interpersonal), and the process facilitator is associated with quadrant B (organizational), as is shown in Fig. 3.

The teacher leads and supervises the teaching-learning process by sharing experiences. The teacher makes the feedback to the learner through online sessions in real-time that are complemented with classroom sessions each week.

The teacher meets the students at the classroom once a week, gives place to doubt solving, make exercises and then a final evaluation is made up to validate the global learning, that is reported as a final note. The role of the teacher is strongly oriented to the cerebral quadrant A (Analytic), under the approach of offering information, solving problems and exercises, among other activities.

On the other hand, the students enrolled in a course are notified of the date, time, and specific classroom to participate in an initial induction session. The students resolve the quizzes to identify their thinking style that allows to conform the learning communities. The student must be registered in a virtual learning environment to be ready for the initial activities that have been programmed previously for the course. The student must assist to all the classroom evaluation that the teacher applies to validate the learning performance. The role of the student is oriented to the cerebral quadrant D (Creative), under the approach of solving problems, make decision, and to propose solutions, among other activities.

The facilitator E, aims to reach a tradeoff between the harmony and the cooperative environment of the learning community, and is focused on the student motivation as an assistant along the formative process. The role of the facilitator E, is oriented to the cerebral quadrant C (Interpersonal), under an approach oriented to offer a motivational support, performs a continuous interaction given by a strong communication with the learner, and must conceive to the student as a valuable person.

Facilitator P focuses on the process, identifies recurrent errors of the student when learning activities are performed, and notifies to the teacher of those errors in order to make corrective activities. The role of facilitator P is oriented to the cerebral quadrant B (Processes), under the approach of supervising the activity execution according to the instructional design, checks the time limits for an opportune activity deliberation, checks the appropriate accomplishment of activities and focuses its attention in the learning process.

The diversity of learning styles is attended with a set of educational resources that includes: animation, audio and interactivity. For this purpose, mental maps, conceptual diagrams, summaries, synopsis, videos, audio, fast reading, chat, blogs, social networks, interactive resources, digital blackboards, games, among others resources are available (see Fig. 4). The didactical contents are elaborated as reusable learning objects (contents).

The learning activities are customized according with the learning styles in such a way that the learner has a large pool of learning activities to make a good choice based on their own thinking styles.

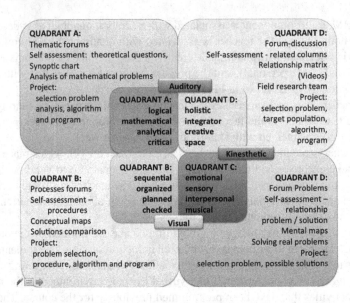

Fig. 4. Customization of learning activities for a language programming course.

5   Case of Study

The case of study consists of experiments that involves to undergraduate students enrolled in Structured Programming courses of the Faculty of Engineering at Autonomous Metropolitan University (UAM) Azcapotzalco in Mexico, Mexico. The main goal is to increase the logical cognitive abilities, to increase the creativity, and to promote the analytic ability for solving problems by proposing solutions, designing algorithms and implementing the corresponding programs in a specific programming language.

We develop five experiments with a duration of twelve weeks each one: at spring 2012 (12S), at autumn 2012 (12O), at winter 2013 (13I), at spring 2013 (13P) and at autumn 2013 (13-O). To validate the proposed model as well as the architecture, the courses were registered with the modality called *Non-Classroom Course (NCC or 100% online)* and with the modality of C*ooperative Learning System (CLS, 50% online, 50% cooperative)*, with a capacity between 70 and 250 students.

5.1   Design of the Learning Activities in the Regulation Model

Now we comment about the learning activities that conform the organization of the Structured Programming course as an example of *forum* design that considers a given quadrant, implements thematic forums, discussion forums, problem forums and process forums.

The orientation for the final project, for specific quadrants define a set of approaches, some oriented to the analysis and the logic, and some other oriented to the procedures, to the creativity or to the benefit of a group of persons. The purpose is to identify mechanisms that allow to a student to be identified with the activity to be developed. However, it could not be applied along all the course, since it must integrate other activities that allow a student to develop other abilities that does not match with the dominant quadrant, in order to achieve global course objectives.

The learner has a set of established activities according to a cerebral quadrant to be stimulated, and simultaneously the learner can choose from a large pool of learning activities.

5.2 Feedback Mechanisms of the Regulation Model

One of the main goals of the Regulation Model is to collect information of all the process that are developed along a course trying to improve the teaching-learning process. All the historical information (positive and negative) is stored to keep records of previous lessons.

Rebeca Anijovich proposes some recommendation to perform an appropriate feedback: (a) to establish a clear and simple communication, by validating what the student understand compared with what the professor teach; (b) to include messages about the product and the collaboration method in the workgroup; (c) to correct the errors with the students and to suggest a mechanism to improve the results; and (d) to provide positive comments.

The learner must be aware of his errors, and to proceed to fix and improve the results considering the feedback, moreover there must exist an *Improvement Planning*. Is

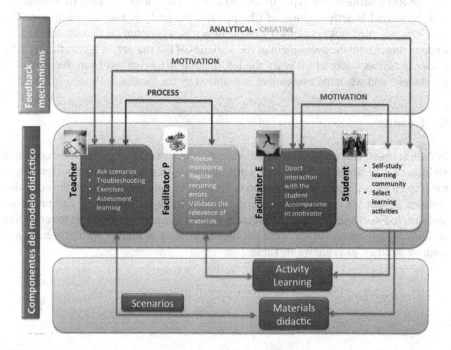

Fig. 5. Feedback mechanisms in the Regulation Model.

convenient to generate a *digital log (keep records)* with all the feedback of all the activities to become a reference for the rest of the participants.

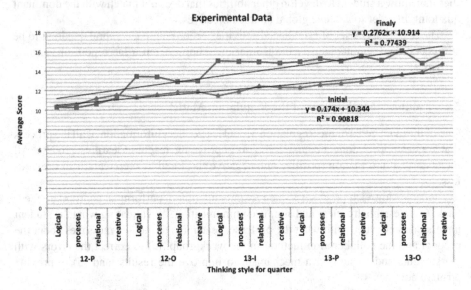

Fig. 6. Curve fitting for experimental data of online courser with SLM.

The RM considers two types of feedback: the first is *user-centered* (motivational) and the second is *activity-centered* (the process, the analysis and the creativity). The *user-centered* feedback is attended with the interaction between the facilitator E and the student, throughout the assessment of the activities of the student. Whereas the *activity-centered feedback* take place when the information is transmitted from the teacher to the student, and when the assessment is followed by the facilitator P (see Fig. 5).

6   Results

In the test cases, the results show an increment in the scoring that measure the cognitive abilities of the learner. In the Experiment 1, there is no a considerable improvement. In the Experiments 2 and 3 we are able to appreciate an improvement in all the cognitive abilities, in fact we can be appreciate the highest score for the logical and processes abilities. In Experiments 4 and 5 the scoring present an improvement in all the cognitive abilities of the learner. In this case the highest scoring is related with processes and creative abilities, as is shown in Table 2.

Table 2. Experimental Results for 5 test cases.

Period	12-P Experiment 1		12-O Experiment 2		13-I Experiment 3		13-P Experiment 4		13-O Experiment 5	
Thinking Style	Initial	Final	Initial	Final	Initial	Final	Initial	Final	Initial	Final
Logic	10.356	10.315	11.290	13.418	11.399	14.987	12.222	14.865	13.353	14.988
Processes	10.548	10.230	11.542	13.372	11.859	14.948	12.481	15.173	13.515	15.965
Relational	11.200	10.635	11.771	12.898	12.371	14.902	12.602	14.913	13.788	14.701
Creative	11.560	11.219	11.824	12.949	12.247	14.732	12.833	15.394	14.658	15.690

In Fig. 6 we show the curve fitting for the experimental data of the 5 experiments which were realized with language programming courses.

7 Conclusions

We have successfully implemented the Regulation Model in 5 experiments involving teachers, undergraduate students as facilitators, and the learning contents have been developed as learning objects, and learning activities were customized according to the thinking and learning styles of the students. Experimental results support the fact of the improvement on the creative, process and logic abilities.

We can conclude that the RM impact positively in the development of the cognitive abilities of the students. Hence, our contribution is the incorporation of the RM that provides the monitoring and feedback necessary to provide a motivation for the students. The RM is the top layer in the Strategic Learning Model, which constitute a learning solution based on cloud computing.

As future work we consider to automatize a reactive layer for the Strategic Learning Metamodel in order to give an adaptive monitoring to the customization of the learning activities.

References

1. Mödritscher, F., Andergassen, M., Lai-Chong, E., García-Barrios, V.: Application of learning curves for didactic model evaluation: case studies. Int. J. Emerg. Technol. Learn. 8(4), 62–69 (2013)
2. Mizoguchi, R., Bourdeau, J.: Using ontological engineering to overcome common AI-ED problems. Int. J. Artif. Intell. Educ. 11(2), 107–121 (2000)
3. Odeh, S., Qaraeen, O.: Evaluation methods and techniques for e-Learning software for school students in primary stages. Int. J. Emerg. Technol. Learn. 2(3), 1–8 (2007)
4. Tedman, R., Loudon, R., Wallace, B., Pountney, H.: integrating regular, on-line evaluation by students into the curriculum review process in an Australian medical program. Int. J. Emerg. Technol. Learn. 4(3), 59–66 (2009)

5. Samarakou, M., Papadakis, A., Fylladitakis, E., Hatziapostolou, A., Tsaganou, G., Gerrit, W.: An open learning environment for the diagnosis, assistance and evaluation of students based on artificial intelligence. Int. J. Emerg. Technol. Learn. **9**(3), 36–44 (2014)
6. Knowles, S., Holton, F., Swanson, A.: Andragogía, El Aprendizaje de los Adultos. Ed. Oxford, México (2001)
7. Peñalosa, E., y Ménez, D.: La apropiación del conocimiento en comunicación y educación para la ciencia: una propuesta de conceptualización. Contextos educativos no-formales: el museo y la apropiación del conocimiento científico. Universidad Autónoma Metropolitana Unidad Cuajimalpa (95,125). México D.F. (2015)
8. Dorrego, E.: Educación a Distancia y Evaluación del Aprendizaje. RED. Revista de Educación a Distancia. Año 5, número monográfico 6 (2005). Recovered from http://www.um.es/ead/red/M6/dorrego.pdf
9. Hoffmann, J.: Evaluación mediadora. Una propuesta fundamentada. In: En Anijovich, R., W. De Camilloni, A., Cappelleti, G., Hoffmann, J., Katzkowicz, R., Mottier, L. (Ed.), La evaluación significativa. Voces de la educación, pp. 73–102. Buenos Aires: Paidós (2010)
10. Peñalosa, E.: Estrategias docentes con tecnologías: Guía práctica. Pearson: Always Learning (2013)
11. Gómez, C.J., Herrera, M., De la Cruz, M., Martínez, J., González, F., Poggioli, L., Herrera, F., Ramírez, M., Ruíz, C., Cazau, P., Martínez, M.: Neurociencia Cognitiva y Educación. Materiales de Posgrado. Perú, Lambayeque: Fondo Editorial FACHSE (2004). Recovered from http://online.upaep.mx/campusTest/ebooks/neurociencia.pdf
12. Gardié, O.: Determinación del perfil de estilos de pensamiento y análisis de sus posibles implicaciones en el desempeño de profesionales universitarios venezolanos. Revista: Estudios Pedagógicos (Valdivia) (26), 25–38 (2000). Recovered from http://www.scielo.cl/scielo.php?pid=S0718-07052000000100002&script=sci_arttext
13. Silva-López, R., Méndez-Gurrola, I., Sánchez-Arias, V.: Strategic learning, towards a teaching reengineering. Res. Comput. Sci. **65**(2013), 133–145 (2013)
14. Silva-López, R.B., Méndez-Gurrola, I.I., Herrera, O.: Metamodelo de aprendizaje estratégico (MAE): Arquitectura de la capa de infraestructura, solución basada en la Cloud Computing. Res. Comput. Sci. **93**(2015), 175–188 (2015)
15. Silva-López, R.B., Méndez-Gurrola, I.I., Alcántara, O.H., Silva-López, M.I., Fallad-Chávez, J.: Strategic Learning Meta-Model (SLM): Architecture of the Personalized Virtual Learning Environment (PVLE) based on the cloud computing. In: Lagunas, O.P., Alcántara, O.H., Figueroa, G.A. (eds.) MICAI 2015. LNCS (LNAI), vol. 9414, pp. 183–194. Springer, Heidelberg (2015). doi:10.1007/978-3-319-27101-9_13
16. Silva-López, R.B., Silva-López, M.I., Méndez-Gurrola, I., Bravo, M., Sánchez, V.: GODeM: a graphical ontology design methodology. Res. Comput. Sci. **84**(2014), 17–28 (2014)
17. Silva-López, R.B., Silva-López, M., Méndez-Gurrola, I.I., Bravo, M.: Onto Design Graphics (ODG): a graphical notation to standardize ontology design. In: Gelbukh, A., Espinoza, F.C., Galicia-Haro, S.N. (eds.) MICAI 2014. LNCS (LNAI), vol. 8856, pp. 443–452. Springer, Heidelberg (2014). doi:10.1007/978-3-319-13647-9_40
18. Anijovich, R., W. De Camilloni, A., Cappelleti, G., Hoffmann, J., Katzkowicz, R., Mottier, L.: La evaluación significativa. Voces de la educación. Buenos Aires: Paidós (2010)
19. Anijovich, R.: La retroalimentación en la evaluación. En Anijovich, R., W. De Camilloni, A., Cappelleti, G., Hoffmann, J., Katzkowicz, R., Mottier, L. (eds.) La evaluación significativa. Voces de la educación, pp. 129–149. Buenos Aires: Paidós (2010a)

Overview of a Framework for Ubiquitous User Models Interoperability

María de Lourdes Martínez-Villaseñor[1](✉) and Miguel González-Mendoza[2]

[1] Universidad Panamericana Campus México,
Augusto Rodin 498, Col. Insurgentes-Mixcoac, México, D.F., Mexico
lmartine@up.edu.mx

[2] Tecnológico de Monterrey, Campus Estado de México, Carretera Lago de Guadalupe km 2.5,
Atizapán de Zaragoza, Edo. de México, Mexico
mgonza@itesm.mx

Abstract. Researchers in the user modeling community have been interested in sharing and reuse profile information from heterogeneous sources. Ubiquitous user model interoperability allows enrichment of adaptive systems obtaining a better understanding of the user, and decreases the effort associated with creating a user model. We present a framework that enables the interoperability between profile suppliers and consumers with a mixed approach that consist in central ubiquitous user model ontology and a process of concept alignment. The central ontology is a flexible representation of a ubiquitous user model to cope with the dynamicity of a distributed multi-application environment that provides mediation between profile suppliers and consumers. The process of concept alignment automatically discovers the semantic mappings in order to interpret the information from heterogeneous sources and integrate them into a ubiquitous user model.

Keywords: User modeling interoperability · User modeling · Schema matching

1 Introduction

User models from commonly used systems, applications and devices are valuable sources of personal information that can be shared and reused to obtain a better understanding of the user, prevent repeated configurations, help deal with the "cold start" problem, and decrease the effort associated with creating a user model. Gathering distributed user information from heterogeneous sources to enable user model interoperability entails handling syntactic and semantic heterogeneity [1]. From literature [2, 3], we see that current research in ubiquitous user modeling has two major approaches: (i) standardization based user modeling founded in defining a common ontology and language for the user model; (ii) mediation-based user modeling using mediation techniques to build semantic bridges between representations. Current solutions for ubiquitous user model interoperability must consider the high degree of dynamism of ubiquitous environments. A possible solution to overcome limitations of standardization and mediation approaches, and leverage their advantages is to integrate elements of both approaches as suggested in [2]. We present an overview of a framework for

© ICST Institute for Computer Sciences, Social Informatics and Telecommunications Engineering 2017
E. Sucar et al. (Eds.): AFI 2016, LNICST 179, pp. 185–188, 2017.
DOI: 10.1007/978-3-319-49622-1_20

ubiquitous user interoperability that enables sharing user model information with a mixed approach to bridge the gap between the mentioned approaches. The proposed framework [4] enables the interoperability between profile suppliers and consumers with central ubiquitous user model ontology to provide formal representation of the user profile, and a process of concept alignment to automatically discover the semantic mappings between the user models. Similar mediation approaches do schema mapping with help of the expert designer [5] or forcing the stakeholders to adopt a syntax format [6]. Standardized approaches, on the other hand use fixed standard representation and every interoperability stakeholder must adder to this model and to an exchange language [7]. Our approach allows the interoperability process with the least intervention of the stakeholders and has the flexibility to accept new stakeholders without modifying current mappings.

2   Overview of the Framework for Ubiquitous User Model Interoperability

The proposed framework is based on a distributed architecture to share and reuse profile information contained in existing heterogeneous user models. The ubiquitous user model is application and system independent. The framework allows gathering information from profile providers, and integrating a user model representation that can evolve over time. It also enables to consume profile information resolving possible semantic conflicts. Due to the great syntactical and structural differences, as well as the profile providers' and consumers' autonomy, it is practically impossible to develop a static commonly accepted ontology for every domain. The main contributions of this work are the central ontology for ubiquitous user model interoperability and the process of concept alignment to deliver quality mappings between concepts of different sources automatically. The framework has been proven gathering profile information of social network applications, personal devices with sensors, personal health records, and learner management systems [4, 10].

2.1   Ubiquitous User Modeling Interoperability Ontology (U2MIO)

The Ubiquitous User Modeling Interoperability Ontology (U2MIO): (a) Provides semantic support for user model overcoming differences between concepts at knowledge level. (b) Represents a flexible user profile structure which provides the possibility for the ubiquitous user model to evolve during time. (c) Provides representation for new stakeholders in the interoperability process without effort of the provider or consumer system. The ontology reuses SKOS ontology; it can be seen as an aggregation of concept schemes each one representing a profile supplier or consumer, and a central ubiquitous user model concept scheme. Semantic mapping relations are established between each supplier/consumer concept scheme and the ubiquitous user model concept scheme at concept level by the process of concept alignment in order to enable interoperability between user models. The ubiquitous user modeling ontology demands the design of concept schemes, one for each profile provider and the ubiquitous user model concept scheme (Fig. 1). Semantic mapping relations were established with SKOS properties.

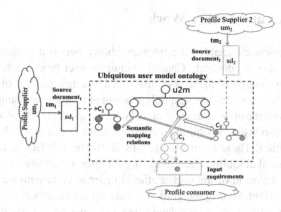

Fig. 1. Interrelations between profile supplier/consumer and ubiquitous user model ontology.

2.2 Process of Concept Alignment

The process of concept alignment is based on a two-tier matching strategy that consists in two phases: element level matching and structure level matching. The process purpose is to determine the mappings between two concept schemes at the granularity of concept elements. This means finding the alignment A' given the pair of schemas X and U where X can be any concept scheme constructed from a profile supplier/consumer document and U will always be the ubiquitous user model concept scheme. One wants to determine all the semantic relations R from the triplet $<c_s, c_t, R>$ from all concepts in X to all concepts in U as shown in Eq. (1):

$$R(c_s, c_t) \forall c_s \in C_s, \forall c_t \in C_T \tag{1}$$

Three types of links are considered between two concepts of different concept schemes based on SKOS mapping properties that establish associative, and interchangeability mappings: *skos:exactMatch*, *skos:closeMatch* and *skos:relatedMatch*. In the element level matching phase, the concepts are directly compared to each other without considering the hierarchy structure and values. The goal of element level matching is given concept c_s of the source concept scheme X_s, finding the best concept label c_{tb} from a set of concept candidates for alignment in the target concept scheme X_T. String similarity, semantic similarity and internal structure similarity techniques are used to determine concept similarity. In the structure level matching step, the context of the source and target concepts (neighbors of the concepts in the hierarchy) are considered. The ultimate goal of this process is determine the one-to-one mappings between the concept c_s of the source concept scheme X_s and the best concept c_{tb} from the set of labels C_t of the target concept scheme X_T. From this phase, decision recommendations can be obtained for the inclusion of new concepts, sub collections and collections in the ubiquitous user model concept scheme allowing it to evolve over time. Details of the process of concept alignment are presented in [8, 10].

3 Conclusions and Future Work

The proposed framework enables the interoperability between profile suppliers and consumers with a mixed approach. Central ubiquitous user model ontology (U2MIO) provides the representation of the user profile, and a dynamic process of concept alignment automatically discovers the semantic mappings to align the supplier/consumer concept scheme with the ubiquitous user model concept schema. The process of concept alignment is also responsible of offering recommendation of concept, sub collection and/or collection addition. These recommendations allow the U2MIO ontology to evolve over time. The central ubiquitous user modeling for interoperability ontology (U2MIO) is a flexible representation of the user profile in order to cope with the dynamicity of ubiquitous environment. Hybrid integration system architecture was proposed in which every stakeholder defines its own schema, but it is mapped to the global ontology U2MIO. In the hybrid approach, new stakeholders (suppliers or consumers) can be easily added without the modification of existing mappings. Specific context in which the service will be provided to the user is not taken into account to determine which values to deliver when consuming profile information. More empirical evaluation is also necessary to refine the model and prove that the solution is practical and generalizable.

References

1. Carmagnola, F.: Handling semantic heterogeneity in interoperable distributed user models. In: Kuflik, T., Berkovsky, S., Carmagnola, F., Heckmann, D., Krüger, A. (eds.). LNCS, vol. 5830, pp. 20–36Springer, Heidelberg (2009). doi:10.1007/978-3-642-05039-8_2
2. Berkovsky, S., Heckmann, D., Kuflik, T.: Addressing challenges of ubiquitous user modeling: between mediation and semantic integration. Adv. Ubiquit. User Model. **5830**, 1–19 (2009)
3. Carmagnola, F., Cena, F., Gena, C.: User model interoperability: a survey. User Model. User-adapt. Interact. **21**(3), 285–331 (2011)
4. de Martinez-Villaseñor, M.L.: Design and Implementation of a Framework for Ubiquitous User Model Interoperability. Ph.D. Thesis. Instituto Tecnológico y de Estudios Superiores de Monterrey, Campus Estado de México (2013)
5. van der Sluijs, K., Houben, G.-J.: A generic component for exchanging user models between web-based systems. Int. J. Contin. Eng. Educ. Life Long Learn. **16**(1/2), 64–76 (2006)
6. Carmagnola, F., Cena, F.: From interoperable user models to interoperable user modeling. In: Wade, V.P., Ashman, H., Smyth, B. (eds.) AH 2006. LNCS, vol. 4018, pp. 409–413. Springer, Heidelberg (2006). doi:10.1007/11768012_60
7. Heckmann, D.: Ubiquitous user modeling. Saarland University, Saarland (2005)
8. de Martinez-Villaseñor, M.L., Gonzalez-Mendoza, M.: An enhanced process of concept alignment for dealing with overweight and obesity. J. Univers. Comput. Sci. (2013)
9. Martinez-Villaseñor, M.D.L., Gonzalez-Mendoza, M., Hernandez-Gress, N.: Towards a ubiquitous user model for profile sharing and reuse. Sensors **12**(10), 13249–13283 (2012)
10. Martínez-Villaseñor, M.D.L.G., González-Mendoza, M.: Process of concept alignment for interoperability between heterogeneous sources. In: Mexican International Conference on Artificial Intelligence, pp. 311–320. Springer, Heidelberg, October 2012

Author Index

Abubakr, Omar M. 22
Aguilar-Noriega, Leocundo 8
Aguirre-Anaya, Eleazar 63
Ahmed, Essam 22
Andrade, Daniel 109

Bareta, David Soasti 103
Bueno Martinez, Monica 128

Cardenas-Osuna, Raúl 8
Castrejón, Luis R. 152
Cervantes, Ofelia 167

de Cote, Enrique Munoz 79, 91
de Lourdes Martínez-Villaseñor, María 185
Del-Valle-Soto, Carolina 91
Derbala, Ahmed H. 22

Enciso-Gonzalez, Angelica 35
Escalante, Hugo Jair 3
Escamilla-Ambrosio, Ponciano Jorge 63

Fallad-Chávez, Jalil 172
Farinelli, Alessandro 39, 79
Funes-Gallanzi, Marcelo 128

Gallardo-Ortíz, Itzell A. 117
García, Francisco Montero 51
García-Macías, J. Antonio 8
Gonzalez-Marron, David 35
González-Mendoza, Miguel 185
Guerrero, Esteban 109

Happa, Jassim 63
Hernández-Franco, Jorge 152
Hernandez-Leal, Pablo 3, 140
Herrera-Alcántara, Oscar 172
Heyer, Patrick 152

Jiménez-Flores, J. Rafael 117
Jung, Youna 12

Lambert, Ana Olivia Caballero 128
Lezama, Fernando 79, 91
Littman, Michael L. 75

Maxhuni, Alban 140
Mayora, Oscar 140
Mejia-Guzman, David 35
Mex-Perera, Carlos 91
Mokhtar, Bassem 22
Morales, Eduardo F. 140
Muñiz, Gerardo 103
Muñoz-Meléndez, Angelica 140
Murguía-Romero, Miguel 117
Mustafa, Ahmad M. 22

Nieves, Juan Carlos 109

Orihuela-Espina, Felipe 152
Orozco-Barbosa, Luis 51
Osmani, Venet 140

Palominos, Jorge 79

Ramos, Antonio Brasa 51
Riquelme, Francisco Montero 51
Rodriguez, Jafet 91
Rodríguez-González, Ansel Y. 79
Rodríguez-Mota, Abraham 63
Roncalli, Michele 39

Sánchez, J. Alfredo 167
Serrano-Estrada, Bernardo 117
Silva-López, Rafaela Blanca 172
Sucar, Luis Enrique 3, 140, 152

Torres Montañez, Cesar Horacio 128

Vera, Fernando 167
Villalobos-Molina, Rafael 117

Wang, Guan 75

Ylizaliturri-Salcedo, Miguel Ángel 8

Printed in the United States
By Bookmasters.

Printed in the United States
By Bookmasters